BTEC

HNC
HND

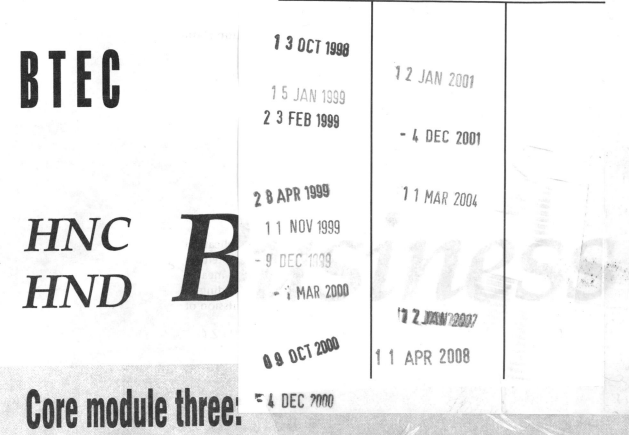

Core module three:

Managing People
and Activities

PUBLISHING

BTEC HNC & HND BUSINESS

First edition December 1995
Second edition June 1996

ISBN 0 7517 7012 4 (previous edition 0 7517 7002 7)

British Library Cataloguing-in Publication Data

A catalogue record for this book
is available from the British Library

Published by

BPP Publishing Limited
Aldine House, Aldine Place
London W12 8AW

11623926

Learning Resources
Centre

Our thanks are due to Genesys Editorial for
additional editorial and production work and to
Rona Marlow for assistance in developing the open
learning aspects of the text.

Printed in England by
DACOSTA PRINT
35/37 Queensland Road
London N7 7AH
0171 700 1000

Contents

Preface   (v)

BTEC Guidelines for Core Module 3   (vi)

Study Guide   (viii)

Part A Managing people   1

  1 Perspectives on management   3

  2 Management style   32

  3 Individual behaviour at work   51

  4 Motivation   73

  5 Interpersonal behaviour at work   87

  6 Teams   108

  7 Monitoring performance   128

  8 Enhancing performance   142

  9 Problem-solving   159

Part B Managing activities   173

10 Planning and organising   175

11 Managing time   191

12 Managing projects   206

13 Communication   225

14 Co-ordination   248

15 Review and monitoring   257

16 Constraints on management   278

Answers to assignments   289

Glossary   297

Index   301

Review form   307

Preface

The HNC and HND qualifications in Business are very demanding. The suggested content, set out by BTEC in guidelines for each module, includes sophisticated topics which are normally only covered at degree level. Students therefore need books which get straight to the heart of these topics, and which relate them clearly to existing knowledge derived from school, college or work experience. BPP's series of textbooks is designed to meet that need.

This book has been written specifically for Core Module 3 *Managing People and Activities*. It covers the BTEC guidelines and suggested content in full, and includes the following features.

(a) The BTEC guidelines.

(b) A study guide, which explains the features of the book and how to get the most out of it.

(c) A glossary and index.

Each chapter contains:

(a) an introduction and study objectives;

(b) summary diagrams and signposts, to guide you through;

(c) numerous activities, topics for discussion and definitions;

(d) a chapter roundup, a quick quiz with answers, answer guidelines to activities and an assignment (with answer guidelines at the end of the book).

BPP Publishing have for many years been the leading providers of targeted texts for professional qualifications. We know that our customers need to study effectively, and that they cannot afford to waste time. They expect clear, concise and highly-focused study material. We believe that this series of study texts for HNC and HND Business students fulfils those needs.

BPP Publishing
June 1996

Other titles in this series:

Core Module 1   Market Relations
Core Module 2   Operating Environment
Core Module 4   Managing Finance and Information
Core Module 5   Organisational Structures and Processes
Core Module 6   Planning and Decision Making
Option Module 1   Finance Accounting Framework
Option Module 5   Marketing
Option Module 9   Personnel Management in the Organisation

For more information, or to place an order, please call 0181 740 2222

If you would like to send in your comments on this book,
please turn to the review form on the last page.

Managing People and Activities

DESCRIPTION OF MODULE

This module is concerned with increasing students' abilities to understand and evaluate processes and techniques for managing people and their activities. The two are interrelated in that effective individuals and teams are essential to the planning, organising, co-ordinating and monitoring of workplace activities.

This module has two sections.

Section One: Managing People

On completion of this section the student should be able to:

● evaluate the effectiveness of alternative styles and approaches to managing people

● analyse the factors influencing the effectiveness of individuals and teams

● evaluate alternative approaches to motivating people at work, improving performance and dealing with staff work problems

● work within a team and identify techniques for team building

● analyse and evaluate the effect of their own and others' behaviour on interpersonal relationships at work.

Suggested content

Management style: major categories of styles, effectiveness and appropriateness of each within different situations; contingency theories; changes in working patterns: flexibility, multi-skilling, team-working, empowerment.

Individual and interpersonal behaviour: motivation theories; personality; perception; attitudes to work, internal and external factors.

Teams: stages in group development; group dynamics; decision-making in teams, team building, team roles and selection, internal and external influences.

Performance at work: coaching skills, training and development; counselling; discipline; monitoring and reporting individual and group performance.

Section Two: Managing Activities

On completion of this section students should be able to:

- use techniques and methods of work planning and organisation
- identify the importance of management information and communications in the effective management of activities
- co-ordinate human, physical and financial resources in carrying out activities
- identify major constraints on effective management of activities
- review effectiveness of self and others and improve the way activities and tasks are organised.

Suggested content

Work planning and organisation: PERT, CPA; method study; flow of work; measures of efficiency and effectiveness; changing and amending plans.

Communications: giving orders and instruction, briefing individuals and teams; giving and receiving feedback.

Co-ordinating: interrelationship of dependent activities; achieving balance between activities.

Constraints: deadlines; regulatory control; scarcity of and internal competition for resources; external changes.

Review and monitoring: value analysis; systems analysis; performance standards and indicators; impact of technology.

Study Guide

As well as giving comprehensive coverage of the BTEC guidelines, this book includes several features which are designed specifically to make learning efficient. The features are these.

(a) At the start of each chapter, there is a summary diagram which maps out the ground covered by the chapter. There are more detailed summary diagrams at the beginning of each main section of each chapter, giving more detail on the contents of that section.

(b) After the summary diagram there is an introduction, which sets the chapter in context. This is followed by learning objectives, which show you what you will have achieved by the time you reach the end of the chapter.

(c) Throughout the text, there are special aids to learning. These are indicated by symbols in the margin as follows.

Signposts guide you through the text, showing how each section is connected with the next one.

Definitions give the meanings of key terms.

Activities allow you to consolidate and test your learning. An indication of the time required for each is given (don't worry too much if you take a longer or shorter time). Answers are given at the ends of the chapters.

Topics for discussion are for use in seminars. They give you a chance to share your views with your fellow students.

(d) The wide margin at the outside edge of each page is for your notes. You will get the best out of this book if you engage in a dialogue with it. Put in your own ideas. Many things in business are matters of opinion, so do not be afraid to disagree with what you read.

(e) At the end of each chapter, there is a chapter roundup, a quiz with answers and an assignment. Use these to consolidate your knowledge. The chapter roundup summarises the chapter. The quiz tests what you have learnt. Brief answers are given, but you can also check many of your answers by going back through the chapter. The very act of going back and searching for relevant details will further improve your grasp of the subject. The assignments, each with a time guide, allow you to put your knowledge into practice – your teacher will let you know how far each assignment you prepare is suitable as actual assessment material. Answer guidelines for the assignment can be found at the end of the text.

(f) The text ends with a glossary of key terms and an index.

Part A

MANAGING PEOPLE

Chapter 1

PERSPECTIVES ON MANAGEMENT

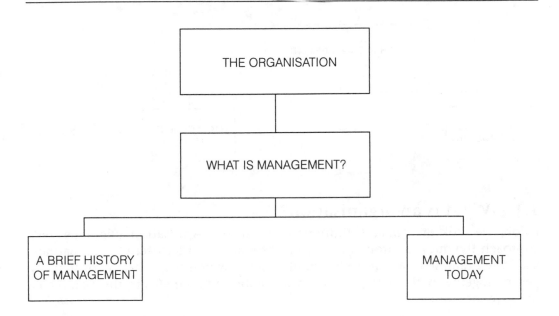

Introduction

Before we can discuss 'managing people and activities', we need to consider what 'managing' is. So we begin this introductory chapter by looking at organisations and why they might need managing. We then look at some of the ideas people have formulated about the nature of management and what it is to be a manager. You will find that managers and writers on management have, over the years, come up with different ideas about how organisations work and what is necessary in order for them to be as efficient and effective as they can be. We look briefly at the five main strands of thinking – the hallmarks of which you may identify in the principles and techniques covered in the rest of this text – and at some of the current 'fashions' in management and organisation.

Your objectives

After completing this chapter, you should:

(a) be able to define the term 'organisation' and explain the need for management of people and activities in business organisations

(b) be able to list some of the activities and roles of a manager, and appreciate the range and complexity of the management task

(c) understand the nature of managerial authority in an organisation, and be able to distinguish between the authority, power and responsibility of managers

(d) be able to outline the principles of the scientific management, classical, human relations and contingency schools of thought

(e) be able to describe an organisation as an open socio-technical system

(f) be able to outline trends in modern management practice, including flexibility, multi-skilling, teamworking and empowerment

1 THE ORGANISATION

1.1 What is an organisation?

Before we look at formal definitions of what an organisation might be, let's approach the question from a purely practical angle. The writer Chester Barnard used the example of a man trying to lift a stone which is too heavy for him. By getting together with another person, and combining their efforts, the man is able to move the stone.

For discussion

Suppose that you are the person wanting to move the stone. Consider how you would go about getting other people to help you: what could you offer them? What are they offering you? Who will be in charge of the operation? What will need organising? Will it make a difference if you are using (a) brute strength, (b) a lever and fulcrum or (c) a bulldozer? You are, in effect, dealing with organisational issues of planning, organising, resourcing, controlling and people management.

Chester Barnard himself described an organisation as 'a system of co-operative human activities'. Another writer described organisations as 'systems of behaviour designed to enable humans and their machines to accomplish goals'. Can you identify in these definitions the features of our rock-rolling organisation?

A simple but precise definition may be given as follows.

Definition

Organisations are 'social arrangements for the controlled performance of collective goals'. (*Buchanan and Huczynski*).

1.2 Social arrangements

An organisation is made up of individuals brought together to carry out different roles within it to enable them to achieve its goals and objectives. This is achieved through the inter-relationships, co-operation and, on occasion, conflict between these individual members.

Banding together in organisations offers:

(a) a greater ability to achieve individual and organisational purposes, by allowing people to pool their knowledge, experience, special expertise and resources.

(b) the satisfaction of the individual's need for relationships with other people.

In order to achieve the goals and objectives, the business organisation must formalise the 'social arrangements' to provide a 'controlled performance' (see Paragraph 1.4). This involves the allocation of functions, tasks and activities to individuals or groups along with clearly defined responsibilities, levels of authority and communication channels. These factors will determine the structure of an organisation.

Organisational structure

Organisation structure implies a framework intended to:

(a) link individuals in an established network of relationships so that authority, responsibility and communications can be controlled;

(b) group together the tasks required to fulfil the objectives of the organisation, and allocate them to suitable individuals or groups; this may be done on the basis of function (sales, production, personnel and so on), geographical area (eg for regional sales territories), product or product type – or whatever is appropriate;

(c) give each individual or group the authority required to perform the allocated functions, while controlling their behaviour and use of resources in the interests of the organisation as a whole;

(d) co-ordinate the objectives and activities of separate units, so that overall aims are achieved without gaps or overlaps in the flow of work;

(e) facilitate the flow of work, information and other resources through the organisation.

We will be discussing some related issues of organisation structure a bit later in this chapter, when we consider the nature of a manager's authority. However, you should be clear in your own mind that 'controlled performance of collective goals' is almost impossible without some kind of deliberate organisational structure. We call this a formal organisation.

Definition

A formal organisation is one which is deliberately constructed to fulfil specific goals. It is characterised by planned division of responsibility and a well-defined structure of authority and communication. The organisation structure provides for consistent functions and roles, irrespective of changes in individual membership.

An *informal organisation* is one which is loosely structured, flexible and spontaneous, fluctuating with its individual membership. Examples of an informal organisation are colleagues who tend to lunch together and 'cliques'. Informal organisations always exist within formal organisations.

Activity 1 [20 minutes]

Jason, Mark, Gary and Robbie set up in business together as repairers of musical instruments – specialising in guitars and drums. They are a bit uncertain as to how they should run the business, but when they discuss it in the pub, they decide that attention needs to be paid to three major areas: taking orders from customers, doing the repairs (of course) and checking the quality of the repairs before notifying the customer.

Suggest three ways in which the boys could structure their business.

NOTES

Organisational culture

The 'culture' of an organisation consists of the shared assumptions, values and beliefs of its members; its collective self-image; its sense of 'the way we do things round here'; its general 'style'. Some aspects of culture are as follows.

(a) Underlying assumptions: belief in quality or the importance of the customer; trust in the organisation to be loyal and provide good rewards; freedom to make decisions, and even mistakes – and so on. These basic ideas guide the behaviour of individuals and groups.

(b) Beliefs and values expressed by the organisation's managers and members. Beliefs and values may emerge as sayings, slogans or mottoes (like IBM's: 'Think'.) They may emerge in a mythology of the organisation: in-jokes, stories about past successes, heroic failures or breakthroughs, legends about past figures and so on. The influential writers Peters and Waterman (who wrote a best-selling book called *In Search of Excellence*) found that a 'handful of guiding values' was often more powerful than rule books and managerial controls – and that those 'guiding values' could be fostered by managers. Managers can encourage the values they want (care for quality, use of initiative, loyalty and so on) by example, by giving the right messages, by rewarding the right attitudes and punishing (or simply not employing) those who are not prepared to be part of the culture.

(c) Visible signs, such as the style of the offices or what people wear, the formality or informality of communication between managers and staff and so on.

1.3 Collective goals

All organisations have collective or shared goals, over and above the individual goals of their members. A chess club, for example, may believe in promoting excellence in the game of chess, or making chess more accessible to ordinary people. It may also have more specific objectives to do with being successful in inter-club chess tournaments, attracting new members, or raising money. Or it may simply fulfil the need for its members to get together with fellow enthusiasts, and to improve their game. In other words, there are different types of goal.

(a) Ideological goals are to do with beliefs and values, and what the organisation has defined as its 'mission'. (For example, the mission or ideological goal of a telecommunications organisation may be to 'get the world talking'.)

(b) Formal goals are those set for the organisation by a dominant individual (the organisation's founder, say) or group (the shareholders or management team). Members work to attain these goals because it is also a means to their personal goals (such as earning pay).

(c) Shared personal goals are pursued when the individual members agree on what they want from the organisation (eg a discussion group, or a group of academics deciding to pursue research).

Activity 2 [30 minutes]

In what areas do you think business organisations might wish to set themselves goals or specific objectives? Suggest five areas

For discussion: case examples

Here are some ideological goals or 'mission statements' of well-known organisations.

Glaxo 'is an integrated research-based group of companies whose corporate purpose is to create, discover, develop, manufacture and market throughout the world, safe, effective

medicines of the highest quality which will bring benefit to patients through improved longevity and quality of life, and to society through economic value.'

IBM (UK): 'We shall increase the pace of change. Market-driven quality is our aim. It means listening and responding more sensitively to our customers. It means eliminating defects and errors, speeding up all our processes, measuring everything we do against a common standard, and it means involving employees totally in our aims.'

Apple Computers: 'Our goal has always been to create the world's friendliest, most understandable, most useable computers – computers that empower the individual...'

Whose goals are these? Who will benefit (inside and outside the organisation) if these organisations achieve their stated goals? (People who stand to gain or lose by the activities of an organisation are called its 'stakeholders': they have a 'stake' or interest in it.)

1.4   Controlled performance

An organisation is responsible to its owners (or shareholders) and other stakeholders for the achievement of its collective goals. It clearly has to find reliable, systematic ways of ensuring that:

(a) its collective goals are known and understood by all members;

(b) the necessary resources (including members' time and effort) are secured and utilised in such a way that goals will be reached without undue risk, disruption or waste;

(c) they can tell whether, or to what extent, they have reached their goals – and if not, why not, and what can be done.

This is called control – hence 'controlled performance'.

Definition

> *Control* is the overall process whereby goals and standards are defined, and performance is monitored, measured against the goals and adjusted if necessary, to ensure that the goals are being accomplished.

At this point, we can suggest that management is the process of achieving controlled performance of the organisation's collective goals. Let's now look in more detail at what that involves.

2 WHAT IS MANAGEMENT?

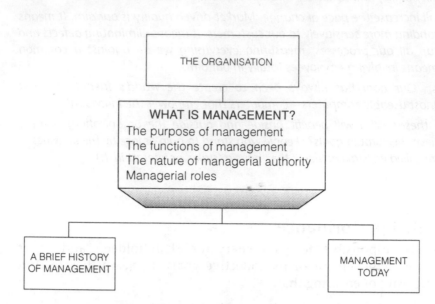

2.1 The purpose of management

Let's look again at our definition of an organisation as 'a social arrangement for the controlled performance of collective goals'. What does it suggest about the purpose of management?

(a) Collective goals have to be set for the organisation, and communicated to its members.

(b) These goals have to be met, and somebody has to ensure that this happens.

(c) The collective goals of the organisation have to be harmonised with the individual goals of its members, in order to secure their co-operation.

(d) Social arrangements – organisational structures and systems – have to be designed and maintained, so that:
(i)   the individual members 'pull' together without gaps or duplicated effort;
(ii) available resources are used to best effect; and
(iii) uncertainty and risk are reduced as far as possible.

(e) The organisation needs a collective or corporate identity in its dealings with its employees and other stakeholders. Somebody has to create and sustain this corporate identity and the shared values or culture that accompany it.

(f) Somebody has to look after the interests of the organisation's stakeholders, especially its owners (if they are not involved in the day to day running of the organisation themselves).

Management can be regarded as the catalyst which is essential for converting the inputs of the operation into valued outputs and, in the process, ensuring that stakeholders' needs are satisfied.

We will now look at what the management process means in terms of its basic functions.

2.2 The functions of management

The process and functions of management have been analysed in various ways by different writers. One of the first, and most influential, accounts of management functions was provided by the French industrialist Henri Fayol. Fayol listed the functions of management as follows.

(a) *Planning*. This essentially means looking to the future. It involves selecting the 'ends' which the organisation wishes to achieve (its objectives) and the 'means' (plans, policies, programmes and procedures) it will adopt in order to achieve them.

(b) *Organising*. The work to be done (in order to fulfil the plans) must be divided and structured into tasks and jobs, within a formal structure of authority and communication. Organising includes work scheduling (what is to be done when) and work allocation (who is to do what).

(c) *Commanding*. Fayol called this 'maintaining activity among the personnel'. It involves instructing and motivating subordinates to carry out tasks.

(d) *Co-ordinating*. This is the task of harmonising the activities of individuals and groups within the organisation, reconciling differences in approach, timing and resource requirements in the interest of overall organisational objectives.

(e) *Controlling*. This is the task of monitoring the activities of individuals and groups, to ensure that their performance is in accordance with the plans, standards and objectives set for them. Deviations must be identified and corrected.

We will be discussing each of these functions in detail in Section 2 of this text.

Activity 3 [10 minutes]

Using Fayol's functions of management, indicate under which of the five headings the activities below fall.

1   Ensuring that the sales department does not exceed its budget.

2   Deciding which products will form the main thrust of advertising during the next financial year.

3   Ensuring that new working practices are communicated to the workforce.

4   Ensuring that the sales department liaises with production on delivery dates.

5   Changing work schedules to reduce idle time.

Peter Drucker worked in the 1940s and 1950s as a business adviser to a number of US corporations. He argued that the manager of a business has another, overarching function: economic performance. In this respect, the business manager is different from the manager of any other type of organisation. The managers of a business can only justify their authority by the economic results they produce, even though as a consequence of their actions significant non-economic results occur as well: employee satisfaction, for example, or an attractive image in the community.

Fayol and Drucker did not suggest that managerial functions were only carried out by 'managers': they could be performed to an extent by any member of the organisation. In most Western companies, however, a separate group of people is responsible for planning, resourcing, co-ordinating and controlling their own work and the work of others. So what gives these people the right to make decisions about people and resources they do not own? Why should anybody listen to them or obey them?

2.3 The nature of managerial authority

Definitions

Power is the ability to do something, or to get others to do it.
Authority is the right to do something, or to get others to do it.
Responsibility is the liability of a person to be called to account for the way he has exercised the authority given to him. It is an obligation to do something, or to get others to do it.

In an organisation, the authority of managers to manage is given to them, or bestowed on them, by the organisation or its owners or stakeholders. A manager is usually given authority from above, by virtue of the position in the organisation hierarchy to which he has been appointed. On the other hand, an elected team leader, for example, is given authority from below. Either way, the scope and amount of the authority being given to a person should be clearly defined.

Authority is, in effect, 'passed' down the organisation structure, by a process called delegation.

Definition

Delegation is the process whereby superior A gives subordinate B authority over a defined area which falls within the scope of A's own authority.

Note from our definition that managers cannot bestow on others the right to make decisions which are outside the scope of their own authority. Managers are simply sharing their own authority. They are also sharing their responsibility – but not giving it away: A remains responsible (and accountable to his own boss) for the results of the tasks and decisions which have been delegated to B.

The delegated authority of a manager of a subordinate in a direct line down the chain of command is sometimes called *line authority*.

Activity 4 [20 minutes]

Bert Close has decided to delegate the task of identifying the reasons for machine 'down' time (when machines are not working) over the past three months to Brenda Cartwright. This will involve her in talking to operators, foremen and supervisors and also liaising with other departments to establish the effects of this down time. What will Bert need to do to delegate this task effectively? List at least four items he will need to cover with Brenda.

Power

You may have noticed that there is a difference between authority and power. It is quite possible for a person to have the right to do something – but not to be able to: to have the right to ask subordinates to perform a task – but to lack the power to make them do so. Within organisations, there may be respect for the authority of a manager's position, but this needs to be backed up by power. Any individual in the organisation may have power, of one or more of the following types.

(a) *Physical power* – the power of superior force. This is not usually used in organisations, but you might recognise elements of it, for example, in the armed forces or prison service – or in cases of physical intimidation or harassment at work.

(b) *Personal power* – the personal charisma and popularity of a particular individual.

(c) *Position power* – the power associated with a particular job or position in the organisation. As well as delegated authority, this may include power from:

(i)   access to information;
(ii) access to other powerful people and groups in the organisation;
(iii) control over rules and procedures, conditions of working and other
      influential factors.

(d) *Resource power* – control over resources which are valued by others. Managers, for
    example, control promotions and pay; trade unions control the availability of
    labour. (Think of strike action.) The amount of a person's power depends on
    how far he or she controls the resource, how much the resource is valued by
    others, and how scarce it is.

(e) *Expert power* – possessing knowledge and expertise which is recognised and
    needed by others. Many people in organisations have no direct line authority
    over operational functions, and have to rely on expert power to influence
    operational managers in matters which fall within their specialist area. For
    example, a personnel manager has no direct authority over sales staff, but when
    disciplinary action is required in the sales department, the personnel manager
    may have more influence than the sales manager, because of his or her training
    and experience in this area. This is sometimes called *staff authority*. If it is
    formalised in the organisation, so that the personnel manager (say) is
    responsible for disciplinary action in all departments of the organisation, this is
    called *functional authority*.

Activity 5 [20 minutes]

What kind of authority – line, staff or functional – do the managers have to secure
compliance with their wishes in the following cases?

(a) The chief accountant tells the production manager that she would like a report on
    the production department's expenditure on raw materials and wages.

(b) The production director tells the production manager that he would like the
    production department's shift-working changed to a more efficient system.

(c) The personnel director tells the production director that she would like the
    production department's shift-working changed to something less stressful to the staff.

We have now looked at the managerial functions required in the organisation, and
the various forms of influence managers require to perform them. Another way of
thinking about management is to observe what managers actually do, and to draw
conclusions about what 'roles' they are called upon to fill or 'act out'.

2.4   Managerial roles

Henry Mintzberg carried out research into how managers actually do their work,
and argued that: 'The classical view says that the manager organises, co-ordinates,
plans and controls; the facts suggest otherwise.' Managers do not spend scheduled
chunks of time analysing formal reports and systematically planning events:
managerial work is disjointed and fragmented, and planning is often conducted on
a day to day basis, in between more urgent tasks. Managers have to wear different
'hats', depending what is going on at the time.

Mintzberg identified ten managerial roles, which may be taken on as appropriate to
the personality of the manager and his subordinates, and to the nature of the task
in hand.

(a) *Interpersonal roles*. Roles adopted in relation to other people.
    (i)   *Figurehead*
          Performing ceremonial and social duties as the organisation's
          representative, for example at conferences. This is mainly the role of
          senior figures.

11

(ii) *Leader*

Selecting and training team members, and uniting and inspiring the team to achieve its objectives.

(iii) *Liaison*

Communicating with people outside the work unit (eg in inter-departmental meetings) or the organisation: building up an informal system of information exchange.

(b) *Informational roles.* According to Mintzberg, 'the manager does not leave meetings or hang up the telephone in order to go back to work. In a large part, communication is his work.' A manager is likely to have a wider network of contacts within and outside the organisation than his subordinates, so he is the best person to gather and spread information.

(i) *Monitor*

Receiving information from the environment and from within the organisation. Much of this may be obtained informally, say from chatting with contacts or subordinates: managers do not rely solely on formal reports.

(ii) *Disseminator*

Passing on information to subordinates.

(iii) *Spokesman*

Transmitting information to interested parties outside the work unit or organisation.

(c) *Decisional roles.* The manager's formal authority and access to information put him in a strong position to take decisions.

(i) *Entrepreneur*

Being a 'fixer', mobilising resources to get things done and to seize opportunities.

(ii) *Disturbance-handler*

Coping with the unexpected, rectifying mistakes and getting operations and relationships back on course when necessary.

(iii) *Resource allocator*

Distributing limited resources in the way that will most efficiently achieve defined objectives.

(iv) *Negotiator*

Bargaining – for example, for resources and influence.

The manager needs to have all these 'hats', putting on the right one(s) for each task and situation. A manager will wear some hats more than others: senior officials, for example, are more likely to be called upon to act as figureheads than team managers, who will be more concerned with resource allocation and disturbance-handling. In modern management theories, particular emphasis has been placed on leadership and entrepreneurship, at team level as well as organisational level: involving and committing employees to achieving goals, and focusing on creative action and resource mobilisation to get things done.

Activity 6 [15 minutes]

The *Telegraph Magazine* asked a cinema manager: 'What do you actually do?' The answer was as follows.

'Everything, apart from being the projectionist and cleaning the lavatories. My office is also the ticket office. If there's a big queue at the confectionery kiosk, I'll help serve and I'll usher people to their seats if we're really busy. Sometimes I go into the cinema before a show and tell the audience about any special events, such as a director coming to give a talk.

'I get in around lunchtime, deal with messages and ensure that the lights and heating are working. I write orders for posters and publicity pictures, popcorn and ice cream and deal with the correspondence for the 2,000 members on our mailing list. I'll brief the projectionist, ushers and kiosk staff and at about 1.45pm the first matinee customers arrive. Our afternoon audience is mainly elderly people and they take some time to settle, so I'll help them to their seats and only start the film when everyone is comfortable. In the evening, more ushers and bar staff arrive and I'll brief them about the programme, seating and timing. While the film is on, I'm selling tickets for the other screen, counting the takings and planning tomorrow. If I get a moment I try to grab something to eat.'

Which of Mintzberg's roles does this manager take on in his 'average' day?

3   A BRIEF HISTORY OF MANAGEMENT

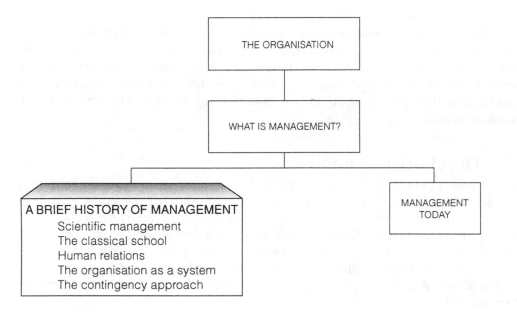

3.1   Scientific management

Frederick W Taylor (1865–1915) was among the first to argue that management should be based on 'well-recognised, clearly defined and fixed principles, instead of depending on more or less hazy ideas'. He pioneered the 'scientific management' movement which suggested that systematic investigation could indicate 'proper' methods, standards and timings for each operation in an organisation's activities. The responsibility of management was to select, train and help workers to perform their jobs 'properly'. The responsibility of workers was simply to accept the new methods and perform accordingly.

The practical application of this approach was to break each job down into its smallest and simplest component parts or 'motions': each single motion in effect became a separate, specialised 'job' to be allocated to a separate worker. Workers were selected and trained to perform such jobs in the most efficient way possible, eliminating all wasted motions or unnecessary physical movement.

its use

For discussion

A summary of scientific management, in Taylor's own words, might be as follows.

(a) 'The man who is fit to work at any particular trade is unable to understand the science of that trade without the kindly help and co-operation of men of a totally different type of education.'

(b) 'It is one of the principles of scientific management to ask men to do things in the right way, to learn something new, to change their ways in accordance with the science and in return to receive an increase of from 30% to 100% in pay.'

How well received do you think Taylor's comments would be by the workers in a modern factory?

Alterations to poor work methods and inefficient movements are used today, both to increase productivity and to reduce physical strain on workers. However, it has now been recognised that performing only one 'motion' within a job is profoundly unsatisfying to workers: operations need to be re-integrated into whole jobs. It has also been recognised that workers can and should take more responsibility for planning and decision-making in connection with their work, as we will see later in this chapter.

Scientific management was concerned primarily with tasks and techniques, but it was an early attempt to address the need for more controlled performance, in response to the increasing pace of change and industrial development in the Western world. A more balanced set of principles for management and organisation was put forward by the founders of modern organisation: the 'classical' school.

3.2   The classical school

Henri Fayol (1841–1925) was a French industrialist who put forward and popularised the concept of the 'universality of management principles': in other words, the idea that all organisations could be structured and managed according to certain rational principles. Fayol himself recognised that applying such principles in practice was not simple: 'Seldom do we have to apply the same principles twice in identical conditions; allowance must be made for different changing circumstances.' Among his principles of rational organisation, however, were the following influential ideas.

(a) *Division of work*, or specialisation. The most effective performance could be obtained by organising activities according to the expertise or resources required – allowing people, in effect, to 'stick to what they do best'. This encouraged functional organisation structures, with separate departments responsible for production, marketing, distribution and so on.

(b) *Matched authority and responsibility*. Managers should be given the authority or official 'right' to carry out the tasks assigned to them. They should always be held responsible for the exercising of that authority.

(c) *The scalar chain of command*. This is a term used to describe a formal organisation structure with a hierarchy from the highest to the lowest rank. Authority passes down the chain, as superiors give orders and instructions to subordinates: subordinates report back up the chain to their superiors. This creates the traditional view of the organisation structure as a pyramid-shaped chain or tree, as depicted in Figure 1.1

Figure 1.1 Organisation chart

(d) *Unity of command.* For any given activity, a subordinate should receive orders from only one boss. Overlap between departments, or missing out a link in the scalar chain causes uncertainty and wasted effort. Similarly, as far as the organisation is concerned, there should be unity of direction: one head and one plan for each area of activity, so that sub-units of the organisation are not pulling in different directions.

(e) *Subordination of individual interests.* The interest of one employee or group of employees should not prevail over the general interest of the organisation.

Fayol also emphasised the qualities of discipline (or outward signs of respect), equity (fairness, or justice towards employees), 'esprit de corps' (unity and a sense of belonging in the workforce) and initiative, which he thought should be encouraged and developed to the full.

Activity 7 [20 minutes]

Borderline Computers use project teams to carry out research, deal with customer needs and to introduce new systems. Identify which of Fayol's principles would clash with this method of working.

In the 1930s, scientific management was heavily criticised for dehumanising workers and treating them like a mere cog in the machine of production. This reflected not just a more enlightened philosophy of work, but a renewed understanding that organisations are made up of people – not just functions. By robbing the worker of any sense of contribution to the total product or task, the organisation was losing out on an important source of energy and creativity. A new approach set out to redress the balance.

3.3 Human relations

The 'human relations' approach emphasised the importance of human attitudes, values and relationships for the efficient and effective functioning of work organisations. Its pioneer, Elton Mayo (1880–1949) wrote: 'We have thought that first-class technical training was sufficient in a modern and mechanical age. As a consequence we are technically competent as no other age in history has been, and we combine this with utter social incompetence.'

Early work focused on the idea that people need companionship and belonging, and seek satisfaction in the social relationships they form at work. This emphasis resulted from a famous set of experiments (the Hawthorne Studies) carried out by Mayo and his colleagues for the Western Electric Company in the USA. The company was using a group of girls as 'guinea pigs' to assess the affect of lighting on productivity: they were astonished to find that productivity shot up, whatever they did with the lighting. Their conclusion was that: 'Management, by consultation with the girl workers, by clear explanation of the proposed experiments and the reasons for them, by accepting the workers' verdict in several instances, unwittingly scored a success in two most important human matters – the girls became a self-governing team, and a team that co-operated wholeheartedly with management.'

Mayo's ideas were followed up by various social psychologists (like Maslow and Herzberg whom we will meet later in this text), who shifted attention towards human beings' 'higher' psychological needs for growth, challenge, responsibility and self-fulfilment. Herzberg suggested that only these things could positively encourage or motivate employees to improved work performance.

This has had a profound affect on the way management is perceived – as we will see later in this chapter, when we look at fashionable concepts such as 'empowerment'.

For discussion

Peter Drucker warned that human relations thinking could manipulate workers just as effectively as bureaucratic rules, dictatorial management or scientific management techniques. It could be used as 'a mere tool for justifying management's actions, a device to "sell" whatever management is doing. It is no accident that there is so much talk in Human Relations about "giving workers a sense of responsibility" and so little about their responsibility, so much emphasis on their "feeling of importance" and so little making them and their work important.'

Do you think managers only pay lip service to 'enlightened' human relations approaches? If so, why?

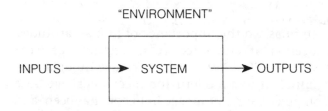

As we have seen, early theorists saw the organisation primarily as a structure of tasks and authority which could be drawn in an organisation chart. But that is like a snapshot of an organisation, showing what it looks like frozen at a particular moment in time. In fact, organisations are neither self-contained nor static: they are open systems.

3.4   The organisation as a system

There is no universally accepted definition of a system, but it can be described as 'an entity which consists of interdependent parts'. Every system has a 'boundary' which defines what it is: what is 'inside' and what is 'outside' the system. Anything outside the system is said to be its 'environment'.

In systems theory, it is possible to have a closed system, which is shut off from the environment and independent of it. An open system, however, is one which is connected to and interacts with its environment. It takes in influences from the environment and itself influences the environment by its activities, figure 1.2.

"ENVIRONMENT"

INPUTS ——→ SYSTEM —|—→ OUTPUTS

Figure 1.2 An open system

Organisations are open social systems. Why? They are social systems because they are comprised of people. They are open systems because those people participate in other social systems in the environment (such as the family or the class system) and bring with them all sorts of influences from the environment: advertising messages, family pressures, government demands (eg for tax), social attitudes and so on. In addition, the organisation itself takes in a wide variety of inputs, or resources, from the environment, and generates outputs to it as a result of its activities.

Activity 8   [20 minutes]

Suggest four inputs and five outputs of an organisational system.

The systems approach also emphasises the existence of 'sub-systems', or parts of a bigger system. An organisation is a 'structured socio-technical system', consisting of at least three sub-systems:

(a) *a structure*, (division of labour, authority relationships and communication channels);

(b) *a technological system* (the work to be done, and the techniques and tools used to do it); and

(c) *a social system* (the people within the organisation, the ways they think and interact with each other).

Looking at the organisation as a system helps managers to remember that:

(a) the organisation is not a static structure as conventional organisation charts suggest: it is continuously reacting to internal and external changes;

(b) sub-systems of the organisation each have potentially conflicting goals which must be integrated, often with some compromise;

(c) an awareness of the environment of the organisation (including competitor activity, technological change and customer needs) is vital if the organisation is to survive.

Activity 9   **[15 minutes]**

Below are a number of statements. Indicate whether they apply to the systems approach. Mark alongside T for True or F for False.

(a) The organisation is static.

(b) People, technology, organisation structure and environment are equally important in the systems approach.

(c) All sub-systems are in complete agreement.

(d) It is important that all employees are happy in their work.

(e) The organisation is aware of change affecting business.

(f) There is interdependence between all aspects of the organisation.

Once you see the organisation as a system, it becomes clear that there can be no 'one best way' to design and manage such dynamic and varied processes. This is where 'contingency theory' comes in.

3.5   The contingency approach

The contingency approach to organisation developed as a reaction to the idea that there are 'universal principles' for designing organisations, motivating staff and so on. Newer research indicated that different forms of organisational structure could be equally successful, that there was no inevitable link between classical organisation structures and effectiveness, and that there were a number of variables to be considered in the design of organisations and their style of management. Essentially, 'it all depends' on the total picture of the internal factors and external environment of each organisation. Managers have to find a 'best fit' between the demands of:

(a) the tasks;

(b) the people; and

(c) the environment

in their own particular situation.

We will note contingency approaches to various aspects of management as we proceed through this module.

Activity 10 [45 minutes]

Cobble and Carter is an accountancy practice. The partners now find that their present, highly bureaucratic methods of organisation are unsatisfactory. Customer needs are wide and varied, decision making is too slow and the staff are becoming demotivated. The partners now have to consider changing their methods to overcome the present difficulties and have decided to use a new approach. This would involve partners being responsible for various companies and they would be assisted by small teams.

(a) Give three advantages if they adopt this approach.

(b) Identify three areas they would need to consider and investigate before making a final decision.

4 MANAGEMENT TODAY

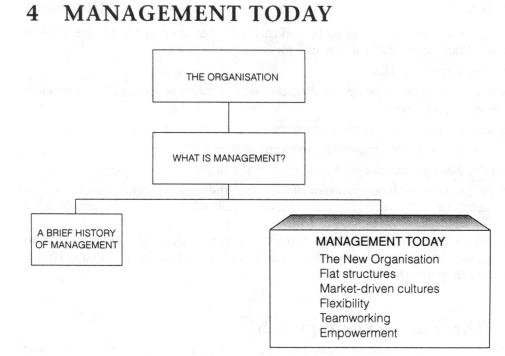

4.1 The New Organisation

In the past, the adoption of classical management principles meant that organisations developed the following characteristics.

(a) *Hierarchical* control through the chain of command.

(b) *Tall structure* with many layers of management and close supervision at each level.

(c) *Single function specialisms* like production and sales, with departments and careers concentrated in these single areas.

(d) *Focus on tasks and responsibilities* within well-defined jobs (as laid out in formal job descriptions) rather than on more flexible concepts such as customer service or using initiative.

(e) *Systems* which were reactive and procedure-bound ('sticking to the rules').

However, the economic downturn or recession, experienced across the world in the late 1980s and early '90s, reduced demand for many organisations' goods and services. This reduced the ability of organisations to carry superfluous staff (people who in Japan are known as 'window-watchers'), under-developed and underutilised. It also created buyers' markets, where the power was on the side of the consumer, who could take their business elsewhere if their needs were not being met.

Meanwhile, the problems associated with the management and performance of large classical organisations were highlighted: such organisations were incapable of the kind of flexibility and responsiveness required in constantly-changing, customer-driven markets.

Nowadays:

(a) *everything is international* – thanks to travel and information technology, we work in what has been described as a 'global village', with a global economy and marketplace;

(b) *everything is new* – organisations have come to appreciate that they are unlikely to survive unless they are responsive to the changing – and more demanding – expectations of their customers;

(c) *everything is faster* – you can order a tailor-made Toyota from a Tokyo car showroom and have it delivered 24 hours later;

(d) *everything is turbulent* – there is no going back to the peace and quiet of organisational stability in a world of slow social and technological change. Organisations must continue to cope with an essentially chaotic environment.

The New Organisation involves structures and cultures which can adapt swiftly to change and respond flexibly to customer demands.

So what is the New Organisation like? Commentators have identified trends towards: flatter organisation structures; market-driven cultures; flexible use of the labour resource; teamworking; and empowerment. Let's look at each of these, briefly, in turn.

4.2 Flat structures

Structures in the New Organisation are moving from tall, many-layered hierarchies to flat structures. This is called 'delayering'. It usually involves removing layers of middle management, whose function has traditionally been administration, supervision and liaison between senior management and front-line workers.

Activity 11 [15 minutes]

List three advantages to the organisation of delayering.

Delayering has been encouraged by:

(a) *improvements in information systems* – senior managers no longer need middle managers, in their informational roles as monitors and disseminators, in order to access the information they require for planning and control;

(b) *the trend towards team-working*, and specifically the development of 'empowered teams' (discussed below), given collective responsibility for directing and controlling their own work. This makes the middle manager's supervisory role redundant.

EXAMPLES

In 1990, the new chairman of BP announced 1,000 job losses, of which 160 were head office managers: a 30% cut.

Harley Davidson, in the US, cut the number of production controllers at one of its plants from 27 – to 1!

Keep an eye out in the press for further examples of this and the other management trends we discuss in this section...

4.3 Market-driven cultures

In the New Organisation values and cultures have changed.

From *'protective'* to *'productive'*.

Workers are encouraged to believe that, ultimately, they work for their customers, not their bosses. Instead of seeing themselves as performing functions, following procedures or holding down jobs, they are urged to focus on the task objectives, and issues such as quality, innovation, customer care and 'added value'.

Definition

Added value is an accounting term for the difference between the cost of raw materials and the sales price of the finished product: in other words, the value that is perceived to have been added to inputs by processing within the organisational system.

There is a focus on ends rather than means – so the means can be as flexible as the ends require.

From competitive individualism to teamwork and co-operation

Individual differences and self-interest are (theoretically) submerged in the focus on collective goals and objectives. This is partly possible because individuals' own needs are (theoretically) being satisfied by the increased challenge, responsibility and autonomy at work.

For discussion

We have used the word 'theoretically' about the benefits of team spirit. Do you think people basically 'look after Number 1', even within a close-knit team culture?

We will look more closely at teamworking below, and in detail in Chapter 6.

From security to flexibility

Workers are being taught to thrive on loose job descriptions, career mobility, continuous learning, training and retraining and so on. Recognition of organisations' need for constant innovation and creativity in order to keep pace with change has led to the development of the concept of the learning organisation.

A learning organisation culture encourages:

(a) continuous learning and knowledge generation at all levels;

(b) the free exchange and movement of knowledge around the organisation; and

(c) the transformation of new knowledge into new action.

This is not just about individual creativity, learning and development: it embraces the idea of groups – and the organisation as a whole – learning together. It also implies the involvement of all members, at all levels of the organisation, in the business of learning and developing in ways required by the market environment.

EXAMPLE

Motorola found themselves trying to compete globally in a market of new technologies and changing demands, with people who, in many cases, had difficulty with reading and basic mathematics. It launched a wide-ranging scheme of education and training (its own 'University') for its employees – and for the employees of suppliers and key customers. Training was designed to develop the person, not just the company and the job. It was aimed at 'creating an environment for learning, a continuous openness to new ideas... We not only teach skills, we try to breathe the very spirit of creativity and flexibility into manufacturing and management.' (Quoted by Pedler, Burgoyne, Boydell: *The Learning Company*).

As we have seen, the new cultural values are directed towards flexibility, co-operation and seeing the 'big picture'. We will now look at ways in which managers can organise for flexibility in its labour resource.

4.4   Flexibility

Re-integration of jobs

In the New Organisation, jobs are changing from simple, well-defined tasks (set out in job descriptions) to more flexible, multi-dimensional work. This new approach recognises that:

(a) performing a whole meaningful job is more satisfying to a worker than performing only one of its component tasks (as in 'scientific' job design);

(b) allowing workers to see the big picture enables and encourages them to contribute information and ideas for improvements, which might not otherwise have come to light;

(c) the focus on the task and overall objectives reduces the need for tight managerial control and supervision over work processes and practices.

Multi-skilling

Multi-skilling is the opposite of specialisation, with its tendency towards rigid job descriptions and demarcation lines between one job and another. It involves the development of versatility in the labour force, so that individuals can perform more than one task if required to do so: workers are being encouraged, trained and organised to work across the boundaries of traditional jobs and crafts. This has been difficult to achieve historically, because craft and occupational groups (such as trade unions) have supported demarcation in order to protect jobs and maintain special skills, standards and pay differentials. This situation is changing now that multi-skilled, flexible labour is highly prized in today's labour market.

> **EXAMPLE**
>
> *SmithKline Beecham*
>
> SmithKline Beecham has introduced multi-skilling at its factory in Irvine. This was accomplished across a great 'divide' of strict demarcation between operators (belonging to the Transport and General Workers' Union, TGWU) and craftsmen (represented by the Amalgamated Electrical and Engineering Union, AEEU). Further problems were posed by deeply-entrenched working practices, and the strong trade union traditions of Western Scotland.
>
> In the past, process operators faced with a blockage in the pipes (carrying materials from one stage of the process to another) had to tell their supervisor, who would tell the engineering foreman, who would send a fitter (a craftsman) to deal with it: meanwhile, production would grind to a halt. Analysis of such situations by working parties (drawn from all groups) resulted in the concept of the 'best person': instead of jobs being 'owned' by particular groups, the most appropriate individual to do a particular job should be trained and skilled to do it!

The benefits of multi-skilling to the organisation are as follows.

(a) It is an efficient use of manpower.
   (i) It smoothes out fluctuations in demand for different skills or categories of worker. As a simple example, take a secretarial services department. If audio typing, say, was in high demand one week, while shorthand dictation was going through a slack period, you would have a problem with specialised staff: there would be a bottleneck in audio typing, while shorthand staff were underutilised. If the secretaries could both type and take shorthand, the inefficiency would not arise.
   (ii) It may be possible to maintain a smaller staff, because you would not need specialists in each skill area.

(b) It puts an end to potentially costly demarcation disputes, where one category of worker objects to others 'invading' their area of work, as defined by narrow job descriptions.

(c) On the other hand, it is less likely that a task will be left undone because it does not explicitly appear on anybody's job description.

Activity 12
[15 minutes]

What does multi-skilling offer the employee?

Flexible working

In the New Organisation there is also increased flexibility in the deployment of the labour resource, or 'man hours'. With the shrinking demand for some categories of labour, ideas about full employment, full-time employment, 'one man, one job' and the '9 to 5' working day have had to be revised. When the demand for labour drops (permanently, seasonally or at random), organisations may be faced either with overmanning and idle time – or with having to lay people off or make them redundant. There are various ways of avoiding this.

(a) The employment of people on short- or fixed-term contracts, or annual hours contracts (an agreement of the number of hours to be worked per year instead of per day or week).

(b) The employment of non-permanent, non-career labour. This was a major growth sector in the 1980s and the trend seems to be continuing. Part-time work, casual labour, temporary working ('temping'), freelancing and consultancy are popular options, both for the workers and for the organisations who benefit from their services without long-term contractual obligations.

(c) Flexitime. Typically, the working day is split into two time zones: a 'core time', when employees must be at their job (commonly 10.00 to 16.00 hours) and a flexible time at the beginning or end of the day, when it is up to the employee to choose which hours to work. Employees may be asked to work a certain number of hours per day ('arrive late, work late'), or per week ('day off, make up the hours'). Annual hours and term-time contracts (allowing parents time off during school holidays) are even more flexible versions of the system.

Activity 13 [20 minutes]

Suggest three advantages to the organisation and to the worker of implementing a flexitime system.

For discussion

How flexible are you ready to be when it comes to:

(a) specialising in a particular knowledge or skill area in your career?

(b) having full-time, long-term employment?

(c) doing more training and learning throughout your working life?

One of the main features of a flexible organisation is focusing workers' attention on whole tasks. But individual workers will not necessarily have the skills or capacity (with only two hands and 24 hours in a day) to perform whole tasks themselves, within the timescales set by the organisation. This is where 'teamworking' comes in.

4.5   Teamworking

The basic work units of organisations have traditionally been specialised functional departments. In the New Organisation, they are more likely to be small, flexible teams. '*Chunking*' is a term coined to describe the breaking up of the organisation into smaller, more autonomous, more responsive, units.

what it is

Teamworking allows work to be shared among a number of individuals, so it gets done faster than by individuals working alone, without people:

(a) losing sight of their 'whole' task; or

(b) having to co-ordinate their efforts through lengthy channels of communication.

A team may be called together temporarily, to achieve specific task objectives (a project team), or may be more or less permanent, with responsibilities for a particular product, product group or stage of the production process (a product or process team).

There are two basic approaches to the organisation of team work.

Multi-disciplinary teams

Multi-disciplinary teams bring together individuals with different skills and specialisms, so that their skills, experience and knowledge can be pooled or exchanged. To an extent, this goes on in any case, at organisational level, but then it requires more elaborate mechanisms for communication and co-ordination. The following chart shows a multi-disciplinary structure, cutting across traditional functional boundaries. In effect, each team member has two bosses: the functional department manager who has line authority over him, and the project manager who has authority over his activity on the project. (This is called a *matrix* structure, see Figure 1.3.)

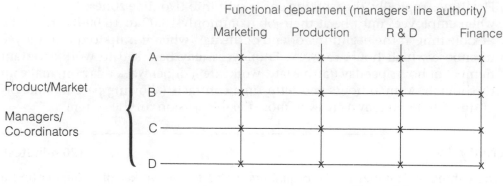

Figure 1.3 Matrix Structure

Teamworking of this kind encourages freer and faster communication between disciplines in the organisation, which:

(a) increases workers' awareness of their overall objectives and targets;

(b) aids co-ordination; and

(c) helps to generate solutions to problems, and suggestions for improvements, since a multi-disciplinary team has access to more 'pieces of the jigsaw'.

Multi-skilled teams

Instead of pooling the skills and knowledge of different specialists, a team may simply bring together a number of individuals, each of whom is functionally versatile or multi-skilled, and who can therefore perform any of the group's tasks. These tasks can then be shared out in a more flexible way between group members, according to who is available and best placed to do a given job at the time it is required.

The recognition that greater autonomy can – and perhaps should – be given to work teams is reflected clearly in the comparatively recent concept of empowerment.

4.6 Empowerment

Definition

Empowerment is the current term for making workers (and particularly work teams) responsible for achieving, and even setting, work targets, with the freedom to make decisions about how they are to be achieved. (In France, empowerment is called '*responsibilisation*'.)

Empowerment goes hand in hand with:

(a) *delayering*, since responsibility previously held by middle managers is, in effect, being given to operational workers;

(b) *flexibility*, since giving responsibility to the people closest to the product and customer encourages responsiveness – and cutting out layers of communication, decision-making and reporting speeds up the process;

(c) *new technology*, since there are more 'knowledge workers' in the New Organisation. Such people need less supervision, being better able to identify and control the means to clearly understood ends. Better information systems also remove the mystique and power of managers as possessors of knowledge and information in the organisation.

For discussion

'The people lower down the organisation possess the knowledge of what is going wrong with a process but lack the authority to make changes. Those further up the structure have the authority to make changes, but lack the profound knowledge required to identify the right solutions. The only solution is to change the culture of the organisation so that everyone can become involved in the process of improvement and work together to make the changes.' (Max Hand).

What does this suggest about the changes needed in the function of managers?

The change in organisation structure and culture as a result of empowerment can be shown as in figure 1.4.

Traditional hierarchical structure: fulfilling management requirements

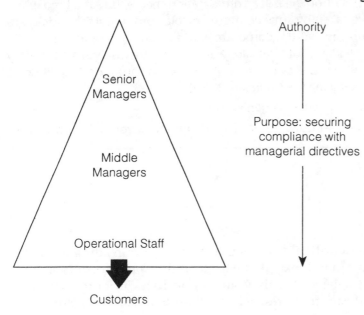

Empowerment structure: supporting workers in serving the customer

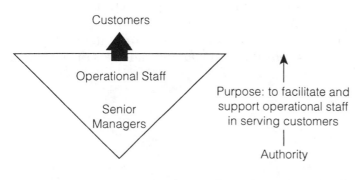

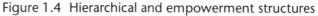

Figure 1.4 Hierarchical and empowerment structures

25

Activity 14 [30 minutes]

Semco is a Brazilian company which makes pumps, dishwashers and cooking units. The company has attracted enormous media and business interest. Here's why.

(a) All managers are rated by their subordinates every six months, on a scale of 1 to 100. Those managers who consistently under-perform are squeezed out.

(b) Workers elect their own boss: 'In a plant where everyone has a financial stake in its success, the idea of asking subordinates to choose bosses seems an eminently sensible way to stop accidents before they are promoted.'

(c) Workers set their own salaries – but they know they might price themselves out of the department's budget if they aim too high.

(d) The workers decide how much of the profits to share and how much to re-invest in the business.

(e) Workers are encouraged to work from home.

(f) Everyone 'from the cleaner upwards' has access to the company's books.

Semco's boss, Ricardo Semler, believes that democracy has been introduced to the work place: this is a radical departure from 'classical' organisation theory, but at a time when firms like IBM are being overtaken by smaller, more flexible competitors, his ideas are gaining currency. 'The trouble is that the corporate world is run by people not exactly busting keen to lose their parking lots, let alone to subject themselves to monthly scrutiny by people whom, currently, they can hire and fire. Even corporate turkeys don't vote for Christmas.' (Victor Keegan, *The Guardian*, 1993).

Compare Semco with a typical 'classical' organisation.

Read points (a) to (f) again and list how the classical organisation would deal with each.

5 WARNING!

This chapter has to conclude with a *caveat* about the danger of reading too much into changes which, when one looks at them carefully, apply to only a small minority of organisations (albeit a highly visible minority). Currently, corporate fashions dictate lean and mean structures, decentralisation of authority, autonomy for teams and a single-minded concentration on innovation and customer needs. But one might be entitled to assume (based on the evidence of the past few decades) that these are only fashions, and will not last forever. In future editions of this text, we may well be talking about the return to impressive corporate headquarters, the folly of fragmented management, the wasting of time on 'the quality of working life' when there is little work to be had, and the way information systems empower managers for closer supervision and control! Keep your eyes and ears open – and a pinch of salt handy.

Chapter roundup

- An organisation is a social arrangement for the controlled performance of collective goals.

- The structure of an organisation establishes how work is allocated and controlled; how people and activities are grouped together; and the channels through which authority and communication are distributed within the organisation.

- The functions of management traditionally include: planning, organising, commanding, co-ordinating and control. More people-centred approaches prefer the terms 'leadership' and 'motivation' to 'commanding' and add functions such as communication. In business organisations, the overall function of management is economic performance.

- A manager's job is not clear-cut and systematic in practice. Managers must be prepared to switch between a number of roles. Mintzberg classified managerial roles as interpersonal, informational and decisional. (If you want to remember the ten roles, you might try the following mnemonic, using the first letter of each: Few Likely Leaders Make Dull Speeches, Especially During Reward Negotiations!)

- Classical organisation and management theories emphasise issues of:
  — hierarchy and structure of authority
  — control by managers and technical specialists over workers and work
  — principles of 'good' organisation.

- Human relations approaches reacted against the impersonal rationality of classical theories and emphasised the importance of people, their relationships and attitudes at work.

- Later theories emphasised the organisation's openness to environmental influences, and its internal complexity. The organisation could be viewed as an open socio-technical system. Given this dynamic, complex nature, there could be no 'one best way to manage': the contingency approach basically says, 'It all depends ...'

- Most of the fashions in management today (including delayering, teamworking, multi-skilling, integrated job design and empowerment) are based on the need for more flexible organisation and management, in the face of change.

- Empowerment is the giving of responsibility or autonomy to workers, and specifically work teams.

Quick quiz

1   Why might people band together to form organisations?
2   What is an informal organisation?
3   Give three examples of things that identify an organisation's culture.
4   Why is management necessary for an organisation?
5   What is the management function of 'control'?
6   What is delegation?
7   Give an example of (a) physical power, (b) expert power and (c) resource power.
8   What is (a) line authority; (b) staff authority; (c) functional authority?

9 List Mintzberg's 'decisional' roles of a manager.

10 Which management theory did Frederick Taylor write about?

11 What is the principle of 'specialisation'?

12 What did the 'Human relations school' recognise?

13 Draw a diagram of the organisation as an open system, listing inputs and outputs.

14 Why is the contingency approach useful?

15 What does a learning organisation culture encourage?

16 What is delayering and what trends have encouraged it?

17 List four ways in which management can deploy the employee resource more 'flexibly'.

18 What are the benefits of multi-skilling to the organisation?

19 Why is empowerment particularly appropriate for teams?

20 What can teamworking in a matrix structure achieve?

Answers to quick quiz

1 To achieve personal and organisational goals and to fulfil personal needs.

2 An informal organisation is a loosely structured, flexible and spontaneous group, such as colleagues who have lunch together.

3 Assumptions, beliefs and values, self image, style.

4 To plan, organise, direct, co-ordinate, control.

5 To plan and monitor activities and correct any deviations.

6 The passing of tasks and responsibilities for which, the manager remains accountable.

7 (a) The army or prison service

(b) A personnel manager's knowledge of employment legislation

(c) Management's control over pay awards.

8 (a) That of a manager over subordinates

(b) Advice/services offered by a specialist

(c) Authority over policies or procedures that affect all departments of the organisation.

9 Entrepreneur, disturbance-handler, resource allocator, negotiator.

10 Scientific management.

11 Organising activities according to the expertise or resources required.

12 The importance of people and their needs at work.

13 Refer to section 3.4.

14 It encourages the organisation to be flexible.

15 Continuous learning and knowledge at all levels.

16 Removing layers of middle management. It was brought on by the trend towards team working and improvements in systems.

17 Short-or fixed term contracts; using part-time, casual or temporary labour; flexitime; freelance workers.

18 It smoothes out fluctuations in demand for different skills. It is possible to employ smaller numbers. It ends demarcation disputes.

19 They are totally involved in improvement, they work together to make changes, they become more flexible and they have power to make decisions.

20 It increases awareness of objectives and targets, aids co-operation and helps generate solutions and improvements.

Answers to Activities _____

1   The boys have identified three major functions of their business (sales, repairs and quality control) and two main product areas (guitars and drums). They might decide to structure the business in the following ways.

(a) Have one 'general manager' (whose responsibilities may include quality control) and three 'operatives' who share the sales and repair tasks.

(b) Divide tasks by function: have one person in charge of sales, one quality controller and two repairers (perhaps one for drums and one for guitars).

(c) Divide tasks by product: have a two-man drums team (who share sales/repair/control tasks between them) and a similar guitars team.

Since there are only four individuals, each (we assume) capable of performing any of the functions for either of the products, the lads may decide to have a looser social arrangement. They may prefer to discuss who is going to do what, as and when jobs come in. A larger organisation would not have this luxury ...

2   Corporate objectives might be formulated for:

(a) profitability;

(b) market standing (being a leader in the market, in relation to competition, and/or having a good reputation);

(c) productivity (efficient use of resources);

(d) innovation (new product development);

(e) public responsibility (involvement in community affairs, compliance with regulations eg on pollution or safety and so on).

3   Fayol's functions would define the activities: 1 = controlling; 2 = planning; 3 = commanding; 4 = co-ordinating; 5 = organising.

4   Your answer should include some of the following.

To delegate, Bert must identify the objectives of the task; explain the limits within which Brenda will work, such as liaising with the sales department but not contacting customers; establish deadlines; indicate in what format the results should be made (oral report, written report, memo); and agree how progress will be monitored (brief weekly meetings, weekly memo or informal chats).

5   Your answer should be similar to ours. Managers secure compliance using:

(a) Functional authority. (The chief accountant is likely to have a formal entitlement to this information, for the benefit of organisational control. It falls within her specialism of financial control, despite having to be prepared by the production department.)

(b) Line authority (within a department, down the chain of command).

(c) Staff authority. (The personnel director is unlikely to have any jurisdiction in the production department in such a matter – although her advice, as an expert in human resource management, may carry some weight.)

6   Your answer may well be that the cinema manager takes on all of Mintzberg's roles, although (a)(i) and (c)(iv) play a very minor part in his day.

7   Borderline Computers' methods would conflict with Fayol's principles of specialisation, the scalar chain of command, and unity of command. Sticking to those principles would prevent rapid decision-making and communication and reduce the efficiency of the teams' performance.

8 Inputs to an organisational system include:

    (a) materials, components and so on;

    (b) labour (ie employees);

    (c) money;

    (d) information and ideas.

    Outputs include:

    (a) goods and/or services;

    (b) trained and/or experienced labour;

    (c) money (dividends to shareholders, wages to employees and so on);

    (d) information;

    (e) environmental consequences of its activities (such as pollution or traffic);

    (f) social consequences of its activities (fashion trends, sensible or dangerous behaviour – wearing seatbelts or smoking – and so on).

9 Systems approach methods, applied to the given statements (True or False), are as follows. (a) F; (b) T; (c) F; (d) F; (e) T; (f) T.

10 Your answer, concerning Cobble and Carter's proposed change from the classical approach, should have included some of the following.

    (a) The advantage of the new approach is that they would be able to respond to different companies in relevant and effective ways. Decision making would be quicker. The smaller teams would feel more responsible for their work, thus increasing motivation. With the improved efficiency, cost savings would be increased.

    (b) They would need to consider staffing levels and redeployment, a logical division of customers, the specialist knowledge required, limits of authority and costs.

11 Delayering cuts costs. It also contributes to the flexibility and responsiveness of the organisation by speeding up communication and decision making, and keeping senior management closer to operations and to the customer. It allows the organisation to give more responsibility to (and get more input from) operational workers, which is a useful source of knowledge and perhaps of extra motivation and commitment.

12 The erosion of rigid specialisation and fragmented job design can offer:

    (a) a higher degree of job satisfaction, through variety of work and a greater understanding of its purpose and importance;

    (b) job security and material benefits, since a versatile, flexible employee is likely to be more attractive to employers, and have a higher value in the current labour market; and

    (c) personal skill development.

13 Benefits to the organisation include: improved staff morale (because of flexibility); less stressed/distracted staff (because problems outside work can be solved without the guilt attached to lateness); less absenteeism (because of the 'I'm late for work: I'd better not go at all' syndrome).

Benefits to the workers include: less frustration in rush-hour commuting; less pressure over needs like the dentist or school sports days; time to shop, socialise etc in off-peak times; satisfaction of choice.

14 Under the classical system (a): managers would be appraised by their managers; (b) managers would be appointed by the board or senior management; (c) salary levels would be set by top management; (d) this would be decided by the board/senior management; (e) this would not be encouraged (lack of management control); (f) not likely! Trade Union officials may be given information prior to wage negotiations.

Assignment 1 [About 1¹/₂ hours]

Six months ago Dawn Reeves, your friend in another section, was promoted to a first line supervisory position. She undertook her new duties enthusiastically and the output of her section has increased. Dawn, however, is not as happy as she used to be when she was an ordinary member of the section. 'I'm not sure I'm the type to be a supervisor,' she confided to you recently. 'There seems to be so much to do, but not a lot of it is what I call proper work.' This seems to be an ideal opportunity to talk to Dawn about 'managerial roles'.

(a) Note, in brief, what you would say to Dawn about managerial roles in general. Try to draw your answer from your own experience (and observation of others) rather than merely listing the traditional roles. Think about a teacher or parent if you have no work experience.

(b) List the key roles which Dawn should play in her current job.

Chapter 2

MANAGEMENT STYLE

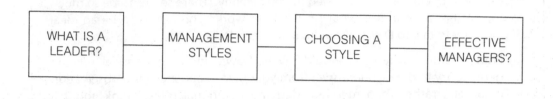

| WHAT IS A LEADER? | MANAGEMENT STYLES | CHOOSING A STYLE | EFFECTIVE MANAGERS? |

Introduction

Having looked at the nature of management in general, we can now turn to *managing people*. This corresponds to the function of management we have called 'commanding', 'directing' or 'leading'. As these varying terms suggest, there are different ways for managers to go about securing the co-operation and controlled performance of their staff. Some managers order people about; others try to persuade them; others encourage them to make their own decisions. So are these different types of manager, or different approaches or 'styles' that any manager can adopt? Is there a right or wrong way to handle people at work? And how does a manager decide which is the best way to go about it in his or her own situation? We will be answering such questions in this chapter.

Your objectives

After completing this chapter, you should:

(a) be able to distinguish between a manager and a leader;

(b) be aware of some of the major classifications of management style;

(c) be ready to adopt a contingency approach, and be able to identify factors which will determine the appropriate management style; and

(d) be able to evaluate the effectiveness of a given management style in a given situation.

1 WHAT IS A LEADER?

WHAT IS A LEADER?
Managers and leaders
Followership
Leadership traits

MANAGEMENT STYLES → CHOOSING A STYLE → EFFECTIVE MANAGERS?

1.1 Managers and leaders

The terms 'management' and 'leadership' are often used interchangeably, and it will not matter much whether you refer to 'management style' or 'leadership style', for example. However, it is worth noting that it is possible to distinguish between the two ideas.

(a) The functions of management, as we discussed in Chapter 1, include planning, organising, co-ordinating and controlling. Management is primarily concerned with logic, structure and control. If done well, it produces predictable results, on time.

(b) Leadership, properly considered, involves a different kind of function, and – it may be argued – a rather different mind set. It involves essentially people-centred activities, with effects potentially beyond the scope of controlled performance. A leader's special function is to:

   (i) *create a vision* of something different to the current status quo;

   (ii) *communicate the vision*. This will be particularly powerful if it meets the needs – conscious or unconscious – of other people, and if the leader can give it credibility in their eyes;

   (iii) *energise, inspire and motivate* others to translate the vision into achievement;

   (iv) *create the culture* that will support the achievement, through shared language, rituals, myths, beliefs and so on.

In other words, while managers have authority by virtue of their position in the organisation to secure the obedience or compliance of their subordinates, leaders direct the efforts of others through vision, inspiration and motivation – forms of *influence*.

Definition

Influence is the process by which an individual or group exercises power to determine or modify the behaviour of others.

For routine work, mere compliance with directives may be sufficient for the organisation's needs. However, if it wishes to secure extra input from its employees – in terms of co-operation, effort and creativity – it may strive for the inspirational quality of leadership, over and above efficient management.

Activity 1   [10 minutes]

We often say that managers (as leaders) should motivate people to put forth extra *effort*. Above, we also use the word *energy*. As it happens, there are lots of words – all beginning with 'E' – which express the kinds of things managers would like to elicit from their staff. Charles Handy called them 'E Factors'. See if you can think of at least five more.

It should be clear that leadership is not merely a function that leaders themselves perform, or a set of techniques that they follow. Like beauty, leadership is largely in the eyes of the beholder: managers can only be called leaders if and when they have an inspiring, energising and motivating influence on their subordinates. A leader must have followers.

1.2 Followership

Some well-known writers on management have suggested that: 'The essence of leadership is followership. In other words, it is the willingness of people to follow that makes a person a leader.'

Leadership requires a conscious intention on the part of the leader to influence others. If you yawn, for example, and others around you feel an urge to do the same, it would more properly be called 'behavioural contagion' than leadership.

Activity 2 [20 minutes]

Suppose you were in a cinema and smelt smoke. How would you categorise the following possible actions on your part? Your options are behavioural contagion, management, and leadership.

(a) You rush to the door screaming 'Fire!' and everyone follows you.

(b) You rush to the door, switch on the lights, hit the fire alarm, and, grabbing a fire extinguisher, start looking for the source of the fire. People start moving towards the exits when they hear the fire alarm.

(c) You rush to the door, switch on the lights, shout for people not to panic but to move towards the exits (which they do) and ask for help to locate the fire and get the fire extinguishers (which you get).

(d) You do any or all of the above, but nobody takes any notice.

It is possible for an isolated individual to be a manager – but a leader requires people to influence: he or she will always be involved with people and groups, sensitive to their needs and behaviour, part of their networks of communication and influence. People tend to follow those whom they see as a means of satisfying their own personal goals. For managers to become effective leaders, they need to understand what motivates their subordinates, and what 'makes them tick'. (We will be looking at several aspects in the following chapters.)

Followership implies – as you may realise from your own experience – that leaders, unlike managers, are not always formally appointed to positions of delegated authority. Leaders *may* be appointed 'heads' – say military officers or business managers. They may, however, *emerge* out of the situations, activities and interrelationships of groups: think of gang leaders, or ringleaders in political protests. All leaders are, in a sense, elected, or at least recognised, by their followers.

For discussion

Select a number of historical (or fictional) figures whom you would identify as 'leaders'.

(a) Why do you think of them as 'leaders' (as opposed to 'heads')?

(b) What qualities in them and/or their context (the task that needed doing, tradition, hereditary 'headship' and so on) attracted followership?

(c) Were they viewed in the same light by everyone – in their own context, and in your discussion group?

It is often said of an influential person that (s)he is (or was) a 'born leader'. But is leadership something you've either got or not? The fact that you are studying management suggests that people can learn to be leaders – and we have already noted that situations can create leaders. On the other hand, your examples of leaders (if you did the discussion exercise above) may have appeared to have certain traits – such as charisma – in common.

1.3 Leadership traits

Early theorists suggested that the capacity to get others to do what you want them to do was an innate characteristic: you either had it, or you didn't. Studies on leadership focused on qualities, personality characteristics or 'traits' which were thought to make a good leader.

It seemed possible to show a significant correlation between leadership effectiveness and the traits of intelligence, initiative, self assurance and individuality – as you might expect.

Other supposed leadership traits included personal magnetism or charisma, (literally, 'gift from God'), interpersonal skills, analytical thinking, imagination, decisiveness, trustworthiness, persuasiveness, self-motivation, flexibility and vision. This list is by no means exhaustive, and various writers attempted to show that their selected list of traits were the ones that provided the key to leadership.

There are, however, several difficulties with the idea of leadership as a bundle of 'traits' or personal characteristics.

(a) The full list of traits is so long that it appears to call for a person of superhuman gifts. Nor, at best, does it help organisations to make better managers or leaders: it merely helps them recognise a leader when they see one.

(b) No two authorities agree on exactly which traits make an effective leader.

(c) Most of the traits listed are positive or desirable characteristics for human beings. Seldom is there any recognition of the possibility that leaders could be flawed individuals, or that their flaws may be the very features which enable them to succeed as leaders: ruthlessness, for example.

(e) Observation of actual successful leaders furnishes unreliable conclusions about leadership traits. If a leader takes risks and succeeds, then he is labelled 'courageous' and 'visionary'; if he takes risks and fails, he is merely 'foolhardy'.

(f) The trait approach does not take into account the individuality of followers, nor other factors in the leadership situation.

Though superficially attractive, and still entrenched in popular thinking, the trait or 'great man' approach to leadership is now largely discredited. Later approaches concentrate on the idea that leadership is a 'style' of relating to people and tasks, and that appropriate styles could be learned and adopted to suit different leadership situations. We will now look at a well-known classification of management style.

2 MANAGEMENT STYLES

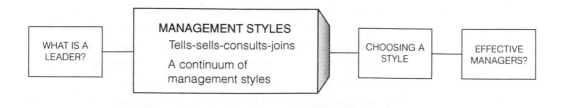

2.1 Tells – sells – consults – joins

Ashridge Management College carried out research in several industries in the UK to develop a classification of management styles. The Ashridge Studies (as the research came to be known) found four broad styles in use.

Style	**Tells** *(autocratic)*
Characteristics	The manager makes all the decisions, and issues instructions which must be obeyed without question.
Strengths	(1) Quick decisions can be made when speed is required.
	(2) It is the most efficient type of leadership for highly-programmed, routine work.
Weaknesses	(1) Communication between the manager and subordinate will be one-way. There may be lack of helpful feedback.
	(2) It does not encourage contribution or initiative from subordinates.
Style	**Sells** *(persuasive)*
Characteristics	The manager still makes all the decisions, but explains them to subordinates, and attempts to motivate subordinates to carry them out willingly.
Strengths	(1) Selling decisions to staff might make them more willing.
	(2) Staff will have a better idea of what to do when unforeseen events arise in their work, because the manager will have explained his intentions.
Weaknesses	(1) Subordinates will not necessarily be committed to decisions in which they have not been involved.
	(2) It may be felt to be a 'tells' style dressed up with pretended concern for employees' views.
Style	**Consults** *(participative)*
Characteristics	The manager confers with subordinates and takes their views and feelings into account, but retains the right to make the final decision.
Strengths	(1) Employees are involved in decisions. This encourages motivation through greater interest and involvement.
	(2) Employees can contribute knowledge and experience, to help in solving problems related to their work.
Weaknesses	(1) It might take longer to reach decisions.
	(2) Subordinates might be limited in their viewpoint on organisational issues.
	(3) If the manager does not take employees' advice, they might perceive the process to be meaningless.
Style	**Joins** *(democratic)*
Characteristics	Leader and followers make the decision together, on the basis of consensus, or compromise and agreement.
Strengths	(1) It can provide high commitment to the decision reached.
	(2) It takes advantage of the knowledge and expertise of individuals in different areas, for high quality, flexible decision-making.
Weaknesses	(1) The authority of the manager might be undermined.
	(2) Decision-making might become a very long process.
	(3) Clear-cut decisions might be difficult to reach.

Activity 3 [15 minutes]

Which of the four Ashridge classifications would you expect:

    (a) to be most popular with subordinates?

    (b) to be perceived by subordinates as the most common style?

    (c) to create most favourable attitudes towards work?

The four-style classification should not be seen as pigeon-holes into which a particular manager's style must fit. In fact, they are points along a 'continuum' or range of styles.

2.2 A continuum of management styles

Looking at management styles as a continuum or 'range' helps us to remember that they are highly flexible, and adaptable according to circumstances. Figure 2.1 shows one model which addresses a range of situations, albeit only in one dimension: the extent to which the manager retains and exercises control.

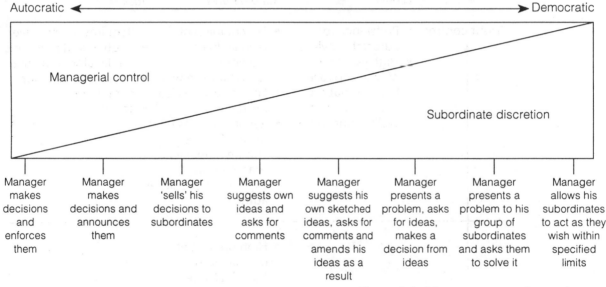

Figure 2.1 Management style continuum

So which style is the 'right' one? Which works best? A contingency approach to management suggests that a style which is appropriate and effective in one situation will not necessarily work in another. 'It all depends' on a number of variables in the leader's situation. In the following section, we will consider what some of those variables might be.

3 CHOOSING A STYLE

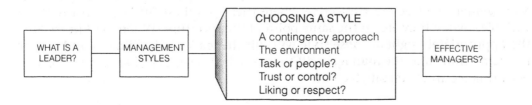

3.1   A contingency approach

Charles Handy suggested a contingency approach to leadership.

According to Handy, the factors in any situation which influence the effectiveness of a particular management style are as follows.

(a) *The leader* (his or her personality, character and preferred style of operating).

(b) *The subordinates* (their individual and collective personalities, and their preference for a style of leadership).

(c) *The task* (the objectives of the job, the technology of the job, methods of working and so on).

(d) *The environment of management* (which we will discuss below).

Handy placed each of his three main variables on a version of the autocratic-democratic continuum, which he called a spectrum, ranging from 'tight' to 'loose' management control. Note that this spectrum (Figure 2.2) does not describe tight and loose styles of management themselves: you can think of them as 'tells' and 'joins' respectively. Instead, it describes the *conditions* in which a tight or loose style would be appropriate.

	Leader	Subordinates	Task
Tight control	• Preference for autocratic style • High estimation of own capabilities • Low estimation of subordinates • Dislikes uncertainty	• Low opinion of own abilities • Do not like uncertainty in work • Like to receive clear instruction • Regard work as trivial • Inclined, through culture or expectation (based on past experience), to accept authority	• Requires no initiative • Routine and repetitive • Predictable outcome • Short time scale for completion • Trivial
Loose control	• Preference for democratic style • Confidence in subordinates • Dislikes stress • Accepts reasonable risk and uncertainty	• High opinion of own abilities • Like challenge • Regard work as important • Prepared to accept uncertainty and longer time scales for results • Inclined, through culture or past experience, to value independence	• Complex and non-routine • Involving problem-solving or decision-making • Long time scales • Important

Figure 2.2 Choosing a management style

Handy argues that leadership style should be tight or loose according to the conditions in each of these areas, reflecting their position on the spectrum. Management will be most effective where there is a 'best fit' between the three variables: when they are on the same point of the spectrum. When 'best fit' occurs, the appropriately tight or loose style will suit the leader, subordinates and task at the same time, and the manager will therefore be successful in all areas: effective performance and team satisfaction.

In practice, there is likely to be a lack of fit, and the leader must decide which factor(s) should be changed to bring all three into line as far as possible. His or her own behaviour and style are easiest to address, in the short term, because they are most within the leader's control: hence the great emphasis on leadership in management literature, Handy argues. However, longer-term benefit might be achieved from tackling the other variables. If a manager wanted to create fit further towards the loose end of the spectrum, for example, (s)he could consult more, *or* could try to develop the confidence and abilities of the subordinates, *or* redefine the task to create more complex, integrated jobs with greater responsibility.

Activity 4 [30 minutes]

Suggest an appropriate style of management for each of the following situations. Think about your reasons for choosing each style in terms of the results you are trying to achieve, the need to secure commitment from others, and potential difficulties with both.

(a) Due to outside factors, the personnel budget has been reduced for your department and one-quarter of your staff must be made redundant. Records of each employee's performance are available.

(b) There is a recurring administrative problem which is minor, but irritating to everyone in your department. Several solutions have been tried in the past, but without success. You think you have a remedy which will work, but unknown problems may arise, depending on the decision made.

(c) A decision needs to be made about working hours. The organisation wishes to stagger arrival and departure times in order to relieve traffic congestion. Each department can make its own decisions. It doesn't really matter what the times are, so long as department members conform to them.

(d) Even though they are experienced, members in your department don't seem to want to take on responsibility. Their attitude seems to be: 'You are paid to manage, we are paid to work: you make the decisions'. Now a decision has come up which will personally affect every person in your department.

3.2 The environment

However appropriate a particular style may be to the leader, subordinates and task, its effectiveness in practice may be constrained by other factors in the organisational context or 'environment' of leadership.

(a) *The position of power held by the leader in the organisation and work group.* A comparatively powerless leader may simply not be allowed to control the variables to achieve best fit, however clear the need to do so.

(b) *Organisational norms, structure and technology.* If the organisation has a tradition of autocratic leadership, for example, it will be difficult to introduce a participative style. If routine and repetitive work is 'built in' to the technology (eg an assembly line), challenging tasks will be difficult to create, and creative, flexible staff difficult to retain.

(c) *The variety of tasks and subordinates.* Placing the nature of the task on the loose-tight spectrum is difficult, if a group's activity varies from routine and simple to complex one-off problem-solving. Similarly, individuals within the work group are likely to be different (and changing, as members leave and arrive through labour turnover): some may require loose control and other tight control. (This is one reason why team building is so important, as we will see in Chapter 6.)

Activity 5 [20 minutes]

List four ways in which an organisation, by dealing with 'environmental constraints' can help its managers to adopt an appropriate management style.

We have already mentioned that managers have a dual responsibility for task achievement and for the satisfaction (or at least co-operative action) of people. Management often seems to involve a compromise, juggling or 'best fit' of these two aims. We will now look more closely at this and other managerial dilemmas: some of the tough choices managers face as they select and adopt a management style.

3.3 Task or people?

Our contingency approach assumes that management effectiveness can be measured according to:

(a) task achievement; or

(b) the fulfilment of individual and group needs; or

(c) both.

In order to adopt an appropriate leadership style, a manager has to ask: *what do I want to achieve?*

Research at Michigan and Harvard appeared to show that there were two distinct types of leader: 'task leaders', who were concerned with results and the structuring of activities, and 'socio-emotional' leaders, who were concerned with supportive and satisfying group practices and relationships.

However, another set of leadership studies (at Ohio State) suggested that, while concern for production/task structures and concern for people were two distinct dimensions, they were not mutually exclusive: a manager could have both concerns at the same time.

Blake's Managerial Grid

Robert Blake and Jane Mouton devised a 'grid' model showing how concern for people and concern for production could be combined in varying proportions, and what kind of management style would result, see Figure 2.3.

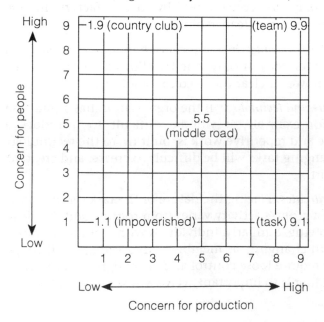

Figure 2.3 Blake and Mouton's managerial grid

Blake defined the extreme cases shown on the grid as follows.

(a) *1.1: impoverished*. The manager is lazy, showing little effort or concern for either staff or work targets.

(b) *1.9: country club*. The manager is attentive to staff needs and has developed satisfying relationships. However, he pays correspondingly little attention to achieving results.

(c) *9.1: task management*. Almost total concentration on achieving results. People's needs are virtually ignored and conditions of work are so arranged that people cannot interfere to any significant extent.

(d) *5.5: middle of the road*. The manager achieves adequate performance through balancing the necessity to meet work targets with maintaining the unity and morale of the group. (There is also a 'statistical 5.5', where the manager averages out at 5.5 by constantly veering between extremes.)

(e) *9.9: team*. The manager achieves high performance by leading people, who are committed to, and satisfied by, fulfilling task objectives.

Clearly, the most efficient manager combines high concern for the task with high concern for people: a 9.9.

The main value of the Managerial Grid is in the appraisal of managers' performance. Individual managers can be placed on the grid, usually using a questionnaire in which they have to choose between statements which represent different points on the grid. (See the Activity below.) A manager should then be able to see in which area his or her performance could be improved: a manager rated 3.8 for decision-making, for example, has further to go in improving the *quality* of his or her decisions than in *involving subordinates* in the decision-making process.

Activity 6 [15 minutes]

Here are some statements about a manager's approach to meetings. Which position on Blake's Grid do you think each might represent?

(a) I attend because it is expected. I either go along with the majority position or avoid expressing my views.

(b) I try to come up with good ideas and push for a decision as soon as I can get a majority behind me. I don't mind stepping on people if it helps a sound decision.

(c) I like to be able to support what my boss wants and to recognise the merits of individual effort. When conflict arises, I do a good job of restoring harmony.

Reddin's 3-D management grid

Professor Reddin argued that a simple task-people model is limited in its usefulness, compared to more thorough contingency approaches which allow for other variables. We may assume that a 1.1 manager is ineffective, because he simply follows rules, with little concern for people or task achievement, but in fact he may be *effective* in certain circumstances: for example, in a bureaucratic organisation, which functions steadily within its framework of rules and procedures.

Reddin therefore added a third dimension to Blake's grid: effectiveness (or ineffectiveness) according to the situation. For each of the combinations of task/people concern, there are two possible management styles. A 1.1 manager in an appropriate situation would be called a 'bureaucrat' and may well be effective: in an inappropriate situation, the same manager would be called a 'deserter', and would be ineffective. A 9.9 manager in an appropriate situation would be called an 'executive' (effective), but in an inappropriate situation he could be viewed merely as a 'compromiser' (ineffective).

You may already have picked up on another managerial dilemma, as we've talked about the range of management styles from autocratic to democratic, or from 'tight' to 'loose'. In order to adopt an appropriate style, a manager has to consider how far he can trust his subordinates to work well without tight control – and whether they will work well with tight control!

3.4 Trust or control?

The trust-control dilemma

Charles Handy identified what he called a 'trust-control dilemma' in management relationships. He expressed it as a simple mathematical equation.

$$T + C = Y$$

where T = the trust the superior has in the subordinate, and the trust which the subordinate feels the superior has in him

C = the degree of control exercised by the superior over the subordinate

Y = a constant, unchanging amount, so that any increase in C leads to an equal decrease in T and vice versa.

If the superior lacks trust (less T) in a subordinate, he will exercise greater control or authority (more C) over his activities, and the subordinate will recognise that he is being trusted less. If the superior wishes to show more trust in the subordinate (more T), he will have to delegate more authority to him, thereby reducing his own control over the work (less C).

Why might this be a problem?

The problem of delegation

In any large or complex organisation, a manager will have to delegate some authority to subordinates because:

(a) there are physical and mental limitations to the work load of any individual;

(b) routine or less important decisions can be passed 'down the line', freeing the superior to concentrate on more important aspects of the work (like planning) which only (s)he has the authority to perform;

(c) employees in today's organisations have high expectations with regard to job satisfaction, including participation in decision-making;

(d) the continuity of management depends on subordinates gaining some experience of management processes in order to be 'groomed' for promotion.

However, in practice many managers are reluctant to delegate and attempt to perform routine tasks and decision-making which could be handed down to subordinates. Among the reasons for this reluctance one can commonly identify:

(a) low confidence and trust in the abilities of the subordinates: the suspicion that 'if you want it done well, you have to do it yourself';

(b) the burden of responsibility and accountability for the mistakes of subordinates;

(c) a desire to stay in touch with the department or team – workload and people: particularly if the manager does not feel at home in a management role and/or misses aspects of the subordinate job, or camaraderie;

(d) unwillingness to admit that subordinates have developed to the extent that they could perform some of the manager's duties: the threat of redundancy;

(e) poor control and communication systems in the organisation, so that the manager feels (s)he has to do everything personally, if (s)he wants to keep track of what is going on;

(f) lack of understanding of what delegation involves: that is, not giving subordinates total control;

(g) a desire to operate with one's personal 'comfort zone', doing familiar, easy jobs and thereby avoiding risky and difficult management tasks.

Activity 7 [20 minutes]

Suggest 4 ways in which senior management (or the organisation) can encourage managers to delegate more.

Assumptions about subordinates

To a large extent, the extent to which a manager trusts subordinates and feels able to delegate authority to them will depend on his or her assumptions about how they will behave. Douglas McGregor formulated perhaps the best-known framework for talking about this. He described the two extremes of attitude that a manager might have about his subordinates, and labelled them Theory X and Theory Y.

Theory X is the assumption that the average human being dislikes work and will avoid it unless he is coerced, controlled, directed and threatened with punishment. He actually prefers to be directed, since he fears responsibility and wants security above all.

A manager who operates on the basis of Theory X will feel he has to direct and control workers with specific instructions, close supervision and rigid task structures. (This is, to an extent, a self-fulfilling prophecy: if a manager controls his subordinates *as if* they are hostile to work and to the organisation, he will usually create conditions in which they will genuinely become hostile to work and to the organisation!)

Theory Y is the assumption that the ordinary person does not naturally dislike work and does not require tight control in order to put in effort. He is motivated by the desire for personal growth and achievement, and will exercise self-direction and self-control and actively seek responsibility, if he is committed to the task.

A manager who operates on the basis of Theory Y will try to integrate subordinates' needs for development and self-expression with the organisation's objectives, so that both can be achieved together. He will tend to use a democratic or consultative style in order to obtain subordinates' involvement and commitment to the task, and will tend to encourage them to take on more responsibility and more challenging work.

For discussion

'Look to the ant, you sluggard; consider its ways and be wise! It has no commander, no overseer or ruler, yet it stores its provision in summer and gathers its food at harvest.' (The Bible, Book of Proverbs 6: 6–9)

What does this ancient idea suggest about the nature of managerial control?

Activity 8 [40 minutes]

Malcolm Ross is head of operations at Disneyland Paris. An article about him in *The Times* (5/8/95) described aspects of the culture and mechanisms of management in the 'Magic Kingdom'.

'Ross cuts an impressive figure on first sighting – red shirt, dark green suit, brown slip-ons, and a large white badge bearing the name Malcolm. He wears a gold-plated Mickey Mouse watch and comes laden with electronic gadgets. Keeping tabs on 6,000 theme park employees – "cast members" in Disney-speak – requires an elaborate communications network. "We keep in touch using mobile phones, beepers and a ten-channel radio system," he says, steering me past immaculate flowerbeds and cascading waterfalls. Cast members are equipped with CIA-style black earpieces, and communicate in code. Ross's call-sign is Magic Kingdom. "There is only one Magic Kingdom", he chuckles....

'Ross spends at least an hour a day mixing with the guests, taking in a show, sampling a ride. "It's management by walking about", he says, stooping to pick up a scrap of litter. "It's very important for me to touch and feel the pulse of the park...".

'Anyone about to enter Ross's office is confronted by the words *Hakuna Matata*, from the film *The Lion King*. "It means 'No Worries'", says Ross's secretary... "whoever goes through that door had better have good news." '

(a) What type of control is being used here?

(b) Is Malcolm Ross a Theory X or Theory Y manager?

(c) Give at least three effects that his style of management may have on the employees.

(You might like to know that the *staff* nicknames for the 'Magic Kingdom' are apparently 'Mouseschwitz' – after a notorious Nazi concentration camp – and 'Neuro-Disney' ...)

3.5 Liking or respect?

This is a tough question. It relates to managerial effectiveness: will the team give more to a manager they like, or to one they respect – or even fear? It also touches on the needs of the manager as a person.

(a) On the one hand, a manager has needs for belonging, relationship and approval. (Self esteem depends to a large extent on being liked by others.)

(b) On the other hand, a manager needs to be in control, in order to achieve objectives.

Managers who are responsible for task performance will inevitably have to make decisions that will be unpopular with all or some of their team members. Individuals have different needs and expectations, only some of which will be in harmony with those of others and with organisational goals. Resources are limited, and individuals are in competition for them. So consensus decisions, even moderately pleasing to everybody, will not always be possible – and unpleasant decisions (such as disciplinary action or redundancies) may be required.

Taking a contingency approach, we can see that how a manager resolves this dilemma will depend on:

(a) *the strength of the individual manager's need to be liked*, which in turn will depend on the availability of other supportive, loving relationships in his or her life;

(b) *the attitude of the team members* – some may take advantage of a boss who tries to be 'one of the lads'; some may feel insecure with a boss who does not seem to exercise authority or face up to responsibility; others may thrive on being treated as a peer;

(c) *the nature of the task or decision* – if the task is basically incompatible with individual/group needs (for example, the work is dangerous or boring), the manager will not be able to fulfil task objectives and stay popular.

Activity 9   **[About 1 hour]**

Scott Peck, a well-known American psychiatrist and writer, was appointed director of psychiatry at the US Army Medical Corps. He was responsible for a department of about forty people, mostly professionals, and mainly young. He had never managed anybody before. He later wrote: 'I was perfectly clear in my own mind about what my management style would be: I was going to be just as different from every authoritarian boss who had ever been in charge of me as I could possibly be... Not only did I never make an administrative decision without consulting everyone involved; I did my very best to see that, within the constraints of professional competence, the people under me made their own decisions wherever possible about the matters that affected their own lives... I discouraged them from addressing me as "Major Peck". Soon everyone was calling me Scotty. I was "Mr Nice Guy". And it worked. The mood was euphoric... The department morale was superb.'

After about six months, however, morale began to suffer; petty bickering broke out; tasks began to be neglected. Things came to a head when the department had to plan a move to a new medical complex: there were fights over who got what office, while the packing process fell way behind schedule. In a confrontational meeting about the problem, someone complained that the department was 'all at sea'. Scott Peck reappraised his leadership.

(a) Identify three main reasons for the breakdown in morale.

(b) What suggestions would you make to Scott Peck to get his department performing effectively?

4   EFFECTIVE MANAGERS?

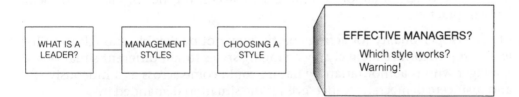

4.1   Which style works?

We have already recommended a contingency approach to this question, which suggests that 'it all depends'. However, it is worth taking note of some major experience-based research into leadership style and effectiveness.

Rensis Likert asked the question: 'What do effective managers have in common?' He found that four main elements are normally present in any effective manager.

(a) *They expect high levels of performance.* Their standards and targets are high and apply overall, not only to their subordinates' performance, but also to other departments and their own personal performance.

(b) *They are employee-centred.* They spend time getting to know their team and developing trust, so that people feel able to air any problems. When necessary, their actions can be hard, but are always fair. They face unpleasant facts in a constructive manner and help their staff to develop a similar attitude.

(c) *They do not practise close supervision.* Effective managers are aware of their team's capabilities and, within those parameters, help them to define their own performance targets. Once this has been done they monitor the results, rather than the activity. In this way, managers develop their team and free themselves for other managerial functions.

(d) *They operate a participative style of management as a natural style.* This means that if a job problem arises, they do not impose a favoured solution, but put the problem to the people involved. They support the team in implementing whatever solution is agreed.

Likert emphasises that all four features must be present for a manager to be truly effective. For example, a manager who is employee-centred, who delegates and is participative will have a happy working environment – but will not produce the required task results unless (s)he also sets the high performance standards.

Activity 10

[20 minutes]

Management style is said to be responsible for subordinates' suffering stress and related health problems – such as high blood pressure, insomnia, coronary heart disease and alcohol abuse.

From your own experience of work, study or even family life, what management behaviours do you think are particularly stressful for employees?

4.2 Warning!

One problem with theories of management approach or style is that studying a concept will not necessarily change an individual's behaviour. Individual managers are unlikely to change their values (which are rooted in past experience, beliefs and attitudes) in response to a theory – especially where it is one of many, often conflicting, frameworks.

Even if a *willingness* to change management style exists, conditions in the organisation may not allow it. It will not necessarily be helpful for managers to model their behaviour on prescriptive formulae which are successful in theory or in a completely different situation: yet more flexible contingency models are difficult to apply in practice.

(a) Managers' personality (or acting ability) may not be flexible enough to utilise leadership theories effectively, by changing styles to suit different situations. A manager who is authoritarian by nature could come across as a hideously stiff and insincere democratic leader, even if the situation demanded it.

(b) Consistency is important to subordinates. If managers practise a contingency approach to leadership, subordinates may simply perceive them to be fickle, or may suffer insecurity, and distrust the unpredictable manager.

(c) 'The essence of leadership is followership' and followers' responses are not necessarily subject to leadership theory, however well supported by research findings from other situations!

For discussion

The Ashridge Studies found that the least favourable attitudes towards work were found – not among subordinates who were subjected to autocratic or 'tells' management styles – but amongst those who were unable to perceive any consistent style of leadership in their boss. In other words, subordinates seemed unsettled by a boss who chops and changes between autocracy, persuasion, consultation and democracy.

Do you think this undermines the basic idea of a contingency approach to management style? What are the main points of value that you have got from your study of management style? Pick at least one thing that you think you could take away and use.

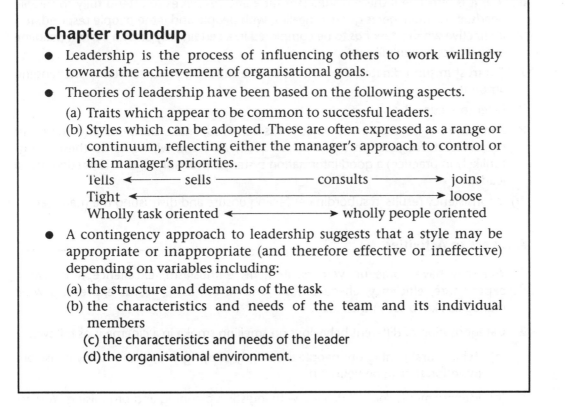

Chapter roundup

- Leadership is the process of influencing others to work willingly towards the achievement of organisational goals.
- Theories of leadership have been based on the following aspects.

  (a) Traits which appear to be common to successful leaders.

  (b) Styles which can be adopted. These are often expressed as a range or continuum, reflecting either the manager's approach to control or the manager's priorities.

  Tells ◄——— sells ——————— consults ———————► joins

  Tight ◄————————————————————————► loose

  Wholly task oriented ◄—————————► wholly people oriented

- A contingency approach to leadership suggests that a style may be appropriate or inappropriate (and therefore effective or ineffective) depending on variables including:

  (a) the structure and demands of the task

  (b) the characteristics and needs of the team and its individual members

    (c) the characteristics and needs of the leader

    (d) the organisational environment.

Quick quiz

1 How do people become leaders in a group or situation?

2 What is the difference between a 'sells' and 'consults' style of management?

3 What might be the disadvantages of a 'tells' style of management?

4 According to Handy, what type of task makes tight control a suitable style?

5 What factors in the environment influence the choice of a tight or loose style?

6 What is the most effective style suggested by Blake's managerial grid, and why is it so effective in theory? Why might it not be effective in practice?

7 Explain the equation T + C = Y.

8 What are Theory X and Theory Y?

9 Do teams need to have a leader? Would they be as effective without one?

10 Why is consistency of management style important – and why might this be a problem?

Answers to quick quiz _____

1 Through different forms of influence such as vision, inspiration and motivation.

2 'Sells' – the manager still makes all decisions but explains them to subordinates to get them to carry them out willingly. 'Consults' – the manager confers with subordinates, takes their views and feelings into account, but retains the right to make the final decision.

3 'Telling' is one-way, there is no feedback. It does not encourage contributions or initiative.

4 Those which lack initiative, are routine, trivial or have a short time scale.

5 The position of power held by the leader, organisational norms, structure and technology, the variety of tasks and subordinates.

6 9.9. It is effective if there is sufficient time and resources to attend fully to people needs, if the manager is good at dealing with people and if the people respond. It is ineffective when a task *has* to be completed in a certain way or by a certain deadline even if people don't like it.

7 T = trust in subordinates; C = control by the superior; Y = a constant, unchanging amount.

8 Refer to section 3.4.

9 Someone has to ensure the objective is achieved, make decisions and share out resources. If everyone on the team is equally able and willing to do these things (unlikely in practice) a good information system is probably all that is needed, not a leader.

10 Inconsistency results in subordinates feeling unsure and distrusting the manager.

Answers to Activities

1 You may have come up with excitement, enthusiasm, excellence, endeavour, expenditure, efficiency, effectiveness – and so on, as 'E' words expressing what managers like to see in their staff.

2 Categorisation of different behaviour on smelling smoke in a cinema is as follows.

   (a) Behavioural contagion: people are simply copying you, without any conscious intention to lead on your part.

   (b) Management. You are dealing with logistics: planning and organising. You are not, however, concerned with influencing the people: they simply respond to the situation.

   (c) Leadership. You intend to mobilise others in pursuit of your aims, and you succeed in doing so.

   (d) Whatever it is, it isn't leadership – because you have gained no followers.

3 The Ashridge researchers found that:

   (a) there was a clear preference for the 'consults' style;

   (b) managers were most commonly thought to be exercising the 'tells' or 'sells' styles;

   (c) the most favourable attitudes were held by subordinates who perceived their boss to be exercising the 'consults' style.

4 Styles of management in the situations described suggest, using the tells-sells-consults-joins model.

   (a) You may have to 'tell' here: nobody is going to like the idea and, since each person will have his or her own interests at heart, you are unlikely to reach consensus. You could attempt to 'sell', if you can see a positive side to the change in particular cases: opportunities for retraining, say.

   (b) You could 'consult' here: explain your remedy to staff and see whether they can suggest potential problems. They may be in a position to offer solutions – and since the problem effects them too, they should be committed to solving it.

   (c) We prefer a 'joins' style here, since the team's acceptance of the decision is more important than the details of the decision itself.

   (d) We would go for 'consult' despite the staff's apparent reluctance to participate. They may prefer you to 'tell' – but may resist decisions they disagree with anyway. Perhaps their reluctance is to do with lack of confidence – or lack of trust that you will take their input seriously, in which case, persistent use of a 'consults' style may encourage them. You could use a 'sells' approach initially, to get them used to a less authoritarian style than they seem to expect.

5   The 'environment' can be improved for leaders if senior management ensure that:

   (a) managers are given a clear role and the power (over resources and information) to back it up;

   (b) organisational 'norms' can be broken without fear of punishment – ie the organisation culture is adaptive, and managers can change things if required;

   (c) the organisational structure is not rigid and inflexible: managers can redesign task and team arrangements;

   (d) team members are selected or developed so that they are, as far as possible, of the same 'type' in terms of their attitudes to work and supervision;

   (e) labour turnover is reduced as far as possible (by having acceptable work conditions and terms, for example), so that the team does not constantly have to adjust to new members, or leaders.

6   Blake's Grid positioning of the given managerial approaches are:

   (a) 1.1: low task, low people

   (b) 9.1: high task, low people

   (c) 1.9: high people, low task

7   To aid delegation, the organisation could:

   (a) increase the perceived 'quality' of staff through selection and training, so the manager can have greater confidence;

   (b) encourage open communication, through organisation culture ('It's good to talk!') or mechanisms such as meetings; if information is freely available to staff and the manager is aware of what is going on, the manager can have more confidence in the staff's decisions and his or her own control;

   (c) ensure that efficient control systems are in place, so that results are monitored at all levels: the 'risks' attached to delegation are lessened;

   (d) make delegation part of the organisation culture by setting the example at senior management level, and by rewarding effective delegation with praise, pay or promotion.

8   Malcolm Ross's control and type of management may be classified as follows. (a) Tight. (b) Theory X. (c) Staff might react by: lack of confidence, demotivation, low opinion of self, fear, lack of trust.

9   (a) Morale has broken down through lack of management control, lack of a cohesive framework, increasing lack of respect for Peck.

   (b) To get his department going again, Scott Peck should start laying proper ground rules, take charge and provide a proper structure within which the department would operate.

Scott Peck actually assigned offices to his team and then informed them of his decision. Although this initially caused dismay, morale began to improve almost immediately. His style of leadership remained relatively nonauthoritarian, but not rigidly so. Morale stayed high.

10 Stressful management practices identified in employee surveys include:

   (a) unpredictability (staff work with uncertainty, or under threat of an outburst);

   (b) destruction of employees' self-esteem (making them feel insecure or inadequate);

   (c) setting up competitive win/lose situations (turning work relationships into battles for control, making work issues personal conflicts);

   (d) providing too much or too little stimulation (work overload or underload);

(e) unfairness (not giving credit where it is due);

(f) failure to define duties and communicate objectives and policies.

Assignment 2 [About 1^1/$_2$ hours]

A new administrative manager has recently been appointed by Metal Stretch Ltd. Peter Curtis is a 29 year old graduate and this is his first management post. His team is made up of five women and three men. Apart from 20 year old Marian, the others are aged between 35 and 52 years. One woman and two of the men also applied for the post but were unsuccessful. The atmosphere in the office is tense and Peter can feel the resentment.

(a) What problems is Peter likely to encounter?

(b) What can he do initially to try to improve the situation?

(c) What management style is likely to be most effective and why?

Chapter 3

INDIVIDUAL BEHAVIOUR AT WORK

Introduction

In order to manage people, you need to understand people. If you understand why people behave as they do, you may be able to encourage – or change – their behaviour. If you know what types of behaviour make people effective as workers, you may be able to encourage or change their behaviour in such a way as to increase their contribution to organisational goals.

Unfortunately, human behaviour is not easy to describe, let alone to explain – let alone to predict! All individuals are different, and so behave differently. Each individual behaves differently over time, in different circumstances and with different people. Interpersonal behaviour (the interaction between two or more people) is different from individual behaviour. Groups of people behave rather differently than their individual members would if they were on their own. (In the following chapters, we will be looking at individual, interpersonal and group behaviour.)

In this chapter, we will be looking at what makes individuals tick and specifically what makes them behave in ways that work organisations might find helpful – or not.

Your objectives

After completing this chapter you should:

(a) be able to describe the nature of personality, perception, attitude and ability and their influence on human behaviour at work;

(b) be aware of the innate needs and goals human beings have;

(c) be able to outline managerial strategies for the diagnosis and control of individual behavioural problems, such as stress and resistance to change.

1 PERSONALITY

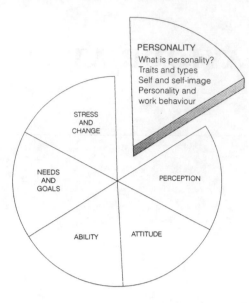

1.1 What is personality?

Individuals are unique. In order to identify, describe and explain the differences between people, psychologists use the concept of personality. Everyday use of the term tends to focus on a single characteristic of behaviour: someone is said to have an 'outgoing personality', for example. It also tends to get confused with charisma and social success, and adds the idea of quantity: TV 'personalities' by implication have 'lots of personality', while other individuals are said to 'lack personality'. Both these ideas are faulty, according to psychologists' more precise definition.

Definition

Personality is the total pattern of characteristic ways of thinking, feeling and behaving that constitute the individual's distinctive method of relating to the environment.

There is a debate about whether or how far the factors of heredity (nature) and environment (nurture) influence personality. There are two main approaches.

- The nomothetic ('law setting') approach suggests that personality is more or less fixed, and that various elements of personality (called traits) are the same from individual to individual. Individuals possess a selection of these traits, which tend to go together in compatible trait clusters, effectively dividing people into personality types.

- The idiographic approach individualises. It suggests that personality develops through interaction with the environment (ie experience), and in accordance with how the individual sees himself. Personality can therefore be studied only as a picture of a particular individual at a particular time.

We will look briefly at each of these approaches, and see how they might be useful to a manager.

1.2 Traits and types

Traits are consistently observable properties, or the tendency for a person to behave in a particular way. If you say someone is generally sweet-tempered or undemonstrative, you are identifying traits in their personality.

Individual personality is simply a 'pick and mix' from a range of possible traits. People are different because individuals possess different traits, and different strengths of the same traits.

However, people who possess a particular trait are likely to possess certain other compatible or related traits: *trait clusters*. Thus a person who is sociable and expressive is (according to H J Eysenck, a leading exponent of this approach) also likely to be impulsive, risk-taking, active, irresponsible and practical. Taken as a whole the trait cluster forms an identifiable *personality type*: in this case, an 'extrovert' personality.

Trait/type theories of personality basically pigeon-hole people, putting them into categories defined by certain common behaviour patterns.

If you find yourself doing this at work, bear the following points in mind.

(a) The ability to make snap assessments of the personality of others, with very little to go on, is an essential part of social interaction: how else could you talk sensibly to a stranger? We treat people as types, on the basis of a few observable traits: a process called stereotyping. The accuracy of such assessments varies widely, according to peoples' powers of observation and judgement, and any prejudices they may have: at best, stereotypes are over-simplified (and at worst wildly inaccurate) – but at least they are a starting point for interpersonal contact.

(b) Such an approach is not, however, an accurate basis for predicting individual behaviour. In particular, the validity and effectiveness of personality trait tests in employee selection is hotly debated.

   (i)   An individual may score highly on desirable traits in testing, but behave rather differently in practice: he may have given false answers in the test (based on what he thought the organisation would want to hear), or the test may have been irrelevant to the real job and work group.

   (ii) It is difficult for organisations to identify which traits are in fact desirable in employees: do you go for conformity to authority, or creative innovation, for example?

Organisations will inevitably make certain generalised assumptions about the personalities of the individuals they employ, about the type of individuals they would like to employ and to whom they would wish to allocate various tasks and responsibilities.

For discussion

Do you think an assessment of personality should form part of an organisation's recruitment process? What traits might it think desirable?

If you completed the above discussion, you may appreciate the difficulty of selecting desirable traits, from the organisation's point of view. In fact, the question: 'What type of person – possessing what traits – will make a successful....?' is naive. As we will see, ability and experience, education and skill training, motivation, job design, sex, age, attitudes, opportunity and many other factors will influence job performance. Research has simply not been able to show significant correlation between any personality trait and successful performance.

We will now turn to the idiographic approach, which attempts to look at whole people, as they are, and as they change over time.

1.3 Self and self-image

According to the idiographic approach, personality is the complex product of a dynamic process whereby the individual interacts with his or her environment and other people, through experience.

Self

George Herbert Mead noted that despite the constraints of social values and norms, people still display originality and individuality. He argued that the 'self' has two components:

(a) 'I' – the unique, active, impulsive part of the individual, which rises above conformity; and

(b) 'Me' – the mental process which reflects objectively on the self and measures it against the social norms, values and expectations which the individual has taken on board as the result of experience in society.

A similar tension is the basis of Sigmund Freud's psychological constructs.

Self-image

People have a subjective picture of what their own self is like: this is called a 'self-image'. Self-image is developed primarily through experience, and interaction with other people – particularly important people, such as our family through childhood, and our peers in adolescence. We evaluate ourselves according to the effect of our behaviour on other people, and how they respond to us. If people regularly praise your hard work, for example, you may have an image of yourself as a conscientious, successful worker. People tend to behave in accordance with their self-image, and how they expect to be treated.

Personality development

As well as an adjustment to the environment, personality development is an internal psychological process. According to most accepted theories, the personality is made up of various psychological forces or 'parts' which combine and interact to shape the behaviour of the whole person. The general trend as people mature is towards increasing diversity and complexity of these 'parts', and usually therefore an increasing sense of selfhood and the need to develop personal potential. They tend, as they mature, to become more actively independent, to take on more equal or superior relationships (moving from child-adult, to adult-adult and adult-child relationships) and to develop self control and self awareness.

These things do not inevitably happen alongside physical ageing. Individuals may remain psychologically immature in some aspects. Indeed, some psychologists consider that classical, efficiency-seeking organisations actively *prevent* people from maturing, by encouraging them to passive compliance with authority!

Whichever approach to personality we adopt, it is clear that the context in which individual and social behaviours emerge or develop is, for very many individuals, a work organisation. So how do you manage personality differences?

1.4 Personality and work behaviour

Obviously, personalities are complex and individual. Nonetheless, if we assume broad consistency in traits or types of personality, we can make some useful observations about individual behaviour at work – at least enough to be going on with in the real world. Adopting a contingency approach, managers will have to consider the following aspects.

(a) *The compatibility of an individual's personality with the task*

Different personality types suit different types of work. Without detailed psychological analysis, a manager should be aware that a person who appears unsociable and inhibited will find sales work, involving a lot of social interaction, intensely stressful – and will probably not be very good at it!

(b) *The compatibility of an individual's personality with the systems and management culture of the organisation*

Some people hate to be controlled, for example, but others (of an 'authoritarian' personality type) want to be controlled and dependent in a work situation, because they find responsibility threatening.

Some people (of a 'need to achieve' personality type) have a strong desire for success and a strong fear of failure. Such people tend to want personal responsibility, moderately difficult tasks and goals (which challenge them but do not present the risk of failure) and clear, frequent feedback on performance.

(c) *The compatibility of the individual's personality with that of others in the team*

Personality clashes are a prime source of conflict at work. An achievement-oriented personality, for example, tends to be a perfectionist, is impatient and unable to relax, and will be unsociable if people seem to be getting in the way of performance: such a person will clearly be frustrated and annoyed by laid-back, sociable types working (or not working) around him. Even attractive traits, like a sunny temper, can get on the nerves of people of a different type.

Where incompatibilities occur, the manager will have to:

(a) *restore compatibility* – this may be achieved by reassigning an individual to tasks more suited to his personality type, for example, or changing management style to suit the personalities of the team;

(b) *achieve compromise* – individuals should be encouraged to:
   (i) understand the nature of their differences. Others have the right to be themselves (within the demands of the team); personal differences should not be 'taken personally', as if they were adopted deliberately to annoy;
   (ii) modify their behaviour, if necessary; if personality develops according to feedback from interaction with others, then people can be encouraged and trained to adopt positive traits and overcome negative ones; you can train people to be more achievement oriented, for example, or to restrain 'natural' aggression or temper;

(c) *remove the incompatible personality* – in the last resort, obstinately difficult or disruptive people may simply have to be weeded out of the team. Team selection should as far as possible ensure that potentially incompatible people never become part of the team in the first place.

Activity 1   [20 minutes]

Look at the following list and number the qualities in priority order. 1 is very important, 2 is quite important, 3 is unimportant.

(a) Good appearance

(b) Ability to do the job

(c) Ability to answer questions clearly

(d) A pleasant speaking voice

(e) Being objective

(f) A pleasant personality

(g) The ability to reason

(h) Being interested in further training

(i) Being used to working in a team

(j) Being a good listener

2   PERCEPTION

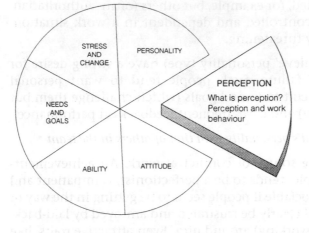

2.1   What is perception?

Different people 'see' things differently. And human beings behave in (and in response to) the world – not 'as it really is', but as they see it. That is why you need to understand perception.

Definition

Perception is the psychological process by which stimuli or in-coming sensory data are selected and organised into patterns which are meaningful to the individual.

Perceptual selection

The sensory apparatus of humans (eyes, ears, skin and so on) has limitations, which filter out certain stimuli: certain pitches of sound, for example, (like a dog whistle) or types of light (infrared). Perception acts as a further screen. We are constantly bombarded by sensory data of all kinds, not all of which is interesting or useful to us. We would not be able to function if we had to deal with every sound, sight, smell and touch. (If you make a real effort to listen to all the sounds in the room where you are sitting now, you will realise that they were only 'background', or that you hadn't noticed them at all, while your attention was focused elsewhere – hopefully, on this study text...)

The filtering process is called *perceptual selectivity*. It means that the world picture that our brains actually hold is not a whole or accurate one. Selection may be determined by any or all of the following.

(a) *The context*. People 'see what they want to see': whatever is necessary or relevant in the situation in which they find themselves. You might notice articles on management in the newspapers, concerning motivation or wage negotiations while studying this module which normally you would not notice.

(b) *The nature of the stimuli*. Our attention tends to be drawn to large, bright, loud, unfamiliar, moving and repeated (not repetitive) stimuli. Advertisers know it...

(c) *Internal factors*. Our attention is drawn to stimuli that match our personality, needs, interests, expectations and so on. If you are hungry, for example, you will pick the smell of food out of a mix of aromas.

(d) *Fear or trauma.* People are able to avoid seeing things that they don't want to see: things that are threatening to their security or self-image, or things that are too painful for them.

Perceptual organisation

A complementary process of *perceptual organisation* deals with the interpretation of the data which has been gathered and filtered. The brain groups, separates and patterns stimuli to make them recognisable, intelligible and useful to the individual. Thus sound waves become music, black and white shapes become writing and so on.

The mind is remarkably resourceful in organising data to give it meaning. It tends to fill in gaps in partial or confusing information, according to its expectations or assumptions about what should be there. This is called closure. (It is partly why speed reading is possible: the mere shape of a familiar word, together with the context, which creates the expectation of what kind of word it must be, is enough for the mind to 'read' the word, without having focused on all the information available.)

For discussion

There is a famous story about a victorious (but unhealthy) French general who was heard to cry: 'Ma sacrée toux!' (My damn' cough!) by his aides. Unfortunately, they were on their way to ask him what he wanted done with all the prisoners taken in battle that day. They heard: 'Massacrez tous!' (Kill everyone!). And they did.

What does this suggest about the process of perceptual organisation?

Like personality, perception is highly complex and highly individual. It is not possible to draw up detailed prescriptions for how people's perceptions can be analysed and utilised by management. However, here are some general principles.

2.2 Perception and work behaviour

Remember that human beings do not respond to the world 'as it really is', but as they perceive it to be. If individuals act in ways that seem illogical or contrary to you, it is probably not because of stupidity or defiance, but because they simply do not see things in the same way you do.

(a) Consider whether *you* might be misinterpreting the situation. Is there any awkward information you are avoiding? Have you jumped to conclusions in your desire for closure? Does your view really fit the facts? What needs and biases colour your perception of things? What are you being sensitive about?

(b) Consider whether *others* might be misinterpreting the situation, or interpreting it differently from you. What might make them see things in a different light? Listen to people, and get to know what their blind spots and biases are. Try and see things through their eyes.

(c) When tackling a task or a problem, get the people involved to define the situation as they see it. Then everyone will know what they mean, and differences of perception can be cleared up before they can cause confusion. (It's the same when you write an essay: define your terms!)

(d) Be aware of the most common clashes of perception at work.
   (i) *Managers and staff.* The experience of work can be very different for managerial and non-managerial personnel, and this has tended to foster 'them and us' perceptions. Efforts to bridge the gap may be viewed with suspicion.

(ii) *Work cultures*. Different functions in organisations may have very different time-scales and cultures of work, and will therefore perceive the work – and each other – in different ways. Consider how a sales team might regard the importance of their work in relation to production workers – and vice versa.

(iii) *Race and gender*. A joke, comment or gesture that one person may see as a 'bit of a laugh' may be offensive – and construed as harassment under the law – to another. Minorities in the workplace are bound to be sensitive to implied discrimination, and may therefore perceive it even where none is intended. Managers should be aware of how their words and decisions may be construed.

Activity 2 [30 minutes]

Identify the perceptual problem(s) in the following cases.

(a) An autocratic manager tries to adopt a more participative style of management, in order to improve the morale of his staff. He tells them they will be given more responsibility, and will be 'judged and rewarded accordingly'. For some reason, morale seems to worsen, and several people ask to transfer to other departments.

(b) A woman has just been promoted to the management team. At the first management meeting, the chairman introduces her to her new colleagues – all male – and says: 'At least we'll get some decent tea in these meetings from now on, eh?' Almost everyone laughs. For some reason, the woman does not contribute much in the meeting, and the chairman later tells one of his colleagues: 'I hope we haven't made a mistake. She doesn't seem to be a team player at all.'

(c) A new employee wanders into the office canteen, and is offered a cup of coffee by a youngster in jeans and a T-shirt, who has been chatting to the canteen supervisor. The youngster joins the man at his table (to his surprise) and asks how he likes working there so far. After a while, glancing uneasily at the man behind the serving counter, the new employee asks: 'Is it OK for you to be sitting here talking to me? I mean, won't the boss mind?' The youngster replies: 'I am the boss. Actually, I'm the boss of the whole company. Biscuit?'

---

3 ATTITUDE

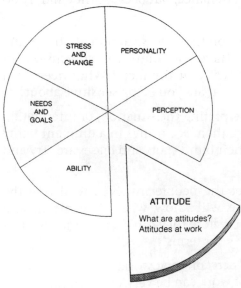

3.1 What are attitudes?

Attitudes are our general standpoint on things: the positions we have adopted in regard to particular issues, things and people, as we perceive them.

Definition

Technically speaking, an *attitude* is 'a mental and neural state of readiness... exerting a directive or dynamic influence upon the individual's response to all objects and situations with which it is related.'

Attitudes are thought to contain three basic components:

- knowledge, beliefs or disbeliefs, perceptions
- feelings and desires (positive or negative)
- volition, will or the intention to perform an action.

So our attitude towards something includes what we think and feel about it – and also predisposes us to behave in a certain way in response to it. This will be of particular interest to a manager, because it suggests that if you can identify people's attitudes to things, you may be able to anticipate how they will behave.

3.2   Attitudes at work

Behaviour in a work context will be influenced by:

(a) attitudes *to* work: the individual's standpoint on working, work conditions, colleagues, the task, the organisation and management;

(b) attitudes *at* work: all sorts of attitudes which individuals may have about other people, politics, education, religion among other things, and which they bring with them into the work place – to act on, agree, disagree or discuss.

Positive, negative or neutral attitudes to other workers, or groups of workers, to the various systems and operations of the organisation, to learning – or particular training initiatives – to communication or to the task itself will obviously influence performance at work. In particular they may result in:

(a) varying degrees of co-operation or conflict between individuals and groups, or between departments;

(b) varying degrees of co-operation with or resistance to management;

(c) varying degrees of success in communication – interpersonal and organisation wide;

(d) varying degrees of commitment and contribution to the work.

Activity 3   [15 minutes]

Suggest four elements which would make up a positive attitude to work. An example might be the belief that you get a fair day's pay for a fair day's work.

Non-work factors that might influence attitudes to work, or affecting work, include the following.

(a) *Class and class consciousness:* attitudes about the superiority or inferiority of others, according to birth, wealth and education; attitudes to money and work (necessity or career?).

(b) *Age.* Attitudes to sexual equality, family and morality (for example) vary widely from one generation to the next. Attitudes in general tend to become less flexible with age.

(c) *Race, culture or religion.* Attitudes about these areas will affect the way people regard each other and their willingness to co-operate in work situations. Culture and religion are also strong influences on attitudes to work: for example, the 'Protestant work ethic', or Japanese concepts of the organisation 'family'.

(d) *Lifestyle and interests*. Attitudes to these areas affect interpersonal relations and self-image, as well as the relative importance of work and leisure to the individual.

(e) *Sex*. Attitudes to the equality of the sexes and their various roles at work and in society may be influential in:

(i) *interpersonal relations at work* (especially where women are in positions of authority over men: sexist attitudes may come into painful conflict with imposed power structures);

(ii) *the self concept of the individual:* women at work may be made to feel inferior, incompetent or simply unwelcome, while men working for female managers might feel threatened; and

(iii) *attitudes to work*. Stereotypical role profiles ('a woman's place is in the home', 'the man has to support the family') may be held by both sexes and may create feelings of guilt, resentment or resignation about wanting or having to work.

4   ABILITY

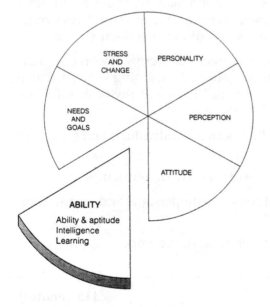

4.1   Ability and aptitude

There have been many attempts to make a useful distinction between:

(a) *abilities* – things that people can do, or are good at – largely believed to be inherited; and

(b) *aptitudes* – the capacity to learn and develop abilities or skill.

There is not always a clear dividing line between the two concepts, however.

Organisations such as schools, colleges and businesses attempt to assess the sphere of individuals' abilities, and the level of required abilities which different individuals possess. It seems obvious that people are 'naturals' at music, drawing or football; some people have 'the gift of the gab', while others are good with numbers; some people are thinkers, while others are 'good with their hands'.

If a certain ability or aptitude is required for an individual to perform his job, or to perform it better, then it would be useful to test for and measure that ability or aptitude. That way the right person can be selected and/or trained for the job – or the task allocated to the person with the right ability or aptitude. However, ability is only one factor of performance in a work context. It may be essential to successful performance in a particular job – but it is unlikely to be sufficient, by itself. Willingness to perform the task, and suitable task design and working conditions, for example, will also be required.

The terms 'ability' and 'intelligence' have often been used interchangeably, and have been rather narrowly defined to denote such things as 'mental dexterity', 'logic' or 'verbal fluency'. Analytical intelligence (the kind measured by IQ tests) is still most frequently used as a measure of 'ability' in children and adults alike. However, there is more to intelligence than this.

4.2   Intelligence

Intelligence is a wide and complex concept. The more scientists explore the idea of creating 'Artificial Intelligence', the more they realise just how complex the nature and processes of human intelligence really are.

Recent work appears to confirm the commonsense observation that intelligence/ability takes many forms, including:

(a) analytic intelligence – measured by IQ tests;

(b) spatial intelligence – the ability to see patterns and connections, most obvious in the creative artist or scientist;

(c) musical intelligence – the 'good ear' that musicians, mimics and linguists have;

(d) physical intelligence – obvious in athletes and dancers;

(e) practical intelligence – some people can make and fix things without theoretical knowledge;

(f) intra-personal intelligence – the ability to know, be sensitive to and express oneself, observable in poets, artists and mystics;

(g) inter-personal intelligence – the ability to relate to and work through others; essential in leaders.

The concept of intelligence has been further complicated by research into the processes of the brain. It has been suggested that the logical, analytical, intellectual functions of the brain – those commonly thought of as intelligence (IQ) – are performed in the left-hand half (hemisphere). The right-hand hemisphere was found to be the seat of less rational processes: intuition, hunches, vision, flair, imagination, emotion and creativity.

For discussion

Do you think management is a left-brain or right-brain activity? Give examples of management functions to support your view.

Do more 'intelligent' people make better managers?

Whatever people's abilities and intelligence, their performance can be improved by extra knowledge, practice and experience – in other words, by learning. We will be covering the organisational aspects of education and training in Chapter 8, but here we will look briefly at how people learn.

4.3 Learning

Learning is how we come to know and do things.

Definition

Learning is the process of acquiring, through experience, knowledge which leads to changed behaviour.

Learning changes behaviour: the test of whether you have learned how to do something is whether you can perform an action, when you could not do so before. This is important because it enables us to define what we want the outcome of learning to be (for example, in designing training programmes) and to measure what people have learned.

There are two main approaches to learning, based on very different theories about how people know things and whether scientists are entitled to make inferences about the internal, unobservable workings of the human mind.

The *behaviourist* or *stimulus-response* approach suggests that we behave in response to sensory stimuli or influences from the environment. Depending whether our experience is positive or negative, we will repeat or modify that response next time. In other words, the result of our responses may be rewarding (*positive reinforcement*) or punishing (*negative reinforcement*) and act as an incentive or a deterrent to similar behaviour in the future. This shaping of behaviour through reinforcement is called *conditioning*. Trial-and-error learning and 'carrot-and-stick' motivation are based on this idea.

Activity 4   [40 minutes]

Give examples of how a manager might use:

(a) positive reinforcement; and

(b) negative reinforcement;

to condition team members' behaviour. Which do you think would be most successful?

The *cognitive* or *information processing* approach to learning suggests that the human mind actively interprets sensory information, analyses experience and takes it into account in making decisions about how to behave in future. Reinforcements do not merely create habits (as conditioning theories suggest): they are one of many factors in our choice of how we will need to behave in order to fulfil our needs and purposes. *Feedback* on the results of our actions is essential so that we can continually adjust our plans and behaviour to fit the situation. In other words, learning is a control process.

The learning cycle

Learning as an information-processing and control activity is modelled in the 'learning cycle', Figure 3.1.

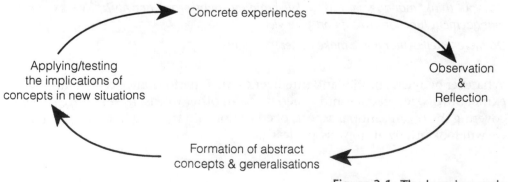

Figure 3.1 The learning cycle

Say a team member interviews a customer for the first time (concrete experience). He observes his performance and the dynamics of the situation (observation) and afterwards, having failed to convince the customer to buy the product, he analyses what he did right and wrong (reflection). He comes to the conclusion that he had failed to listen to what the customer really wanted and feared, underneath her general reluctance: he realises that the key to communication is listening (abstraction/generalisation). In his next interview he applies his strategy to the new set of circumstances (application/testing). This provides him with a new experience with which to start the cycle over again.

Earlier in this chapter, we said that the way we perceive things is influenced by our needs and goals at the time. Above, we noted that we learn and make decisions about our behaviour in pursuit of needs and goals. We will be looking at their central role in employee motivation in Chapter 4. Here, we will look at what needs and goals people have, and some of the many ways in which they influence individual behaviour.

5 NEEDS AND GOALS

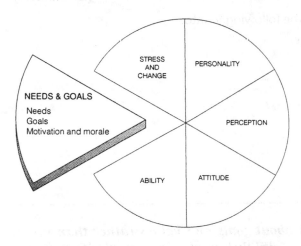

5.1 Needs

Individual behaviour is partly influenced by human biology, which requires certain basics for life: oxygen, food, water, shelter, sleep, self-preservation and so on. When the body is deprived of these essentials, biological forces called *needs* or *drives* are activated, and dictate the behaviour required to end the deprivation: eat, drink, flee and so on. We do not learn these drives, we cannot make them go away, and they are very powerful. However, we retain freedom of choice about *how* we satisfy our drives: they do not dictate specific or highly predictable behaviour. (Say you are hungry: how many specific ways of satisfying your hunger can you think of?)

We also behave in ways that make no direct contribution to our physical survival or health: people study, enjoy art, and make sacrifices for causes they believe in. This suggests that as well as physical drives, we have emotional and psychological needs. The American psychologist Abraham Maslow suggested that people have certain innate needs, as shown in Figure 3.2.

Learning Resources
Centre

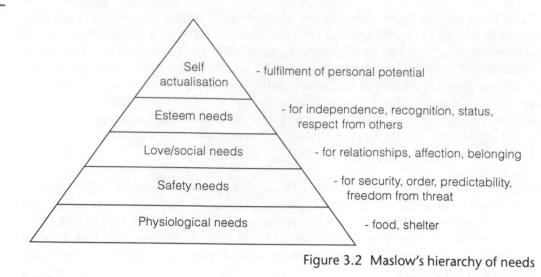

Figure 3.2 Maslow's hierarchy of needs

Maslow also suggested that 'freedom of inquiry' and 'knowledge and understanding' were two further needs and that these were the channels through which we could satisfy all the other needs. Freedom of speech and expression and to gain knowledge, explore and experiment are the bases of satisfaction.

Activity 5 [20 minutes]

Decide which of Maslow's categories the following fit into.

(a) Receiving praise from your manager

(b) A family party

(c) An artist forgetting to eat

(d) A man washed up on a desert island

(e) A pay increase

(f) Joining a local drama group

(g) Being awarded the OBE

(h) Buying a house.

It has become fashionable to talk about goals and values rather than needs. People pursue goals which promise to fulfil their needs. For example, if you have a need for achievement, you might have an HNC or HND in Business as your goal. If you have a need for love and belonging, your goal may be to start a family – or join a religious community! As you can see, goals are more specific and more various than needs. Let's look at some of the factors that influence an individual's choice of goals.

5.2 Goals

Each individual has a different set of goals. The relative importance of those goals to the individual may vary with time, circumstances and other factors, including the following.

(a) *Genetic inheritance, childhood environment and education.* Aspiration levels, family and career models and so on are formed at early stages of development.

(b) *Experience.* This teaches us what to expect from life: we will either strive to repeat positive experiences, or to avoid or make up for negative ones.

(c) *Age and position.* There is usually a gradual process of 'goal shift' with age, as well as more radical re-evaluations of one's life, in cases of illness, redundancy, death in the family, birth of a child and so on. Recognition may have high priority for a child, while relationships and exploration may preoccupy teenagers. Career and family goals tend to conflict in the 20-40 age group: career launch and 'take-off' may have to yield to the priorities associated with forming permanent relationships and having children. Power and autonomy goals tend to be essential to an individual's self image in mature years, or 'career peak' time. Retirement usually forces a reappraisal of relationships, purpose in life and security.

(d) *Culture.* Compared to European worker goals, for example, Japanese goals show a greater concern for relationships at work and a lesser preoccupation with power and autonomy.

(e) *Self-concept.* All the above factors are bound up with the individual's own self-image. The individual's assessments of his own abilities and place in society will affect the relative strength and nature of his needs and goals.

You should now be able to identify some of the needs and goals that people might have, where they might come from and why they might change. So why are they relevant to a manager?

5.3 Motivation and morale

We will not say much about this here: motivation is such a complex and important matter for a manager that we will be covering it in more detail in Chapter 4.

Here are some general points.

(a) People behave in such a way as to satisfy their needs and fulfil their goals.

(b) An organisation is in a position to offer some of the satisfactions people might seek: relationships and belonging, challenge and achievement, progress on the way to self-actualisation, security and structure and so on. Pay, or money, does not directly feature in any need lists, but it represents a means of obtaining all sorts of satisfactions of other needs: from food and shelter to personal development courses, power and recognition and so on.

(c) The organisation can therefore influence people to behave in the ways it desires (to secure work performance) by offering them the means to satisfy their needs and fulfil their goals *in return for* that behaviour. This process of influence is called motivation.

Definition

Motivation (in this context) is the process by which the behaviour of an individual is influenced by others, through their power to offer or withhold satisfaction of the individual's needs and goals.

(d) If people's needs are being met, and goals being fulfilled, at work, they are likely to have a positive attitude to their work and to the organisation. The term *morale* is used to denote the state of mind or spirit of a group, particularly regarding discipline and confidence. Satisfaction at work may thus be associated with high morale. And high morale can (sometimes) be associated with committed performance at work.

For discussion

'Motivation sounds just like "bribery", with a more respectable name.' Do you agree?

6 STRESS AND CHANGE

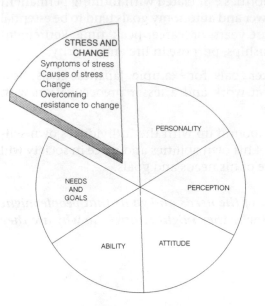

6.1 Symptoms of stress

Stress is a term which is often loosely used to describe feelings of tension or exhaustion – usually associated with too much, or overly demanding, work. In fact, stress is simply the product of demands made on an individual's physical and mental energies: boredom can be just as stressful as pressure. Demands on an individual's energies may be stimulating, as well as harmful, and most people require some form of stress to bring out their best performance. Executive stress, however, can be damaging. This is why we talk about the control or management of stress, not its elimination: it is a question of keeping stress to helpful proportions.

Harmful stress or 'strain' can be identified by its effects on the individual and his or her performance. Symptoms usually include:

(a) *nervous tension* – this may manifest itself in various ways: irritability and increased sensitivity, preoccupation with details, a polarised ('black and white') view of issues, or sleeplessness; various physical symptoms, such as skin and digestive orders, are also believed to be stress-related;

(b) *withdrawal* – this is essentially a defence mechanism, which may show itself in unusual quietness and reluctance to communicate, abuse of drugs or alcohol, or physical withdrawal by absenteeism, poor time-keeping or even leaving the organisation;

(c) *low morale* – low confidence, dissatisfaction, poor discipline, frustration amongst other symptoms.

6.2 Causes of stress

Stress may be caused by a number of work and non-work factors.

(a) *Too many demands on the individual:* overwork, or pressure, too much responsibility or too little time.

(b) *Too few demands on the individual:* monotony (or 'sameness'), boredom – in short, frustration.

(c) *Uncertainty and therefore insecurity,* especially where the outcome is important to the individual, or his responsibility. (This is why career change, redundancy, retirement, innovations at work, moving house and change of family circumstances are highly stressful.)

(d) *Personality factors.* People who are naturally 'laid back' are simply better able to handle stress than those who are dynamic and competitive. The amount of stress people of either type will be able to cope with depends on factors such as:
  (i) emotional sensitivity (can you shrug off unpleasantness?);
  (ii) flexibility (do you bend – or snap – under pressure?);
  (iii) inter-personal competence (do you draw strength from others in a crisis?);
  (iv) sense of responsibility (do you have an 'easy come, easy go' attitude, or do you fear letting people down?)

Activity 6 [20 minutes]

See if you can suggest ways of controlling stress that arises from each of the causes listed in section 6.2. (Look for the logical solution. There's no great 'mystique' to stress management...)

6.3 Change

Change affects individuals in all sorts of ways. A change in shift-work patterns or work conditions, for example, may affect workers' bodies. Office relocation will affect their circumstances. Changes in office layout or work organisation may change their network of relationships.

Most importantly, change affects individuals psychologically.

(a) It may create feelings of disorientation or 'lostness' before new circumstances have been absorbed.

(b) This may threaten the individual's self-concept, because (s)he may no longer feel competent to cope in the new circumstances: most people feel guilty and inadequate as 'beginners'.

(c) Change involves uncertainty, which creates insecurity – especially at work, where there are great pressures for continuity (of employment, and of performance).

(d) The support offered by established relationships is likely to have been disrupted, and the need to start all over again with a new group of people can be daunting.

(e) Change can be particularly threatening if it is perceived as an outside force against which the individual is powerless.

Resisting change means attempting to preserve the existing state of affairs – the *status quo* – against pressure to alter it. Despite the possibly traumatic effects of change *per se*, most people do not in fact resist it on these grounds alone. Where people do resist change itself, it may be partly because of inflexibility (which may or may not be related to age) or strong needs for security and structure.

Activity 7 [30 minutes]

Resistance to particular proposed changes will depend on the circumstances. Read through some newspapers and give examples of resistance based on:

(a) attitudes or beliefs;

(b) habit or custom;

(c) loyalty to a group;

(d) politics or holding onto power.

So what do managers do about resistance to change? Here are a few ideas.

6.4   Overcoming resistance to change

The pace of change

Changes ought if possible to be introduced slowly. The more gradual the change, the more time is available for questions to be asked and answered, relationships to be adjusted, old ways unlearned, new ways learned and got used to, and individuals reassured that they will be able to cope. Timing will also be important: those responsible for change should be sensitive to incidents and attitudes that might indicate that 'now is not the time'.

The scope of change

Total transformation will create greater insecurity than moderate change – but also greater excitement, if the organisation has the kind of innovative culture that can stand it. Management should be aware of how many aspects of their employees' lives they are proposing to alter – and therefore on how many fronts they are likely to encounter resistance. There may be 'hidden' changes to take into account: a change in technology may necessitate changes in work methods, which may in turn result in the breaking up of work groups.

The manner of change

The manner in which a change is put across is vital: if possible the individuals concerned should be positively encouraged to adopt the changes as their own.

(a) Resistance should be welcomed and confronted, not denied or swept under the carpet. Talking through areas of conflict may give useful insights.

(b) There should be free circulation of information about the reasons for the change, its consequences and expected results. This information should appear sensible, consistent, realistic and trustworthy – not an attempt to 'pull the wool over the eyes' of people, or to 'blind them with science'.

(c) The change must be sold to the people as important, necessary or desirable – for them, if possible. (Changes in a crisis often face less resistance than changes of a routine nature.)

(d) People must be reassured that they have or will be given the skills and resources to implement the change successfully.

(e) The effects of insecurity may be lessened if people can be consulted or involved in the planning and implementation of the change. Successful change will usually be *initiated* from the top (otherwise the politics are too complicated), but will harness the knowledge and experience of those affected in the 'nitty gritty' of the change programme.

Chapter roundup

- Personality is the total pattern of an individual's thoughts, feelings and behaviours. It is shaped by a variety of factors, both inherited and environmental.

- Perception is the process by which the brain selects and organises information in order to make sense of it. People behave according to what they perceive – not according to what 'really is'.

- People develop attitudes about things, based on what they think, what they feel and what they want to do about it. Attitudes are formed by perception, experience and personality, which in turn are shaped by wider social influences.

- Ability is the capacity to do something. It is often equated with intelligence. It is now recognised that there are many types of ability/intelligence, not all of which are based about mental dexterity or verbal fluency.

- Learning is the process whereby we acquire knowledge through experience, which changes our behaviour.

- People have certain innate needs: both physical needs and emotional/psychological needs. Maslow has categorised needs as physiological, security, love/social, esteem and self-actualisation. People also have goals, through which they expect their needs to be satisfied.

- Stress is the product of mental and physical demands on the individual. It becomes 'strain' if excessive or uncontrolled.

- Change poses a threat to individuals in many areas of their lives, and is often resisted. The change must be carefully managed to overcome this resistance.

Quick quiz

1 What is a trait cluster, and why might it be useful in everyday social interaction?

2 List three factors for a manager to consider in managing 'personality' at work.

3 Give three examples of areas where people's perceptions commonly conflict.

4 What are the three components of an 'attitude'?

5 Give three examples of non-work factors that might influence attitudes to work.

6 Indicate the difference between 'abilities' and 'aptitudes'.

7 Give four examples of non-analytical or non-intellectual intelligence.

8 What is (a) 'positive reinforcement' and (b) self actualisation?

9 Draw the 'learning cycle'.

10 List the five categories in Maslow's Hierarchy of Needs.

11 How do an individual's goals change with age?

12 Define motivation.

13 List three ways in which an organisation can offer motivational satisfaction.

14 List some symptoms of stress.

15 Outline a five-point plan for introducing change.

Answers to quick quiz

1 A number of related or compatible traits which form a personality type.

2 The compatibility of an individual's personality with the task, with the systems and culture of the organisation and with other members of the team.

3 Managers and staff, work culture, race and gender.

4 Knowledge, feelings and desires, volition.

5 Class, age, race, culture or religion, interests and sex.

6 Abilities are things people can do or are good at. Aptitude is the capacity to learn and develop abilities and skills.

7 Spatial, musical, physical, practical, inter-personal, intra-personal.

8 (a) Encouraging a certain type of behaviour by rewarding it.

(b) Personal growth and fulfilment of potential.

9 Refer to section 4.3 Figure 3.1.

10 Physiological, safety, love/social, esteem, self-actualisation.

11 Increasingly they include forming permanent relationships, having children, power and autonomy.

12 Motivation is the process by which the behaviour of an individual is influenced.

13 Relationships, belonging, challenge, achievement, progress, security.

14 Nervous tension, physical symptoms, withdrawal, drink/drugs, low morale.

15 Sell change, give information and reasons, reassure, consult, deal with resistance.

Solutions to activities

1 You probably felt as we did that none of the qualities listed were unimportant. You probably had similar priorities to ours, as follows:

1 = b, c, e, g, j. 2 = a, d, f, h, i.

2 The perceptual problems in the situations given are as follows.

(a) The manager perceives himself as 'enlightened', and his style as an opportunity and gift to his staff. He clearly thinks that assessment and reward on the basis of more responsibility is a positive thing, probably offering greater rewards to staff. He does not perceive his use of the word 'judged' as potentially threatening: he uses it as another word for 'assessed'. His staff obviously see things differently. 'More responsibility' means their competence – maybe their jobs – are on the line. Feeling this way, and with the expectations they have of their boss (based on past experience of his autocratic style), they are bound to perceive the word 'judged' as threatening.

(b) The chairman thinks he is being funny. Maybe he is only joking about the woman making the tea – but he may really perceive her role that way. He lacks the perception that his new colleague may find his remark offensive. From the woman's point of view, she is bound to be sensitive and insecure in her first meeting and with all male colleagues: small wonder that, joke or not, she perceives the chairman's comment as a slap in the face. The chairman later fails to perceive the effect his joke has had on her, assuming that her silence is a sign of poor co-operation or inability to communicate.

(c) This is a case of closure leading to misinterpretation. The new employee sees the informal dress, the position behind the counter, and the offer of coffee: his brain fills in the gaps, and offers the perception that the youngster must be the tea-boy. Perceptual selectivity also plays a part, filtering out awkward information that does not fit his expectations (like the fact that the 'tea-boy' comes to chat with him).

3 Elements of a positive attitude to work may include a willingness to:

(a) commit oneself to the objectives of the organisation, or adopt personal objectives that are compatible with those of the organisation;

(b) accept the right of the organisation to set standards of acceptable behaviour for its members;

(c) contribute to the development and improvement of work practices and performance;

(d) take advantages of opportunities for personal development at work.

4 Managers may use positive and negative reinforcement;

(a) Positive reinforcement: praise; pay (or extra pay, such as a bonus); promotion; prizes.

(b) Negative reinforcement: warnings; loss of pay; threat of dismissal; the cold shoulder.

A person who has been punished may simply learn how to avoid punishment! Positive reinforcement is generally thought to be more effective, as well as more pleasant. However, if we take a contingency approach, we must recognise that negative reinforcement can be effective in certain situations – for example, if the punished person himself feels that the punishment was deserved.

5 Maslow's categories for the listed circumstances are as follows.

(a) Esteem needs.

(b) Social needs.

(c) Self-actualisation needs.

(d) He will have physiological needs.

(e) Safety needs initially; esteem needs above in a certain income level.

(f) Social needs or self-actualisation needs.

(g) Esteem needs.

(h) Safety needs or esteem needs.

6 (a) Overload and underload could both be addressed by management, in consultation with the individual. Tasks and responsibilities could be reallocated, or clarified. Training in delegation, planning and assertiveness (eg learning to say 'no') may help those who have problems tackling excessive workloads. Jobs may have to be redesigned, if the issue of stress is important enough and the workers are too valuable to be allowed to leave.

(b) Uncertainty can be alleviated to an extent by the provision of relevant information and counselling. Management style will be important in offering accessibility in the event of problems (an 'open door' policy, for example) and in showing confidence in the individual, to counteract the effects of insecurity.

(c) There is little you can do about personality, but inter-personal competence and flexibility, for example, might be improved by training. In addition, greater awareness of stress may be helpful. Stress management techniques such as rest breaks, relaxation techniques (breathing exercises, meditation), physical exercise and so on may be helpful.

7 Resistance to changes of attitudes, habit, loyalty and retaining power, include the following examples.

(a) Resistance to changes in the law on Sunday trading.

(b) 'You can't teach an old dog new tricks' (especially on computers!).

(c) Resisting merger with another team or company.

(d) Resisting multi-skilling in what has been a specialist area.

Assignment 3 [About 1½ hours]

During the annual holiday shutdown, the senior management of Treadmills decided to modernise the office accommodation. The small offices, which had housed two or three members of staff, were knocked down and the whole office complex became open plan, housing around twenty people.

When the staff returned to work, they were horrified and soon began to complain about noise, heat, lack of privacy, furniture in the wrong place and many other things.

The senior management team had a meeting to identify the problems, to establish how they had arisen and how they could be overcome.

(a) Other than the complaints, what problems do you think there are and what caused them?

(b) What steps would you take to overcome them?

(c) If you were going to introduce change like this in the future, how would you do it?

Chapter 4

MOTIVATION

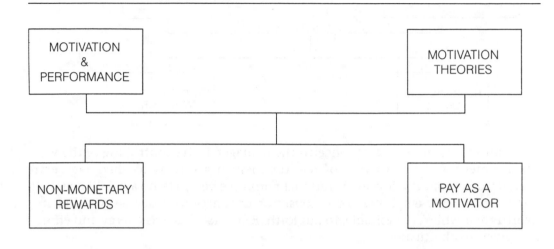

Introduction

The word motivation is commonly used in different contexts to mean:

(a) goals or outcomes that have become desirable for a particular individual, as in: 'he is motivated by money';

(b) the mental process of choosing a goal and deciding whether and how to achieve it, as in: 'he is motivated to work harder';

(c) the social process by which the behaviour of an individual is influenced by others, as in: 'the manager motivates his team'.

In this chapter, we cover some basic motivation theories (which explain the first two meanings), then concentrate on 'motivation' in the third sense, which is the practical responsibility of the manager.

Your objectives

After completing this chapter you should:

(a) be able to define motivation and discuss its impact on work performance;

(b) be able to outline the need theory, two factor theory and expectancy theory of motivation;

(c) appreciate the range of rewards and incentives that might act as motivators;

(d) be able to outline how 'job satisfaction' might be offered to employees;

(e) be able to discuss the significance of pay as a motivator.

NOTES

1 MOTIVATION & PERFORMANCE

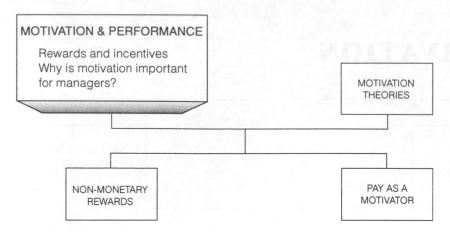

Motivation, as it most nearly concerns the manager, is the controlling of the work environment and the offering of rewards in such a way as to encourage extra performance from employees. As rational purposive beings (who act deliberately in pursuit of goals), employees consciously or unconsciously decide whether it is 'worth their while', or desirable, to put forth 'E factors' – such as energy and effort – in a given work situation.

The decision of whether more 'E' is worth putting in is reached by considering what rewards or incentives are available for doing so. We discussed some of the needs and wants of individuals in Chapter 3: effective incentives offer the satisfaction of those needs and wants. Let's recap, briefly.

1.1 Rewards and incentives

Definitions

A *reward* is a token (monetary or otherwise) given to an individual or team in recognition of some contribution or success.

An *incentive* is the offer or promise of a reward for contribution or success, designed to motivate the individual or team to behave in such a way as to earn it. (In other words, the 'carrot' dangled in front of the donkey!)

Not all the incentives that an organisation can offer its employees are directly related to *monetary* rewards. The satisfaction of *any* of the employee's wants or needs may be seen as a reward for past or incentive for future performance.

Different individuals have different goals, and get different things out of their working life: in other words they have different *orientations* to work. There are any number of reasons why a person works, or is motivated to work well.

(a) The 'human relations' school of management theorists regarded *work relationships* as the main source of satisfaction and reward offered to the worker.

(b) Later writers suggested a range of 'higher' motivations, notably:
   (i) *job satisfaction*, interest and challenge in the job itself – rewarding work; and
   (ii) *participation* in decision-making – responsibility and involvement.

(c) *Pay* has always occupied a rather ambiguous position, but since people need money to live, it will certainly be part of the reward 'package' an individual gets from his work.

74

You may be wondering whether motivation is really so important. It could be argued that if a person is employed to do a job, he will do that job and no question of motivation arises. If the person doesn't want to do the work, he can resign. So why try to motivate people?

1.2 Why is motivation important for managers?

Like 'leadership' as opposed to 'management', motivation is about getting extra levels of commitment and performance from employees, over and above mere compliance with rules and procedures.

It is suggested that if individuals can be motivated, by one means or another, they will work more efficiently (and productivity will rise) or they will produce a better quality of work.

For discussion

'If all those who may be considered potential contributors to an organisation are arranged in order of willingness to serve it, the scale descends from possibly intense willingness through neutral or zero willingness to intense opposition or hatred. The preponderance of persons in a modern society always lies on the negative side with reference to any existing or potential organisation.' (Chester Barnard).

Do you think this is true? What does it suggest about the importance of motivation?

Managers need to be aware, however, that motivation is not an exact science. In particular the case for *job satisfaction* as a factor in improved performance is not proven. You should be clear in your own mind that although it seems obviously a Good Thing to have employees who enjoy their work and are interested in it, there is no reason why the organisation should want a satisfied work force unless it makes the organisation function better: it is good for human reasons, but it must be (at least plausibly) relevant to organisational efficiency or effectiveness.

We will now look at how motivation works, in theory.

2 MOTIVATION THEORIES

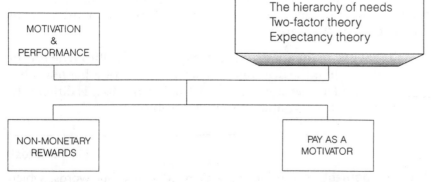

One way of grouping the major theories of motivation is by distinguishing between:

(a) *content theories;* and

(b) *process theories.*

Content theories assume that human beings have an innate package of 'motives' which they pursue; in other words, that they have a set of needs or desired outcomes and will act in such a way as to fulfil them. Maslow's need hierarchy theory and Herzberg's two-factor theory are two of the most important approaches of this type.

Process theories explore the process through which outcomes become desirable and are pursued by individuals. This approach assumes that people are able to select their goals and choose the paths towards them, by a conscious or unconscious process of calculation. Expectancy theory is the major approach of this type.

Activity 1 [10 minutes]

What do you think is your main 'motive' for studying this module? In other words, what is the main thing you expect to get out of it?

2.1 The hierarchy of needs

Need theories suggest that the desired outcome of behaviour in individuals is the *satisfaction of innate needs*.

If you need to refresh your memory of what we mean by innate needs, turn back briefly to Chapter 3 and reread our discussion of Abraham Maslow.

In his motivation theory, Abraham Maslow put forward certain propositions about the motivating power of needs. He suggested that Man's needs can be arranged in a 'hierarchy of relative pre-potency'. This means that there are levels of need, each of which is dominant until it is satisfied; only then does the next level of need become a motivating factor. See Chapter 3, Section 5.1, Figure 3.2, for a diagram of Maslow's theory.

There is a certain intuitive appeal to Maslow's theory. After all, you are unlikely to be concerned with status or recognition while you are hungry or thirsty – but once your hunger is assuaged, the need for food is unlikely to be a motivating factor. Unfortunately, research does not bear out the proposition that needs become less powerful as they are satisfied, except at this very primitive level: how much recognition or friendship is 'enough'? The theory is too vague to be used to predict behaviour. Different people emphasise different needs (and some people are clearly able to suppress even their basic physiological and safety needs for the sake of a perceived 'higher cause', or for the sake of other people). Also, the same need may cause different behaviour in different individuals. (Consider how many ways of achieving self-esteem or fame there are!)

Application of the theory in work contexts presents various difficulties. The role of pay is problematic, since it acts as the instrument of a wide range of other rewards – status, recognition, independence and so on. Self-actualisation, too, is difficult to offer employees in practice, since its nature is so highly subjective.

Activity 2 [10 minutes]

Where are you, at the moment, in the hierarchy of needs? In other words, which category of needs (if any) is uppermost in your mind and in the way you are directing your activities?

2.2   Two-factor theory

In the 1950s, the American psychologist Frederick Herzberg interviewed 203 Pittsburgh engineers and accountants and asked two 'critical incident' questions. The subjects were asked to recall events which had made them feel good about their work, and others which made them feel bad about it. Analysis revealed that the factors which created satisfaction were different from those which created dissatisfaction.

Herzberg saw two basic needs of individuals:

(a) the need to avoid unpleasantness, satisfied (temporarily, and in a rather negative way) by 'environmental factors'; and

(b) the need for personal growth, satisfied at work only by 'motivator factors'.

Environmental factors

Herzberg suggests that: 'when people are dissatisfied with their work it is usually because of discontent with the environmental factors'. Herzberg also calls these *'hygiene' factors* because at best they prevent or minimise dissatisfaction but do not give satisfaction, in the same way that sanitation minimises threats to health, but does not give good health.

These environmental, or hygiene, factors include:

(a) company policy and administration;

(b) salary;

(c) the quality of supervision;

(d) interpersonal relations;

(e) working conditions; and

(f) job security.

Satisfaction with environmental factors is not lasting. In time, dissatisfaction will occur. For example, an individual might want a pay rise which protects his income against inflation. If he is successful in obtaining the rise he wants, he will be satisfied for the time being, but will swiftly take his new level of income for granted, and want more.

Motivator factors

Motivator factors, on the other hand, create job satisfaction and can motivate an individual to superior performance and effort. These factors fulfil the individual's higher need for a sense of self-actualisation or personal growth, and include:

(a) status (although this may be a hygiene factor as well as a motivator factor);

(b) advancement;

(c) gaining recognition;

(d) being given responsibility;

(e) challenging work;

(f) achievement; and

(g) growth in the job.

Activity 3   [20 minutes]

Note down:

(a) the things you regard as the 'basics' you would expect from a study course; and

(b) the things you positively like about studying for this course at this college.

Do the factors you have listed in (a) correspond to Herzberg's 'hygiene' factors: are they things that make studying 'comfortable' but don't really 'switch you on' to extra effort?

Do the factors you have listed in (b) correspond to Herzberg's 'motivator' factors: do they make you want to work harder, for their sake?

Herzberg encouraged managers to study the job itself (nature of tasks, levels of responsibility) rather than conditions of work. 'Dissatisfaction arises from environment factors – satisfaction can only arise from the job.' If there is sufficient challenge, scope and interest in the job, there will be a lasting increase in satisfaction and the employee will work well; productivity will be above 'normal' levels. The extent to which a job must be challenging or creative in order to provide motivation will depend on each individual, his ability, his expectations and his tolerance for delayed success.

We will discuss job satisfaction as a motivator in more detail, later in this chapter.

Maslow's hierarchy and Herzberg's two factors are content theories. We will now look at a major process theory. There are various theories based on ways of calculating whether extra 'E factors' are worth expending in the pursuit of goals. One of the earliest and most influential is expectancy theory.

2.3   Expectancy theory

Essentially, expectancy theory states that the strength of an individual's motivation to do something will depend on the extent to which he expects the results of his efforts, if successfully achieved, to contribute towards his personal needs or goals.

In 1964 Victor Vroom (another American psychologist) worked out a formula by which human motivation could actually be assessed and measured, based on expectancy theory. Vroom suggested that the strength of an individual's motivation is the product of two factors.

(a) *The strength of his preference for a certain outcome.* Vroom called this *valence.* It may be represented as a positive or negative number, or zero – since outcomes may be desired, avoided or considered with indifference.

(b) His *expectation that that outcome will in fact result from a certain behaviour.* Vroom called this *subjective probability*: it is only the individual's expectation, and depends on his perception of the link between behaviour and outcome. As a probability, it may be represented by any number between 0 (no chance) and 1 (certainty).

In its simplest form, the expectancy equation therefore runs: $F = V \times E$.

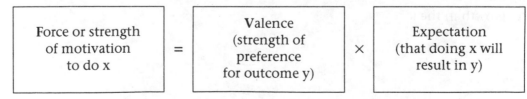

| Force or strength of motivation to do x | = | Valence (strength of preference for outcome y) | × | Expectation (that doing x will result in y) |

This is what you might expect: if either valence or expectation have a value of zero, there will be no motivation.

(a) An employee may have a high *expectation* that behaviour x (increased productivity) will result in outcome y (promotion) – because of past experience, or a negotiated productivity deal, for example. So E = 1. However, if he is *indifferent* to that outcome (perhaps because he doesn't want the responsibility that promotion will bring), V = 0. And 0 x 1 = 0: the individual will not be motivated to more productive behaviour.

(b) If the employee has a *great desire* for outcome y (promotion) – but doesn't have high *expectations* that behaviour x (increased production) will secure it for him (say, because he has been passed over previously), E = 0. He will still not be highly motivated.

(c) If V = -1, (because the employee actively fears responsibility and doesn't want to leave his work group), the value for motivation may be negative: the employee may deliberately *under*-produce.

Activity 4 [15 minutes]

Read the following statements and analyse the force of each individual's motivations.

(a) Raj has seen how people can progress within the organisation and is studying at evening classes to gain further qualifications.

(b) Mary is good at her job but knows there is little chance of promotion.

(c) John is frightened by new challenges.

Now analyse the force of your motivation to pass this module.

Expectancy theory attempts to measure the strength of an individual's motivation to act in a particular way. It is then possible to compare 'F' (force of motivation) values for a range of different behaviours, to discover which behaviour the individual is most likely to adopt. It is also possible to compare 'F' values for different individuals, to see who is most highly motivated to behave in the desired (or undesirable) way.

3 NON-MONETARY REWARDS

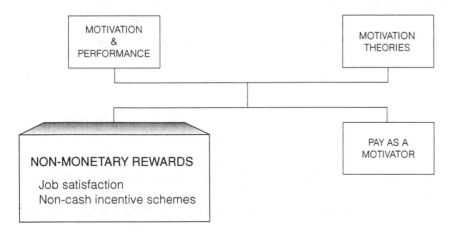

3.1 Job satisfaction

More satisfying job design

Job design is the way in which tasks are fragmented or grouped to form a given job, and what decisions are made about specialisation, discretion, autonomy, variety and other job elements. It acquired its prominence when human relations theorists became interested in the role of job satisfaction in employee performance. It was recognised that jobs made up of low-skilled, repetitive tasks (of which there will inevitably be some in any organisation's operations) could offer little satisfaction to the workers performing them. Such tasks came to be seen as socially isolating, meaningless and monotonous. They were identified as the cause of stress, low morale, fatigue, inattention – causing errors and accidents – and resentment against management.

Activity 5 [15 minutes]

How, other than by *asking* employees (through feedback, interviews or attitude surveys), might an organisation assess whether its employees were satisfied or not?

A systematic approach to job design as a source of job satisfaction was first put forward by Frederick Herzberg, who coined the term 'job enrichment'.

Definition

Job enrichment is planned, deliberate action to build greater responsibility, breadth and challenge of work into a job.

Job enrichment is, in effect, a 'vertical' extension of the job design. It might include:

(a) removing controls;
(b) increasing accountability;
(c) creating natural work units, teams or client relationships;
(d) providing direct feedback on performance; or
(e) introducing new tasks or special assignments.

For discussion

'Even those who want their jobs enriched will expect to be rewarded with more than job satisfaction. Job enrichment is not a cheaper way to greater productivity. Its pay-off will come in the less visible costs of morale, climate and working relationships'. (Handy).
Who really gains from job enrichment?

Job enlargement is frequently confused with job enrichment, though it should be clearly defined as a separate technique.

Definition

Job enlargement, as the name suggests, is the attempt to widen jobs by increasing the number of operations in which a job holder is involved.

Arguably, job enlargement is limited in its ability to improve motivation since, as Herzberg points out, to ask a worker to complete three separate tedious, unchallenging tasks is unlikely to motivate him more than asking him to fulfil one single tedious, unchallenging task!

Empowerment

We have already discussed empowerment, in Chapter 1. To recap, in the words of a human resource practitioner (quoted in *Personnel Management*):

'The purpose of empowerment is to free someone from rigorous control by instructions and orders and give them freedom to take responsibility for their ideas and actions, to release hidden resources which would otherwise remain inaccessible.'

The prevailing view of empowerment as a motivator is very much in line with that of the neo-human relations theorists such as Maslow and Herzberg, who believed that organisational effectiveness is determined by the extent to which people's 'higher' psychological needs for growth, challenge, responsibility and self-fulfilment are met by the work that they do. Empowerment is, in effect, a form of job enrichment.

3.2 Non-cash incentive schemes

Incentive and 'recognition' (or reward) schemes are increasingly focused not on cash, but on non-cash awards. Traditionally aimed at sales people, gifts and travel incentives may be offered to staff:

(a) as prizes for workable suggestions on quality improvements or cost reductions;

(b) as rewards for performance improvement, achievement, loyalty, teamwork and so on;

(c) to encourage internal competition.

EXAMPLES

British Telecom – in the wake of large scale voluntary redundancies – launched an up-beat 'Living our values' initiative, including the awarding of gifts to employees exemplifying the organisation's values and being role models to others.

ICL used to offer symbolic awards of bronze, silver and gold medals, but has now replaced these with a gift catalogue (called the 'Excellence Collection') from which nominees choose rewards they value.

Abbey Life's top performers are given the opportunity to attend conventions in exotic foreign locations, with partners (and without an onerous work content): length of stay and luxury of location depend on performance.

Trusthouse Forte has launched a drive to cut employee turnover through an incentive scheme which awards air mileage in return for staff loyalty ... THF is also offering further incentives to staff, including 500 miles for the employee of the month and 1,000 for employee of the year, with another 200 miles for staff receiving a complimentary letter from a guest.

Such schemes can be effective as incentives, team-building exercises, and, perhaps more fundamentally, ways of expressing recognition of achievement – without which staff may feel isolated, undervalued or neglected.

Activity 6 [10 minutes]

The general secretary of the staff union at *Sun Alliance* has been quoted as saying: 'I have worked for a firm which rewarded its top salespeople with a cruise. I can't imagine anything worse than being trapped on a yacht with a lot of other life assurance salesmen'!

What other demotivating effects may result from non-cash incentive schemes?

---

4   PAY AS A MOTIVATOR

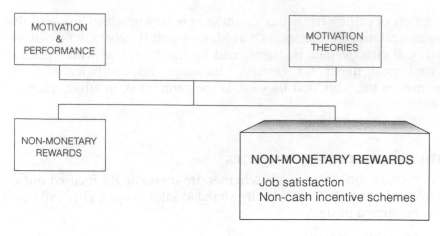

4.1   What do people want from pay?

The most important functions of pay for the organisation are attracting, keeping and motivating staff. But does it work? Pay has a central – but ambiguous – role in motivation theory. It is not mentioned explicitly in any need list, but it may be the means to an infinite number of specific ends, offering the satisfaction of many of the various needs. The assumption that people will adjust their effort if offered money is the basis of payment-by-results schemes, bonuses, profit-sharing and other monetary incentives. However, individuals may have needs unrelated to money, which money cannot satisfy, or which the pay system of the organisation actively denies. So to what extent is pay an inducement to better performance: a motivator or incentive?

Employees need income to live. The size of their income will affect their standard of living. However, people tend not to be concerned to maximise their earnings. They may like to earn more, but are probably more concerned:

(a) to earn *enough* pay; and

(b) to know that their pay is *fair* in comparison with the pay of others both inside and outside the organisation.

Payment systems then have to tread the awkward path between *equity* (the perceived fairness of pay rates and structures) and *incentive* (an offered reward to stimulate extra effort and attainment by particular individuals and groups).

Pay as a hygiene factor

Pay is one of Herzberg's hygiene rather than motivator factors. It gets taken for granted, and so is more usually a source of dissatisfaction than satisfaction. (In the absence of information about how much colleagues are earning, individuals tend to guess – and usually over-estimate. This then leaves them dissatisfied because they resent earning less than they think their colleagues are getting!)

However, pay is the most important of the hygiene factors. It is valuable because:

(a) it can be converted into a wide range of other satisfactions (perhaps the only way in which organisations can – at least indirectly – cater for individual employee's needs and wants through a common reward system);

(b) it represents a consistent measure of an individual's worth or value to an employer, allowing people to compare themselves with other individuals and occupational groups inside and outside the organisation.

The only reason to work?

The Affluent Worker research of Goldthorpe, Lockwood et al (1968) investigated highly-paid Luton car assembly workers who experienced their work as routine and dead-end. The researchers concluded that they had made a rational decision to enter employment offering high monetary reward rather than intrinsic interest: they were getting out of their jobs what they most wanted from them.

The Luton researchers, however, did not claim that all workers have this kind of orientation to work, but suggested that a person will seek a suitable balance of:

(a) the rewards which are important to him; and

(b) the deprivations he feels able to put up with.

Most people have limits to their purely financial aspirations, and will cease to be motivated by money if the deprivations – in terms of long working hours, poor conditions, social isolation or whatever – become too great: in other words, if the 'price' of pay is too high.

For discussion

How do you (and others) feel personally about pay as a motivator? Where would you draw the line between extra money and the hardships required to earn it?

Organisations are obliged to reward or remunerate employees for the amount and standard of work agreed in the contract of employment: to give a fair day's pay for a fair day's work. In addition, the organisation may wish to offer monetary incentives (or 'carrots') to employees, if they will work longer or more productively. Monetary incentives include performance-related pay, bonuses, and profit-sharing. So do they work?

4.2 Cash incentives

Following our discussion of the limitations of pay as a motivator, you should be aware of a number of difficulties associated with incentive schemes based on monetary reward.

(a) Workers are unlikely to be in complete control of results, because of other variables such as resource availability, or market conditions. The relationship between an individual's efforts and a results-related reward may therefore be indistinct. This will affect the expectancy calculation, and reduce the motivating effect of the incentive.

(b) Increased earnings simply may not be an incentive to some individuals. An individual who already enjoys a good income may be more concerned with increasing his leisure time, for example.

(c) Even if employees are motivated by money, the effects may not be altogether desirable. Individual bonuses, for example, may encourage self-interest and competition at the expense of teamwork. Payment by results may encourage attention to output at the expense of quality, and the lowering of standards and targets (in order to make bonuses more accessible).

(d) Workers often suspect that if they regularly achieve high levels of output (and earnings), they will make it look too easy (and costly) so that management will set higher performance targets to reduce future earnings. Work groups therefore tend to restrict output to a level that they feel is 'fair', but 'safe'.

> ## Chapter roundup
>
> - *Content* theories of motivation suggest that man has a package of needs: the best way to motivate an employee is to find out what his needs are and offer him rewards that will satisfy those needs.
>   - Abraham Maslow identified a hierarchy of needs which an individual will be motivated to satisfy, progressing towards higher order satisfactions, such as self-actualisation.
>   - Frederick Herzberg identified two basic need systems: the need to avoid unpleasantness and the need for personal growth. He suggested factors which could be offered by organisations to satisfy both types of need: 'hygiene' and 'motivator' factors respectively.
> - *Process* theories of motivation do not tell managers what to offer employees in order to motivate them, but help managers to understand the dynamics of employees' decisions about what rewards are worth going for. They are generally variations on the expectancy model: F = V x E.
> - Various means have been suggested of improving job satisfaction but there is little evidence that a satisfied worker actually works harder.
> - Pay is the most important of the hygiene factors, but it is ambiguous in its effect on motivation.

Quick quiz

1 What is the difference between a reward and an incentive?
2 List five motivator and five hygiene factors.
3 Explain the formula 'F = V x E'.
4 Distinguish between job enrichment and job enlargement.
5 What is 'empowerment'?
6 Give two examples of non-cash incentives and two examples of monetary incentives.
7 'People will work harder and harder to earn more and more pay.' Do you agree? Why (or why not)?
8 List three potential problems of cash incentives.

Answers to quick quiz

1 A reward is given for some contribution or success. An incentive is a promise or offer of reward.
2 Motivation – status, advancement, recognition, responsibility, challenging work, achievement, growth. Hygiene – company policy and administration, salary, quality of supervision, relationships, job security, working conditions.
3 Force of motivation = Valence x Expectation
4 Refer to section 3.1, Definitions.
5 Empowerment frees staff from rigorous control to let them take responsibility for their ideas and actions.
6 Non-cash incentives include gifts, awards, travel. Cash incentives include bonuses, results related rewards, profit sharing.
7 People work to earn enough pay which can then be converted into other satisfactions. If they enjoy a good income, they become more concerned with increasing leisure time.

8 Workers are not in control of results, individual bonuses can encourage self-interest, payment by results emphasises output rather than quality.

Answers to Activities

1 Your answer probably indicates that your motives for studying for this qualification are to improve yourself and your opportunities.

2 We do not usually think consciously about which category of needs we have reached. If you are a student on a low income, your main needs may be in the lower categories such as security and safety. Once those have been taken care of, you will probably move to the need for esteem and recognition.

3 (a) Possibly some of the basics you wish to get from a study course are gaining knowledge, experiencing the 'learning' environment of the college and enjoying the company of colleagues, all of which correspond to Herzberg's hygiene factors.

　　(b) Apart from individual subjects which you may particularly enjoy, you might also like the feeling of achievement when you receive good marks, knowing there will be a better opportunity for work or higher education, challenge and growth.

4 The force of motivation in the three situations is:

　　(a) $V = 1, E = 1; F = 1 \times 1 = 1$ (Highly motivated towards success)

　　(b) $V = 0, E = 1; F = 0 \times 1 = 0$ (Low expectations)

　　(c) $V = -1, E = 0; F = -1 \times 0 = 0$ (Totally negative and probably under-producing).

5 (a) There is little evidence that a satisfied worker actually works harder – so increased productivity per se will not imply satisfaction on the part of the work force. They may be motivated by fear, or work methods may have been improved.

　　(b) There is, however, support for the idea that satisfied workers tend to be loyal, and stay in the organisation.
　　　　(i) *Labour turnover* (the rate at which people leave an organisation) may therefore be an indication of dissatisfaction in the workforce – although there is a certain amount of natural wastage.
　　　　(ii) *Absenteeism* may also be an indication of dissatisfaction, or possibly of genuine physical or emotional distress.

　　(c) There is also evidence that satisfaction correlates with mental health – so that symptoms of stress or psychological failure may be a signal to management that all is not well.

6 Non-cash incentive schemes can be regarded as manipulative, irrelevant (awards may be seen as being given for things that ought to be part of the job, with no special effort required), or just plain gimmicky.

Assignment 4 [About 1/2 hour]

JC Ltd manufacture garden furniture. It is a very successful company with a good reputation for the goods it produces. There are wage and salary grades, job descriptions and firm rules and procedures. The rates of pay are competitive and it is easy to attract external applicants when supervisory or management jobs are advertised (it is company policy to recruit from outside the company). There is a bonus scheme for shop floor operatives and generous overtime payments are paid. Communication is 'top down' with little or no encouragement for feedback.

Over the past year there has been a steady increase in labour turnover and absenteeism. Time keeping has worsened and there has been an increase in reported grievances. It is also becoming more difficult to encourage operatives to work overtime.

(a) What do you think are the reasons for this unrest and dissatisfaction?

(b) What can JC Ltd do about it?

Write a memo to J Cross, the Managing Director.

Chapter 5

INTERPERSONAL BEHAVIOUR AT WORK

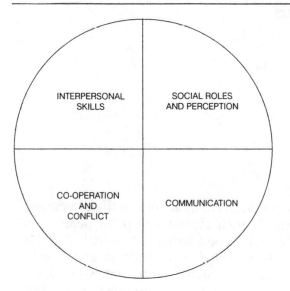

Introduction

'Interpersonal behaviour' simply means behaviour 'between people' and specifically between two or more individuals. (Behaviour in and between groups of people is slightly different, and we'll be covering it in Chapter 6.)

Interpersonal behaviour is crucial in organisations because – as you may remember – they involve 'social arrangements for the controlled performance of collective goals'. People have to deal with each other, communicate with each other and co-operate with each other – and handle situations where they are not communicating or co-operating well. This is why interpersonal skills are so highly prized, particularly in managerial jobs.

Interpersonal behaviour includes *interaction between people:* two-way processes such as communication, co-operation or conflict, persuasion and influence. However, it also includes our *individual behaviour in relation to other people.* For example, the way we perceive others (rightly or wrongly) and the way we perceive ourselves in relation to others (the 'roles' we adopt with them).

Your objectives

After completing this chapter you should:

(a) be aware of the roles that you may adopt in relation to other people at work;

(b) be aware of the tendency to perceptual bias and distortion in your assessment of others;

(c) be able to outline the process of interpersonal communication, identify potential barriers, and suggest how communication might be improved;

(d) be able to analyse the causes and nature of conflict, and to suggest means of controlling conflict and encouraging co-operation in a work situation;

(e) be able to analyse and evaluate the effect of your (and others') behaviour in interpersonal relationships at work.

1 SOCIAL ROLES AND PERCEPTION

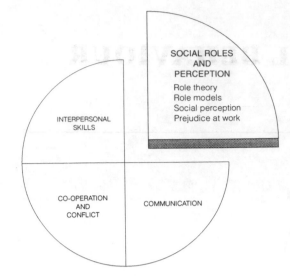

1.1 Role theory

Role theory is concerned with the roles that individuals act out in their lives, and how the assumption of various roles affects their attitudes to other people. An individual may, for example, consider himself to be a father (when he is with his children) and husband (with his wife). He may also be an amateur golfer (with other golfers), a Christian (at church) and a research scientist (at work). Each organisation to which the individual belongs provides him with one or more such roles to perform, and he will behave with other people according to the particular role(s) he is 'in' at the time, in relation to those people.

The people who relate to a particular person in a particular role are called a *role set*. For example, in her role as business manager, an individual may deal with a role set consisting of her bosses, subordinates, and other colleagues, and the suppliers and customers with whom she comes into contact. All these people will relate to the manager as a manager – rather than as a wife, mother, tennis enthusiast or whatever.

People adopt *role signs* to indicate what role they are in at a particular time: in other words, which 'hat' they have on. This might actually involve wearing a hat (the role sign of a chef, for example) or other clothes, so that when someone puts on a uniform, a white coat or a business suit, they adopt the behaviour appropriate to the associated role. Role signs also include manners or styles of behaving: if you worked with your partner in an office, you would (hopefully) act rather differently, in your role as a colleague or supervisor/subordinate, than you would in your role and relationship outside work.

If an individual (or members of his role set) are not sure exactly what his role is in a given situation, there is a problem of *role ambiguity*. Managers who are very informal with their staff may encounter problems in this area: are they relating to their staff as friend, or as boss? Which do their staff *see* them as? It may also be a problem where a person's responsibilities are not clearly defined: what role does the organisation (or family, or whatever) *expect* him to adopt?

Different people may have different expectations about what role an individual should be in, in a particular situation: this is called *role incompatibility*. A classic example is the demands of an individual's work and non-work roles: do you work late, or spend more time with your family? If incompatible roles actually clash, this may cause *role conflict*.

Activity 1 [20 minutes]

Choose one role in which you regularly interact with other people. (The role of 'student', say?)

(a) Identify your role set and role signs.

(b) Identify any areas of ambiguity, incompatibility or conflict the role presents. What could be done about each (if anything)? Could the other members of your role set help?

We noted in Chapter 3, on personality, that our self-image is partly developed through interaction with other people. We compare ourselves with others, and adapt our image of what we are and what we want to be, accordingly. The people we compare ourselves with are called our role models.

1.2 Role models

Individuals consciously or unconsciously select models for the various roles that are relevant to their lives: other individuals that are perceived to be successful or admirable in those roles. We tend to model our own behaviour in a given role on that of the relevant role model. Boys learn what it is to be a man/father/husband/worker from their observation or experience of their father, older brother, a male teacher, or a sports hero, for example.

An individual's attraction as a role model may come from our perception of that person's:

(a) charisma, or personal charm;

(b) expertise, or knowledge – the appeal of the parent, teacher, boss, guru;

(c) demonstrated success – as with a manager, hero or famous person; or

(d) moral or physical ascendancy, strength or personal domination.

The role model may therefore not represent an ideal or socially helpful example of the role in question. Teenagers may, for example, model themselves on charismatic rebels, whose behavioural style may not be appropriate in a family or work context.

Activity 2 [15 minutes]

Managers could exert a powerful influence over team members if they could establish themselves as role models. What kind of example could they set that might be helpful for the team members and for the organisation?

We covered the process of perception in Chapter 3. Here, we look at some of its implications for the way we relate to other people at work.

1.3 Social perception

The way in which we *perceive* other people is crucial to how we relate to them and communicate with them in any context. It is the root of all attempts to motivate and manage people at work, and the basis from which individuals develop (by comparison with others, as they perceive them). However, we noted that the process of perception means that we rarely see things and people as they 'really are'.

Definitions

Bias is a mental tendency or inclination to see things in a particular way. It is used mainly to refer to irrational preferences or dislikes, usually a form of prejudice.

Prejudice is a 'pre-judgement', an opinion formed before all the relevant facts are known – particularly an unfavourable opinion.

There are two important forms of bias in our everyday perception of other people:

● the 'halo effect'; and
● 'stereotyping'.

The halo effect

The halo effect is the term relating to our first highly selective judgements about people – based on immediately obvious characteristics like dress, manner or facial expression. These colour our later perception of other features of those people, to positive or negative effect. Further information that does not agree with the first assessment, and the expectations based on it, tends to be filtered out (perceptual selectivity).

This presents a problem because the characteristics on which we base our first impressions may be:

(a) irrelevant to the judgement we are actually trying to make (consider how physical attractiveness colours your perception of a person's personality, intelligence and so on); and/or

(b) highly superficial, and usually the characteristics that we possess ourselves – since these are most readily recognisable and esteemed.

The halo effect operates, favourably or unfavourably, in all sorts of situations (such as job interviews) where 'first impressions count'. You have probably been told at some point that well-groomed, smiling people with firm handshakes do well in interviews.

Stereotyping

Stereotyping can have the same practical implications as the halo effect, but operates through perceptual organisation rather than selectivity. We tend to group together people who share certain general characteristics: say, nationality, occupation, age, race, gender or physical characteristics (like baldness or obesity). We attribute certain qualities or traits to the group – based on personal experience of particular individuals, common misconceptions or pure prejudice. We then assume (illogically) that each individual member of our (artificial) 'group' possesses our (arbitrary) traits.

So, for example, in a recent survey to find the most boring group of people in Britain, statisticians 'won' by a large majority! Dumb blondes, thick Irishmen and other stereotypes tend to be spread and perpetuated by jokes and popular culture. (At the time of writing, there is protest over an advertisement for a chunky, masculine, 4-wheel drive off-road vehicle, with a headline saying 'Hairdressers need not apply'!)

Stereotypes are obviously over-generalisations, and although, as we suggested in Chapter 3, they may be a convenient shortcut to interpersonal relations, they should be consciously checked for accuracy in each case.

For discussion

What traits come to mind when you think of the following? Brainstorm some adjectives – being as honest as you can – and then discuss where any prejudices or assumptions might have come from.

● *Scotsmen*
● *Female shot putters*
● *Football supporters*
● *Trainspotters*
● *Grannies*
● *Sports car drivers*

Keeping an eye on hasty assumptions and bias is not just a matter of getting at the truth or reality. 'Prejudice' means pre-judging an issue: it also means intolerance of, or dislike for, people of a specific race, religion or other group. Such prejudice, where it is offensive or harmful to a person of that group, may well be an offence under the law. This is a management issue!

1.4 Prejudice at work

'Discrimination' occurs when one group is treated less favourably than another, particularly in regard to access to opportunities at work: selection for jobs or promotion, training, equal pay for equal work, selection for redundancy and so on.

Three main Acts of Parliament deal with this issue in the UK.

(a) The Sex Discrimination Act 1975, outlawing certain types of discrimination on the grounds of sex or marital status (whether someone is married or single).

(b) The Race Relations Act 1976, outlawing certain types of discrimination on grounds of colour, race, nationality, or ethnic or national origin.

(c) The Disability Discrimination Act 1995, outlawing discrimination on the grounds of physical or mental impairment.

Activity 3 [15 minutes]

Why do you think there has traditionally been discrimination against women in regard to job opportunities? Try to think of at least three reasons.

Apart from sex and race, you should be aware of the implications of your attitudes towards:

(a) *marital status* – it is unlawful to discriminate against married people, for example, if you believe a single man will devote more time to the job;

(b) *age* – the Institute of Personnel Development has urged that age-related criteria be challenged in every aspect of employment decision-making;

(c) *sexual orientation* – British Airways, for example, has extended its concessionary travel scheme to partners of gay employees, as well as husbands and wives.

2   COMMUNICATION

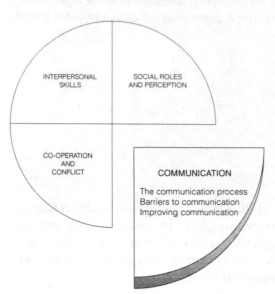

Definition

Communication is basically the transmission or exchange of information.

Communication is a universal human activity, which may be directed at:

(a) initiating action – eg by request, instruction or persuasion;

(b) making known needs and requirements;

(c) exchanging information, ideas, attitudes and beliefs;

(d) establishing understanding – and perhaps also exerting influence or persuasion;

(e) establishing and maintaining relationships.

Communication therefore embraces a wide spectrum of interpersonal activities in organisations, both in the way the organisation as an entity communicates or projects itself to people who come into contact with it, and in the way that individuals within and around the organisation communicate with each other.

2.1   The communication process

Effective communication is a two-way process, perhaps best expressed as a cycle. Signals, or messages are sent by the communicator and received by the other party, who sends back some form of confirmation that the message has been received and understood, see figure 5.1.

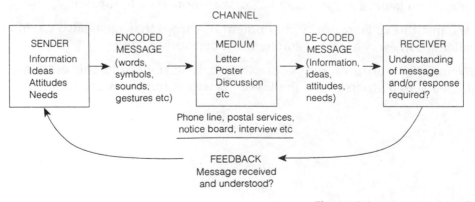

Figure 5.1 A communication cycle

A number of points should be noted.

(a) *Coding and de-coding.* The code or language of a message may be:
   (i) verbal (in words), whether oral (spoken) or written; or
   (ii) non-verbal: in pictures, diagrams, numbers or body language, facial expression, gestures and so on.

The important thing is that the code should be shared by the sender and receiver – otherwise the receiver will not be able to translate the message correctly.

(b) *Media.* The choice of an appropriate medium for communication depends on a number of factors.
   (i) A phone call, for example, is *quicker* than a letter.
   (ii) *Complexity.* A written message, for example, allows the use of diagrams, figure workings etc and time for perusal at the recipient's own pace, repeated if necessary.
   (iii) The *need for a written record*, eg for the confirmation of business transactions.
   (iv) The *need for interaction* or the immediate exchange of information or questions and answers. Face-to-face discussion is often used to solve complex problems or sell the benefits of a service.
   (v) *Confidentiality* (eg a private interview or personal letter) or, conversely, the *dissemination* of information widely and quickly (eg via a notice board or public meeting).
   (vi) *Cost*, in relation to all the above, for the best possible result at the least possible expense.

(c) *Feedback.* Feedback makes communication a two-way process or cycle, and indicates to the sender whether or not his message has been successfully received and interpreted. Failure to seek or offer feedback, and ignoring feedback offered, are a source of major problems in communication. Feedback may be:

Positive	*Negative*
● Action being taken as requested	● No action or wrong action being taken
● A letter/note/memo confirming receipt of message and replying in an appropriate way	● No written response where expected
	● Request for more information, clarification or repetition
● Accurate reading-back of message	● Failure to read back message correctly
● Smile, nod, murmur of agreement, 'I've got that' etc	● Silence, blank look, sound or gesture of protest or perplexity

Non-verbal communication

People generally learn, and are taught, to use words to communicate: to speak articulately and to write intelligibly. Much less attention is given to the more complex, and more ambiguous area of 'non-verbal communication': communication without words, or other than in words. The way we stand, where we position ourselves in relation to other people, our tone of voice, gestures and facial expressions all communicate something.

We may use such signals deliberately:

(a) *instead* of words, for example storming from a room, or pointing something out; or

(b) to *confirm or add* to the meaning of our words (nodding and saying 'yes', pointing something out and saying 'look!');

(c) to provide appropriate *feedback* to the sender of a message (a yawn, applause, a clenched fist, fidgeting);

(d) to create a desired *impression* or atmosphere (smart dress, firm handshake, informal manner, respectful distance).

We may also be using such signals, *unconsciously*, in a way that undermines our verbal message (saying 'I'm fine' with a grim expression, pallor or shaking hand).

If we become more aware of non-verbal messages, we can:

(a) pick up feedback from our listeners, and modify our message accordingly;

(b) recognise people's real feelings below their words, which may be particularly useful if the 'surface' of the communication is constrained by politeness or formality, or if there are signs of personal or interpersonal problems;

(c) 'read' situations in order to control our own communication and response strategy – is the potential customer convinced? (make the sale); – is the interviewee on the point of hysteria? (be soothing);

(d) control our own signals, to reinforce the messages we want to give – and disguise those we do not!

Activity 4 [15 minutes]

From your own experience, list at least four non-verbal messages you have recognised as contradicting what is being said.

Our outline of the communication cycle should have alerted you to how complex the process is, and how open to problems. Consider the nature of 'coding' and 'uncoding', for example. It is easy to misinterpret the surface meaning of words and numbers (eg for a layman who is not familiar with technical language or jargon), let alone the underlying meaning conveyed only by tone of voice, sarcasm, metaphorical language and so on. Let us look in more detail at barriers to effective communication.

2.2 Barriers to communication

Potential problems in the communication process include the following.

(a) *Not* communicating. (Bear in mind that even 'tactful' or 'thoughtful' silences are open to misinterpretation).

(b) *Pointless* communicating: sending a message that is meaningless, irrelevant or unsuitable to the purpose and recipient of the communication.

(c) *Distortion:* a technical term for the way in which the meaning of a communication is lost in handling. It occurs mainly at the 'encoding' and 'decoding' stages of the process, where:
  (i) the intention of the sender fails to translate itself accurately into language that is suitable for its purpose and its intended recipient, so that the wrong message is being sent; (examples include lack of clarity, and using technical language or jargon); or
  (ii) the language used is not translated properly by the receiver, so the wrong message is being received. (Remember perceptual selectivity – people hear what they want or expect to hear.)

(d) *Noise* refers to distractions and interference in the environment in which communication is taking place. It may be physical noise (passing traffic), technical noise (a bad telephone line), social noise (differences in the personalities, background and attitudes of the parties) or psychological noise (anger, frustration, tiredness and other feelings).

(e) *Non-verbal signals* (gestures, facial expression, appearance, posture are examples) contradicting the verbal message, confusing the recipient. (If someone is saying, 'That's very interesting', as they visibly stifle a yawn, what are you to think?)

(f) *'Overload'* – giving the recipient more information than he can digest or use in the time available – or, on the other hand, insufficient or incomplete information for its purpose.

Activity 5 [20 minutes]

Before reading on, what problems are suggested by the following?

(a) [On the noticeboard] 'P Brown. Your complaint about the behaviour of your colleague S Simms is being looked into. Manager.'

(b) 'Prima facie, I would postulate statutory negligence, as per para 22 Sec three et seq. Nil desperandum.' 'Eh?'

(c) 'Smith – you've been scratching your head and frowning like mad ever since I started the briefing half an hour ago. I've tried to ignore it but – have you got fleas or something?'

(d) 'Sorry, this line's terrible – how many? how much? – what was that? NO, it's OK: I'll remember it all. We'll deliver on Monday – no, MONDAY: no, M-O-N ...'

(e) Date: 11 March. Report on communication: 463 pages. Please read for staff meeting: 12 March.

(f) 'Look. Nobody pays you to think: leave that to us professionals. Just do your job.'

There may be additional, particular problems in a work situation.

(a) Hostility or resentment of subordinates towards management, resulting in deliberate attempts to sabotage communication.

(b) Subordinates otherwise giving superiors incorrect or incomplete information (eg to protect a colleague, to avoid bothering the superior or to avoid giving 'bad news').

(c) People from different levels in the hierarchy, jobs or specialisms, being on a different wavelength: with different perceptions, attitudes, technical vocabulary and so on.

(d) Lack of opportunity, formal or informal, for subordinates to say what they think or feel.

(e) Employees simply not taking an interest in organisational matters which do not affect them personally.

(f) An organisation culture which shares information only on a functional or 'need to know' basis: common in bureaucracies.

(g) Organisational politics and conflict: since 'knowledge is power' people may be reluctant to share information with each other.

2.3 Improving communication

It may be apparent from the preceding paragraphs that communication problems fall into three broad categories.

● There may be a bad formal communication system hindering or discouraging the exchange of information. (We will be discussing this in Chapter 13.)

● Noise or distortion may be causing misunderstanding about the content and meaning of messages.

● Interpersonal differences may be causing a break-down in communications.

Some interpersonal communication difficulties can therefore be overcome by:

(a) encouraging people to be aware of the problems;

(b) training people in communication techniques; and

(c) creating a trusting and communicative organisation culture.

Activity 6 [10 minutes]

Indicate the most effective way in which the following situations should be communicated.

(a) Spare parts needed urgently.

(b) A message from the managing director to all staff.

(c) Fred Bloggs has been absent five times in the past month and his manager intends taking action.

(d) You need information quickly from another department.

(e) You have to explain a complicated operation to a group.

---

3 CO-OPERATION AND CONFLICT

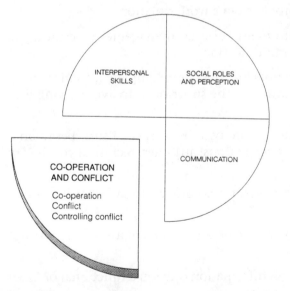

3.1 Co-operation

Definition

Co-operation is working or acting together.

Right at the beginning of this text, we noted that organisations exist through and for people working or acting together. Organisations are co-operative structures and systems. In a sense, all the management functions and techniques covered in this module are about encouraging and facilitating co-operation.

Co-operation is a common cultural belief.

(a) It has a rational appeal. A number of people co-operating on a task will often achieve better results than the same number of individuals working alone. This 2 + 2 = 5 effect is called synergy.

(b) It has an emotional appeal. It incorporates values about unity, teamwork, comradeship, being insiders (versus outsiders) and so on.

Some cultures encourage this more than others. In the UK, individualism is a major aspect of the national culture – despite stated views on the virtues of co-operation. Studies of German, Japanese and Swedish cultures demonstrate a greater emphasis on co-operation and inter-dependence.

For discussion

'Any business must mould a true team and weld individual efforts into a common effort. Each member of the enterprise contributes something different, but they must all contribute towards a common goal. Their efforts must all pull in the same direction, without friction and without unnecessary duplication of effort.' Drucker.

'The history of all ... society is the history of class struggles. Freeman and slave, patrician and plebeian, lord and serf ... in a word, oppressor and oppressed, stood in constant opposition to one another, carried on an uninterrupted, now hidden, now open fight.' Marx and Engels: The Communist Manifesto.

Is an organisation a 'happy family' – or a 'theatre of war'? (Note that while it is difficult to argue against co-operation as a Good Thing, actually it depends on what you are asking people to co-operate with! Does co-operation reflect their real views and interests?)

The opposite of co-operation is conflict. We will now look at conflict, and how (or whether) a manager can avoid or control it in the work team.

3.2   Conflict

You might assume that, as the opposite of co-operation, conflict is a Bad Thing. Indeed, conflict can be destructive, or negative. It may:

(a) distract attention from the group's task (to personal objectives, like scoring points off other group members);

(b) polarise views and fragment – or even destroy – the group;

(c) encourage defensive or 'spoiling' behaviour;

(d) stimulate emotional, win-lose arguments and hostility.

However, conflict can also clarify issues and revitalise relationships – as you may know if you 'enjoy a good argument'! Conflict can be helpful or *constructive* when its effect is to:

(a) introduce new solutions to problems, as people 'spark' ideas off each other;

(b) define relationships more clearly;

(c) encourage the testing of ideas to see whether they are valid;

(d) focus attention on individual contribution and responsibility rather than allowing people to hide behind group decisions;

(e) provide opportunity for the release of hostile feelings and attitudes that have been, or may be, repressed otherwise.

Sometimes, what appears to be a rather painful argument can have very positive outcomes: a strike, for example, may normally be seen as destructive and hostile. In fact it can provide an impetus to problem-solving, and a way of clearing the air. Too much co-operation and agreement may conversely produce a 'love-in', where task objectives become secondary to the group's enjoyment of its interpersonal relationships.

So how is a manager to get the best out of conflict in his team – and not the worst?

3.3   Controlling conflict

Charles Handy redefined the term 'conflict' to offer a useful way of thinking about destructive and constructive conflict and how it might be managed.

(a) Organisations are political systems within which there is *competition* for scarce resources and unequal influence.

(b) *Differences* between people are natural and inevitable. Differences emerge in three ways:
  (i)   argument;
  (ii) competition; and
  (iii) conflict – which alone is harmful.

Argument and competition are potentially beneficial and fruitful; both may degenerate into conflict if badly managed.

Argument

Argument means resolving differences by discussion. This can encourage the integration of a number of viewpoints into a better solution. Handy suggests that in order for argument to be effective:

(a) the arguing group must have leadership, mutual trust, and a challenging task to focus on; and

(b) the logic of the argument must be preserved: the issues under discussion must be clear, the discussion must concentrate on available information (not guesswork or fantasy), and all views must be heard and taken into account.

If such argument is frustrated, or if the argument itself is merely the symptom of underlying, unexpressed hostility, then conflict will be the result.

Competition

Competition can:

(a) set standards, by pointing to the 'best' performance achieved by one of the competing parties;

(b) motivate individuals to better effort; and

(c) 'sort out the men from the boys'.

In order to be fruitful, competition must be seen to be *open*, rather than *closed*. 'Closed' competition is a win-lose (or 'zero-sum') situation, where one party's gain will be another party's loss: one party can only do well at the expense of another, in competition for resources, recognition and so on. 'Open' competition exists where *all* participants can increase their gains together: for example, if bonuses are available to *all* teams which produce more or better output, not just the 'best' team.

If competition is perceived to be open, the rules are seen to be fair, and the competitors feel that the factors leading to success are within their control, then competition can be extremely fruitful.

Activity 7 [10 minutes]

What *symptoms* might indicate to you that *conflict* was becoming a problem in a team?

Conflict

Charles Handy suggests two types of strategy which may be used to turn harmful conflict into constructive competition or argument, or to manage it in some other acceptable way.

(a) *Environmental ('ecological') strategies* involve creating conditions in which individuals may be better able to work co-operatively with each other. Such strategies include:
  (i) agreement of common objectives;
  (ii) reinforcing the group or 'team' nature of organisational life;
  (iii) providing feedback information on progress;
  (iv) providing adequate co-ordination and communication mechanisms;
  (v) sorting out territorial/role conflicts in the organisational structure.

(b) *Regulation strategies* are directed to the *control of conflict* when it arises. Possible methods include:
  (i) the provision of arbitration to settle disputes;
  (ii) the establishment of detailed rules and procedures for conduct by employees;
  (iii) using confrontational inter-group meetings to hammer out differences, especially where territorial conflicts occur;
  (iv) separating the conflicting individuals; and
  (v) ignoring the problem, *if* it is genuinely likely to go away, and there is no point in opening fresh wounds.

Activity 8 [30 minutes]

In the light of the above, consider how conflict could arise and how it might be resolved in the following situations.

(a) Two managers who share a secretary have documents to be typed at the same time.

(b) A company's electricians find out that a group of engineers have been receiving training in electrical work.

(c) Department A stops for lunch at 12.30 while Department B stops at 1 o'clock. Occasionally the canteen runs out of puddings for Department B workers.

(d) The Northern Region and Southern Region sales teams are continually trying to better each other's results, and the capacity of production to cope with the increase in sales is becoming overstretched.

4 INTERPERSONAL SKILLS

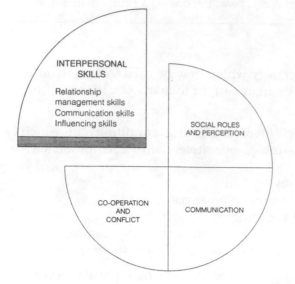

Interpersonal skills are those which are needed by an individual in order to:

- *understand and manage the roles, relationships, attitudes and perceptions operating in any situation in which two or more people are involved;*

- *communicate clearly and effectively; and*

- *achieve his or her aims from an interpersonal encounter (ideally, allowing the other parties to emerge satisfied too).*

We will look at each of these in turn.

4.1 Relationship management skills

Roles and relationships are emotional, perceptual and political processes. They are obviously very complex. A manager will need to be skilled in:

(a) interpreting behaviour and role signs;

(b) empathising with the feelings, attitudes, needs and perceptions of others, in order to understand their behaviour;

(c) giving appropriate role signs to establish the nature of the relationship with others.

Here are some factors to consider in any interpersonal situation.

Goals	What does the other person want from the process? What do you want from the process? What will both parties need and be trying to do to achieve their aims? Can both parties emerge satisfied?
Perceptions	What might be distorting the way both parties see the issues and each other?
Roles	What roles are the parties playing? (Superior/subordinate, customer/server, complainer/soother?) What expectations does this create of the way they will behave?

Resistances   What may the other person be sensitive to or afraid of? What may he be trying to protect? (Self-image? Attitudes?) Tread carefully in these areas.

Attitudes   What sources of difference, conflict or lack of understanding might arise from attitudes and other factors which shape them (sex, race, specialism, hierarchy)?

Relationships   What are the relative positions of the parties and the nature of the relationship between them? (Superior/subordinate? Formal/informal?) What 'style' is appropriate?

Environment   What factors in the situation might affect the issues and the people? (Business competition: remember the customer is always right! Pressure of disciplinary situation: nervousness?)

4.2   Communication skills

Communication skills include the following. (You might like to use our list as a study/practice checklist.)

Skills in the selected medium of communication:

Oral	*Written*	*Visual/non-verbal*
☐ Clear pronunciation	Correct spelling	Understanding of/
☐ Suitable vocabulary	Suitable vocabulary	control over 'body
☐ Correct grammar/syntax	Correct grammar/syntax	language' and
☐ Fluency	Good writing or typing	facial expressions
☐ Expressive delivery	Suitable style	Drawing ability

General skills in sending messages

☐ *Selecting and organising your material:* marshalling your thoughts and constructing your sentences, arguments and so on.

☐ *Judging the effect of your message* on the particular recipient in the particular situation.

☐ *Choosing language and media* accordingly.

☐ *Adapting your communication style* accordingly: putting people at their ease, smoothing over difficulties (tact), or being comforting/challenging/informal/formal as the situation and relationship demand.

☐ *Using non-verbal signals* to reinforce (or at least not to undermine) your spoken message.

☐ *Seeking and interpreting feedback.*

Skills in receiving messages

☐ *Reading* attentively and actively: making sure you understand the content, looking up unfamiliar words and doubtful facts if necessary; evaluating the information given: is it logical? correct? objective?

☐ *Extracting relevant information* from the message, and filtering out inessentials.

☐ *Listening* attentively and actively; concentrating on the message – not on what you are going to say next, or other matters; questioning and evaluating what you are hearing.

☐ *Interpreting the message's underlying meaning*, if any, and evaluating your own reactions: are you reading into the message more or less than what is really there?

☐ *Asking questions* in a way that will elicit the information you wish to obtain. This will usually involve *open* questions ('What ...?', 'Why ...?', 'Who ...?', 'When ...?' etc) requiring the respondent to answer in his own words in complete sentences. *Closed* questions are those which elicit only 'yes' or 'no' answers ('Did you ...?', 'Have you ...?', 'Were there ...?'), which may not be so helpful. *Leading* questions are those which push the respondent to answer in a particular way, because he thinks that is what you want to hear ('Surely you don't ...?', 'I hope you agree that ...'): this may force apparent agreement, but won't elicit real views!

☐ *Interpreting non-verbal signals*, and how they confirm or contradict the spoken message.

☐ *Giving helpful feedback*, if the medium is inappropriate (eg a bad telephone line) or the message is unclear, insufficient or whatever.

4.3 Influencing skills

As we discussed in Chapter 1, there are many factors involved in a person's power and influence over others. However, there are two major skills which will come in handy if you want to achieve your purposes through interpersonal encounters.

Persuasion

Being persuasive may involve skills in the following areas.

(a) *Using logical argument:* starting with points (called 'premises') with which others can readily agree, and showing how together they lead to the conclusion you want to draw.

A logical argument goes: X is true and Y is true, therefore X + Y must be true. ('We don't promote people with poor disciplinary records. And your record is appalling. So you're just not going to get anywhere by behaving like this, are you?')

Bear in mind that you can also make an argument *look* logical, even if it isn't:
(i) if one of your premises (X or Y) is untrue, but is sufficiently plausible to be accepted by an unwary listener/reader; or
(ii) if your premises are correct, but you draw a conclusion that does not really follow from them.

Activity 9
[20 minutes]

What is illogical or dishonest about the following arguments?

(a) 'Well, she's a woman, isn't she? And we all know women are terrible drivers. So there's no sense in letting her have the driver's job, is there?'

(b) 'Look, files have been going missing ever since January. And Jo joined us in January. There's got to be a connection there, hasn't there? Jo's obviously our culprit.'

(c) 'I'm afraid we've simply got to make these changes. All the other departments can't be wrong, can they?'

(b) *Appealing to the needs and wants of other people.* Persuasion is a form of motivation. If you can make it look as if going along with your viewpoint or plans will offer others some benefit to them, they will have a better reason to be persuaded. Persuasion in this sense may be positive reinforcement (offering satisfaction of a need or desire, or the solution to a problem) or negative reinforcement (confronting people with the unpleasant consequences of not going along with you).

(c) *Appealing to emotion*, which may enthuse people, or support a logical argument – or simply override considerations of whether your argument is logical or not! You will have your own views about how valid or honest this is, but advertisers (for example) seem to think it works ...

Assertiveness

Assertiveness may be described as clear, honest and direct communication. It is not to be confused with 'bossiness' or aggression. Aggressive behaviour is competitive and directed at beating someone else: assertion is based on equality and co-operation. Assertion is a simple affirmation that every individual has certain rights and is entitled to stand by them in the face of pressure from other people. It means:

(a) not being dependent on the approval of others for your self-esteem;

(b) not feeling guilty if you do not put other people's needs first all the time (being able to say 'no');

(c) having the confidence to receive criticism openly and give it constructively;

(d) avoiding conflict without having to give up your own values and wants;

(e) being able to express your own values and feelings without guilt or fear;

(f) making clear requests for what you want.

For discussion

Swap some stories about 'best' and 'worst' interpersonal encounters you have had:

(a) as a customer of an organisation, with a representative of an organisation (say, a shop assistant or waiter); and

(b) with a person in authority over you, when they wanted you to do something you did not want to do (a teacher? parent? employer?)

What do these stories reveal about good and bad ways to deal with other people in a work context?

Chapter roundup

- Interpersonal behaviour is behaviour between one or more individuals and the behaviour of one individual in relation to others.
- Individuals assume roles in relation to each other and to the situation: these are the 'hats' that people wear.
- Individuals perceive other people with a certain bias, due to:
  - perceptual selectivity, causing a 'halo effect', which colours the individual's perception, based on superficial characteristics; and
  - perceptual organisation, causing 'stereotyping', or the pigeon-holing and labelling of people according to generalised assumptions.
- Communication is a two-way process involving the transmission or exchange of information, and the provision of feedback. Individual differences, poor communication skills and situational factors may create barriers to effective communication which must be overcome.
- Co-operation is widely considered to be desirable and necessary in organisations, but conflict may also be either destructive or constructive. Differences should be encouraged, and channelled into argument and competition, not destructive conflict.

> ### Chapter roundup *continued*
> - Interpersonal skills which should be developed include:
>   — skills in role and relationship maintenance;
>   — communication skills; and
>   — influencing skills.

Quick quiz

1 What are (a) role signs and (b) role ambiguity?

2 How do we stereotype people?

3 Draw a simple diagram of the communication process, using dotted or broken lines where 'distortion' may be a problem.

4 Give five examples of non-verbal communication, and suggest what they might be used to indicate.

5 Give three examples of good communication practice.

6 Suggest three positive effects of conflict.

7 What is 'zero-sum' competition?

8 Suggest three potentially effective methods of controlling harmful conflict.

9 What is (a) an open question and (b) a closed question?

10 What is the difference between aggression and assertiveness?

Answers to quick quiz

1 (a) How someone dresses and behaves to match the role.

  (b) If an individual is unsure of what his/her role is in a certain situation.

2 By grouping people together who share certain general characteristics.

3 Refer to section 2.1. The dotted lines would run alongside all the arrows.

4 A nod of agreement, a smile to encourage, a frown to disapprove, a yawn to show boredom, turning away to discourage.

5 Using a shared code, choosing an appropriate medium, and providing feedback. Try to think of specific examples.

6 Conflict can introduce new solutions, define relationships more clearly and focus attention on individuals.

7 A competition where one party wins and the other loses.

8 Arbitration, establishing rules and procedures, separating conflicting individuals.

9 (a) Open questions require the respondent to answer in his or her own words;

  (b) closed questions only need 'yes' or 'no'.

10 Aggressive behaviour is competitive; assertion means that every individual has certain rights, and is entitled to stand by them.

Answers to Activities

1 Your answer might be along the following lines.

  (a) If you chose 'student' your role set would consist of fellow students, lecturers, library and administrative staff. Your role signs may included dressing and acting informally with your colleagues, but being rather more formal with the others.

(b) Lecturers who dress and act informally with their students may cause problems. Mature students with partners and children may find role incompatibility when study interferes with personal life.

2 You may have your own views on examples managers could set. Basically, successful managers provide an aspirational model: showing junior staff that it is possible for them to achieve organisational success and the lifestyle that may go with it. A manager may also model the roles of popular leader, a person who combines work and home/leisure life, a person who does not panic in a crisis, a person who is developing their skills and so on. Models are, after all, in the eye of the beholder!

3 Reasons for discrimination against women traditionally include:

(a) social pressures on women to bear and rear children and on men to make a lifetime commitment to 'breadwinning';

(b) child-bearing and family responsibilities interrupting career development;

(c) the nature of early industrial work, which was physically heavy;

(d) the reinforcing of 'segregation' at home and school: for example, lack of encouragement for girls to study maths, science or engineering;

(e) career ladders which do not allow for 'fast-tracking' women

4 Non-verbal contradictions to what is actually said may include someone saying 'I've plenty of time', but looking continually at their watch, avoidance of eye contact, arms folded aggressively, turning away, drumming fingers on a surface or foot tapping.

5 Problems suggested by the statements made may be summed up as follows.

(a) A complete lack of tact and diplomacy. It may be that the manager is deliberately alerting 'S Simms' to the complaint by 'P Brown' but, of course, by putting the information on the noticeboard the whole department will be aware of it too.

(b) Here is someone from a specialist background talking in a jargon which will mean virtually nothing to the average recipient.

(c) At least the speaker has noticed Smith's body language! Even if the suggestion about fleas is an attempt to be facetious, the speaker appears to have misunderstood the nature of feedback: Smith is giving clear signals that (s)he is perplexed by the briefing.

(d) Technical 'noise', plus a further problem, which you may have spotted: the speaker has chosen an inappropriate medium, since he is not writing down the details which are clearly important and will require reference and confirmation later.

(e) A 463-page report to be read for the following day sounds like overload; (and since it's on 'communication', it sounds like a contradiction in terms!)

(f) Status differentials (real or imagined) are the principal source of difficulty here, the speaker evidently wishing to 'put down' the listeners and 'keep them in their place'. S(he) is potentially losing valuable contributions.

6 Communicating the situations given might best be done as follows.

(a) Telephone, confirmed in writing (order form, letter)

(b) Noticeboard or general meeting.

(c) Face-to-face conversation. It would be a good idea to confirm the outcome of the meeting in writing so that records can be maintained.

(d) Either telephone or face to face.

(e) Face to face, supported by clear written notes. You can then use visual aids or gestures. This will give the opportunity for you to check the group's understanding. The notes will save the group having to memorise what you say.

7 Symptoms of conflict in a team might include:

(a) poor communications;

(b) interpersonal friction;

(c) inter-group rivalry and jealousy;

(d) low morale and frustration;

(e) proliferation of rules and norms; especially widespread use of arbitration, appeals to higher authority, and inflexible attitudes towards change.

8 The situations described might lead to the following kinds of conflict, each resolved as shown.

(a) Competition for scarce resources. There would need to be negotiated compromise (someone's documents would wait), borrowing of resources from elsewhere (an extra typist), or a decision on priorities by the two managers' joint boss.

(b) Inter-group rivalry, and dispute about power/job security/'territory'. The electricians will fight against the 'invasion' of their specialist area, and the implied threat to their jobs. Not easy to resolve – especially since the electricians have 'found out' rather than 'been informed'. Confrontation with management (if not the engineers) will bring fears and anger to the surface: reassurance, negotiation (eg cross-training for electricians too) and other conciliation methods will have to be tried. Meanwhile, the conflict may challenge the electricians to better performance – or cause a walkout! One to watch ...

(c) Similar to (a), but less important. It might not be worth stirring up resentment – unless Department B staff already feel very strongly about the issue.

(d) Excessive competition or rivalry. Managers will need to re-emphasise the common objectives (and capacity) of the organisation. Meetings of sales and production team representatives might help clarify the issues: production capacity might be increased! The causes of rivalry should be looked at (North/South attitudes?), as should pay incentives, which may be competitive (win-lose) rather than generally motivating.

9 The given statements are illogical or dishonest because:

(a) One true premise + one false premise (on unsupported 'evidence') = false conclusion.

(b) One true premise + one true premise, but false conclusion because X and Y does not necessary mean X *therefore* Y. ('There's got to be a connection there, hasn't there?' No, actually ...)

(c) 'All the other departments can't be wrong can they?' Yes, they can.

Assignment 5 [About 1$^{1}/_{2}$ hours]

Due to changes in market demand, a massive re-organisation will have to take place in Fleece & Rook Ltd. Some machines will be sold, new ones will be purchased, one production line will close and new methods of packaging will be introduced. This will involve the work force in retraining, changes in work practices and some redundancies. It will also mean that shift working will be introduced.

The managing director, Chris Connor, has to decide the most effective method of communicating these changes to the whole workforce.

(a) How should Chris tell the workforce?

(b) What barriers and reactions is he likely to encounter?

(c) What further communication methods will be necessary to overcome at least some of the barriers and reactions?

Chapter 6

TEAMS

```
                    ┌──────────────────────┐
                    │  WHAT IS A WORK TEAM? │
                    └──────────┬───────────┘
           ┌───────────────────┼───────────────────┐
   ┌───────┴───────┐                       ┌────────┴───────┐
   │  FORMING A     │                       │     TEAM       │
   │  TEAM          │                       │   DYNAMICS     │
   └───────┬───────┘                       └────────────────┘
           │
   ┌───────┴───────┐
   │     TEAM      │
   │ EFFECTIVENESS │
   └───────────────┘
```

Introduction

We have already studied how individuals behave in and by themselves (intra-personal behaviour) and in relation to other individuals (interpersonal behaviour). You may, however, have noticed yourself that people behave differently in a group or crowd than they do on their own or when talking to one or two others: think about a gang of friends on an outing, or a crowd of people at a football match. The interplay and influences within groups that create this behaviour are called 'group dynamics'.

Groups in business organisations are, in effect, sub-*organisations*, and they require management for 'controlled performance of collective goals': not only *their* own collective goals, but those of the business organisation as a whole. This is especially important if the organisation wishes to empower work teams. (See Chapter 1 if you need to refresh your memory.) This chapter looks at what goes on, and why, when people work together in teams.

Your objectives

After completing this chapter, you should:

(a) be able to identify areas in which teamworking may be more or less effective;

(b) be able to identify which stage of development a team has reached, and predict what comes next;

(c) be able to describe the types of people and behaviour required for an effective team;

(d) be able to identify techniques for teambuilding and be aware of the dangers of too much 'team spirit';

(e) be able to outline the dynamics of groups, with regard to behaviour, communication and decision-making;

(f) be able to analyse the factors influencing the effectiveness of teams, and take a contingency approach to team management;

(g) be able to assess the effectiveness (or otherwise) of a team.

1 WHAT IS A WORK TEAM?

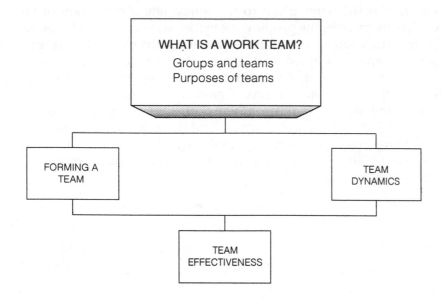

WHAT IS A WORK TEAM?
Groups and teams
Purposes of teams

FORMING A TEAM

TEAM DYNAMICS

TEAM EFFECTIVENESS

1.1 Groups and teams

Definition

A *group* is any collection of people who *perceive* themselves to be a group.

The point of this definition is that there is a difference between a random collection of individuals and a 'group' of individuals who share a common sense of identity and belonging. Groups have certain attributes that a random 'crowd' does not possess.

(a) *A sense of identity*. Whether the group is formal or informal, its existence is recognised by its members: there are acknowledged boundaries to the group which define who is 'in' and who is 'out', who is 'us' and who is 'them'.

(b) *Loyalty to the group*, and acceptance by the group. This generally expresses itself as conformity, or the acceptance of the norms of behaviour and attitudes that bind the group together and exclude others from it.

(c) *Purpose and leadership*. Most groups have an express purpose, whatever field they are in: most will, spontaneously or formally, choose individuals or sub-groups to lead them towards the fulfilment of those goals.

You should bear in mind that although an organisation as a whole may wish to project itself as a large group, with a single identity, loyalty and purpose, any organisation will in fact be composed of many sub-groups, with such attributes of their own. People will be drawn together into groups by a preference for smaller units, where closer relationships can develop and individual contributions are noticed; by the combined power of a group which individuals may not possess; and by the opportunity to share problems and responsibilities.

(a) *Informal* groups will invariably be present in any organisation. Informal groups include workplace cliques, and networks of people who regularly get together to exchange information, groups of 'mates' who socialise outside work and so on. The purposes of informal groups are usually related to group and individual member satisfaction, rather than to a task.

(b) *Formal* groups, put together by the organisation, will have a formal structure and a function for which they are held responsible: they are task oriented, and become teams. Leaders may be chosen within the group, but are typically given authority by the organisation.

A *primary working group* is the name given to the immediate social group of an individual worker: in other words, the people (s)he works with directly and most of the time. This group is the smallest unit of the organisation: the close relationships on which it depends cannot be formed among more than about a dozen people. People tend to be drawn into groups of this size, and if the organisation does not formally provide for them, informal primary groups – whose aims will not necessarily be in harmony with those of the organisation – will spring up. It is only comparatively recently that organisations have realised the importance of primary working groups for harnessing the energy and team-spirit of employees. With the concept of empowerment, attention is being given to enhancing the purpose and leadership of such groups.

Activity 1 [20 minutes]

Anthony Jay has identified a primary workgroup of ten people as the descendant of the primeval hunting band, working together for mutual survival. He suggests that such a small band balances:

(a) the individuality which is necessary to generate new ideas; with

(b) the support and comradeship necessary to develop and put those ideas into action.

What primary groups are you a member of in your study or work environment(s)? How big are these groups? How does the size of your class, study group, work-team – or whatever – affect your ability to come up with questions or ideas and give you the help and support to do something you couldn't do alone?

We have suggested that a small group can allow people to generate ideas, and encourage action. How might the organisation utilise these benefits? What might it use teams for?

Definition

Where a group is informal, a *team* is formalised to achieve particular objectives.

1.2 Purposes of teams

From the organisation's point of view, the advantages of teams may be as follows.

(a) Teams allow the performance of tasks that require the skills and time of more than one person, without involving co-ordination across structural boundaries. They are mechanisms for co-ordinating the efforts of individuals within a controlled structure.

(b) Teams encourage exchange of knowledge and ideas, and the creation of new ideas through 'hitchhiking': one person's idea or information sparks off an idea in someone else's head. They are thus particularly useful for:
   (i)   increasing communication;
   (ii)   generating new ideas;
   (iii) evaluating ideas from more than one viewpoint;
   (iv)   consultation, where a cross-section of views may help to produce better, or more acceptable, decisions;
   (v)   job-related training, since they allow the testing of ideas in a realistic work-group context;
   (vi)   resolving conflict, since argument can lead to agreement, compromise or consensus which will be reinforced by the group's sense of solidarity.

(c) The power of the team over individual behaviour can be both:
   (i)   a method of control – or, better still, self control; and
   (ii) a powerful motivator, if the aims of the group can be harmonised with the aims of the organisation.

All of these factors have encouraged the empowerment of teams, as opposed to individuals.

Examples of teamworking

Specific applications of teamworking may include the following.

(a) Brainstorming groups

Definition

> *Brainstorming* is a process whereby people produce spontaneous, uncensored ideas, sparked off by a particular problem or task.

A brainstorming group would typically involve six to twelve people. The idea of brainstorming is to 'throw out' ideas, however irrelevant or impractical they may seem. The ideas are not, at this stage, criticised or examined, so people are free to think creatively and take risks, and to feed or 'hitchhike' on each other's ideas. The next stage would be for the ideas to be considered individually, and a decision made. Such an approach might be used to solve specific production problems, for example, or to come up with marketing or new product ideas.

For discussion

In a small group, imagine you are the advertising agency creative team given the task of recommending a new name for the charity Oxfam. This was a real task set by The Spastic Society, who felt that the word 'spastic' for sufferers of cerebral palsy has taken on unfortunate connotations. Also, the name does not sound dynamic enough, and does not express the Society's purpose: to raise awareness of prejudice against sufferers, to emphasise their underutilised potential in the workplace, and to support their aspirations.

Oxfam may feel their title, although well known, is misunderstood (where's the famine in Oxford?). Brainstorm some ideas for a catchy and expressive new name. If you do this in class, you might like to have 'competing' groups of 6-10 people, and get each to present what it considers its best idea. Remember to look for quantity, not quality, at the brainstorming stage, though: the real job candidates were observed spending too much time discussing single ideas, with not enough ideas on the table ...

The Spastic Society's new name is SCOPE. Do you think this is a good name?

(b) Quality circles

Definition

> *Quality circles* are groups of (typically 6-10) employees from different levels and/or disciplines, who meet regularly to discuss problems of quality and quality control in their area of work.

In these days of *empowered teams*, quality improvement is only one area in which responsibility is given to groups of employees – but it is still one of the most important. Quality circles are said to result not only in improved product quality, but also in higher morale among employees, higher productivity and a better level of awareness about organisational issues.

(c) *Project or product/service teams*, set up to handle:
  (i) strategic developments, such as new product development, or the introduction of computer systems;
  (ii) tasks relating to particular 'cases' or customer accounts, products or markets;
  (iii) tasks relating to a particular process within the production system (design, purchasing or assembly of components, say);
  (iv) special audits or investigations of current procedures or potential improvements and opportunities.

(d) *Training or study groups*

Training groups (sometimes called 'T-groups') are often used to develop individuals' awareness of how they behave in relation to others, and particularly within a team: members are encouraged to observe and give feedback on the group's behaviour and how they respond to it. T-groups develop skills in identifying and controlling group dynamics in a 'live' context and are sometimes used when new groups are formed due to reorganisation.

(e) *Employee representative committees*, such as the local branch of a trade union or staff association, or less formal groups which meet to discuss matters of interest or concern to staff. Such groups may meet jointly with representatives of management for the purposes of consultation and negotiation.

(f) *Other committees and 'panels'* – for example, employee selection panels; investigatory panels for disciplinary or grievance procedures; task forces set up to investigate and/or make decisions on a particular task or problem; advisory committees on specialist areas (a legal team, say) and so on.

Small departments or sections might also be organised and managed as a team: we will look further at this area in Section 2 of this chapter, on teambuilding.

2   FORMING A TEAM

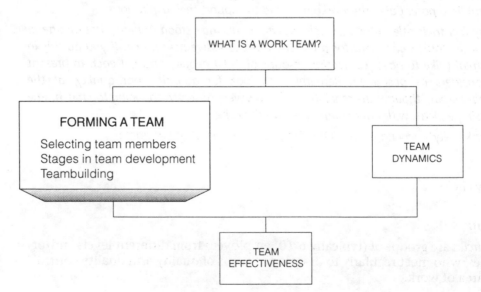

2.1   Selecting team members

Team membership may already be dictated by:

(a) *existing arrangements:* a long-standing committee, section or department;

(b) *organisation:* a task force or project/product team may require a representative from each of the functions involved in the task, for the sake of co-ordination;

(c) *politics:* representatives of particular interest groups in the organisation might need to be included, so that they feel their interests are protected and so that decisions reached (if any) are likely to find broad acceptance;

(d) *election:* for example in the case of a staff association committee.

Where a manager is able to select team members, however, (s)he should aim to match the attributes or resources prospective members are able to bring to the group with the requirements of the task.

(a) *Specialist skills and knowledge* may be required, from different areas in the organisation (or outside it).

(b) *Experience* may be helpful, especially if other team members are relatively inexperienced, and are therefore less likely to anticipate and know how to handle problems.

(c) *Political power in the organisation* may be a useful attribute in a member, particularly if the team is in competition for scarce resources, or its collective authority is unclear. The team leader may, for example, wish to co-opt a senior manager as the team's 'champion' in the organisation.

(d) *Access to resources*, such as use of equipment in other departments or information through specialist or personal contacts, may be helpful.

(e) *Competence* in the tasks likely to be required of the team member will be desirable, whatever other resources (s)he brings to the team.

In addition, both task performance and team maintenance (keeping the group together and satisfied) will require a mix of personalities and interpersonal skills.

Activity 2 [15 minutes]

Before reading on, list five 'types' of people that you would want to have on a project team, involved (say) in organising an end-of-term party.

Team roles

RM Belbin researched business-game teams at the Carnegie Institute of Technology. He developed a picture of the character-mix in a team, which many people find a useful guide to team selection and management. Belbin suggests that an effective team is made up of people who fill, between them, the following eight roles.

(a) The *co-ordinator* – presides and co-ordinates; balanced, disciplined, good at working through others.

(b) The *shaper* – highly strung, dominant, extrovert, passionate about the task itself, a spur to action.

(c) The *plant* – introverted, but intellectually dominant and imaginative; source of ideas and proposals but with disadvantages of introversion (unsociability, inhibition, need for control).

(d) The *monitor-evaluator* – analytically (rather than creatively) intelligent; dissects ideas, spots flaws; possibly aloof, tactless – but necessary.

(e) The *resource-investigator* – popular, sociable, extrovert, relaxed; source of new contacts, but not an originator; needs to be made use of.

(f) The *implementer* – practical organiser, turning ideas into tasks, scheduling, planning and so on; trustworthy and efficient, but not excited; not a leader, but an administrator.

(g) The *team worker* – most concerned with team maintenance; supportive, understanding, diplomatic; popular but uncompetitive; contribution noticed only in absence.

(h) The *finisher* – chivvies the team to meet deadlines, attend to details; urgency and follow-through important, though not always popular.

Belbin has also identified a ninth team-role, the specialist, who joins the group to offer expert advice when needed. Examples are legal advisers, PR consultants, finance specialists and the like.

For discussion

What role would you, and each of your study group or class-mates, fill in a working group, do you think?

Supposing that you are putting together a team from scratch, at what point do they stop being a collection of individuals and become a group or team? Of course, they will have to 'get to know one another', but there are more complex processes at work in team formation and development ...

2.2 Stages in team development

Groups mature and develop. Tuckman identifies four stages in this development, which he gives the catchy names: forming, storming, norming and performing.

(a) *Forming*. The group is just coming together, and may still be seen as a collection of individuals. Each individual wishes to impress his or her personality on the group, while its purpose, composition, and organisation are being established. Members will be trying to find out about each other, and about the aims and norms of the group, without 'rocking the boat'.

This settling down period is essential, but may be time-wasting.

(b) The second stage is called *storming* because it frequently involves more or less open conflict. Changes may be suggested in the group's original objectives, leadership, procedures and norms. Whilst forming involved toeing the line, storming brings out team members' own ideas and attitudes. This may encourage disagreement, as well as creativity.

(c) The third or *norming* stage is a period of settling down. There will be agreements about work sharing, output levels and group customs. The enthusiasm and creativity of the second stage may be less apparent, but norms and procedures may evolve which enable methodical working to be introduced and maintained. This need not mean that new ideas are discouraged, but that a reasonable hearing is given to everyone and 'consensus' or agreement (often involving compromise) is sought.

(d) Once the fourth or *performing* stage has been reached the group concentrates on its task. Even at earlier stages some performance wili have been achieved, but the fourth stage marks the point where the difficulties of growth and development no longer get in the way of the group's task objectives.

It would be misleading to suggest that these four stages always follow in a clearly-defined progression, or that the development of a group must be a slow and complicated process. Particularly where the task to be performed is urgent, or where group members are highly motivated, the fourth stage will be reached very quickly while the earlier stages will be hard to distinguish. Some groups never progress beyond storming, however, because their differences are irreconcilable.

It is often the case that after a team has been performing effectively for a while it becomes complacent. In this phase, which has been called *'dorming'* (so that it sounds like the other phases in Tuckman's model), the team goes into a semi-automatic mode of operation, with no fresh energy or attention focused on the task – even if it changes – and with efforts devoted primarily to the maintenance of the team itself.

Activity 3 [15 minutes]

Read the following statements and decide to which category they belong (forming, storming, norming, performing, dorming).

(a) Two of the group arguing as to whose idea is best.

(b) Progress becomes static.

(c) Desired outputs being achieved.

(d) Shy member of group not participating.

(e) Activities being allocated.

A manager might want to speed up the process of team development to the performing stage. Given the uncertainties and conflict of the storming stage, it might also seem apparent that team spirit and solidarity should be developed as soon as possible. So how do you build a team?

2.3 Teambuilding

Teambuilding involves:

(a) giving a group of people a greater sense of their *identity* as a team; this is sometimes called *'esprit de corps'* or 'team spirit';

(b) encouraging group loyalty or *solidarity*, so that members put in extra effort for the sake of the group; and

(c) encouraging the group to commit themselves to shared work *objectives*, and to co-operate willingly to achieve them.

Activity 4 [30 minutes]

Why might the following be effective as team-building exercises?

(a) Sending a project team (involved in the design of electronic systems for racing cars) on a recreational day out 'karting'.

(b) Sending a project team on an 'Outward Bound' style course, walking in the mountains from A to B, through various obstacles (rivers to cross and so on).

(c) Sending two sales teams on a day out playing 'War Games', each being an opposing combat team trying to capture the other's flag, armed with paint guns.

(d) Sending a project team on a conference at a venue away from work, with a brief to review the past year and come up with a 'vision' for the next year.

These are actually commonly-used techniques. If you are interested, you might locate an activity centre or company near you which offers outdoor pursuits, war games or corporate entertainment and ask them about team-building exercises and the effect they have on people.

Team identity

A manager may be able to increase his work group's sense of itself as a team by any or all of the following means.

- *Giving the team a name.* A group name or nickname can express a lot about the team and encourage its members to identify with it: if the nickname naturally emerges from the group, as the way it refers to itself, even better. What sort of qualities of a group do names like 'The Monarchs', 'The Crazy Gang', 'The Gangstas' or 'The A Team' express?

- *Giving the team a badge or uniform.* 'Uniform' may sound offputting – but basically suggests any kind of shared dress norms. If a team has a distinctive identifying style or insignia, it will be expressing its boundaries: who is out and who is in. Think about how teams you know use baseball caps or T-shirts, badges or ties in this way. What do you notice about the crews in MacDonalds, say, or the Guardian Angels?

- *Expressing the team's self-image.* One way of doing this is by identifying key phrases which tend to be repeated in the group, and turning them into group mottoes, or slogans. Think about the effect of slogans such as: 'You don't have to be crazy to work here, but it helps', or 'The impossible takes a bit longer'.

- *Building a team mythology.* Collecting and repeating stories about past successes and failures (funny or heroic) develops the group's self-image in the same way that experience shapes an individual's. Classic cock-ups make just as good team-building myths as hard-won successes or lucky breaks, as long as there is the sense that the team came through it together.

Activity 5   [45 minutes]

Consider the group of people you are studying with. Do you feel you are a team? Appoint a leader – someone you think is a 'co-ordinator' type, who will keep the discussion on track and under control – and try another brainstorming session. This time you are going to organise the end of term party.

Team solidarity

Another term for solidarity is 'cohesion' (literally, sticking together). Here, again, are some practical suggestions.

- *Expressing solidarity.* This is one of the more important uses of a team slogan. 'One for all and all for one' and 'United we stand' may be clichés now, but they caught on, to good effect, in their day. If you were a Polish trade union leader, why might you want to call a movement 'Solidarnosc' ('Solidarity')?

- *Encouraging interpersonal relationships.* Team members need to trust each other and be willing to work together – at the very least. Informal relationship-building activity should be encouraged and even provided (within reason, obviously: the main everyday focus of the group should be on its work objectives). Rallying round in times of need can be particularly powerful – but a team leader might want to pay attention to comparatively trivial things like members' birthdays, too.

- *Controlling conflict.* Personality clashes and disagreements should be dealt with immediately, and in the open – not left to fester and infect the whole team. The team leader needs to mediate between conflicting members, not to act as judge between them. In other words, (s)he needs to guide them in expressing and understanding their disagreement, and in finding ways of resolving the conflict that will be acceptable to both, if at all possible: a win-win situation.

- *Controlling intra-group competition.* Team members should all feel that they are being treated fairly and equally. The team leader should not show favouritism – which means that if there are inequalities of status, pay or 'say' in decisions, all members should be able to see that they are both reasonable and necessary to the success of the team as a whole. (You might give more of a say to someone who is an acknowledged expert.) Getting team members competing among themselves for bonuses and so on may spur them to better individual performance, but will not build the team.

- *Encouraging inter-group competition.* Competition with other teams, however, has been shown to increase cohesion within the competing groups, as they face what they perceive to be a threat from outside. The team closes ranks, and submerges its differences, demanding loyalty: it also focuses its collective energies more closely on the task. If a team lacks cohesion, or a task is particularly demanding of effort and loyalty, the team leader might pull the team together by finding an 'enemy', competitor or other perceived threat to face them with. (Warning: don't try this if it is important to the organisation as a whole to have teams working together!)

Activity 6 [30 minutes]

Can you see any dangers in creating a very close-knit group? Think of the effect of strong team cohesion on:

(a) what the group spends its energies and attention on;

(b) how the group regards outsiders, and any information or feedback they supply;

(c) how the group makes decisions.

What could be done about these dangerous effects?

Commitment to shared objectives

The purpose of teambuilding is, ultimately, not to have a close-knit and satisfied team, but to have a close-knit and satisfied team that fulfils its task objectives. In fact, a cohesive and successful task-focused team may be more supportive and satisfying to its members than a cosy group absorbed only in its own processes and relationships.

Getting a team behind its objectives involves:

(a) clearly setting out the team's objectives, and their place in the activity of the organisation as a whole;

(b) involving the team in setting specific targets and standards, and agreeing methods of organising work, in order to reach the objectives;

(c) providing the right information, resources, training and environment for the team to achieve its targets – involving the team in deciding what its requirements are;

(d) giving regular, clear feedback on progress and results – including constructive criticism – so the team can celebrate what they have achieved, and be spurred on by what they have not yet achieved;

(e) encouraging feedback, suggestions and ideas from the team, and doing something about them: helping team members believe that they can make an impact on their work and results, and that that impact is appreciated by the organisation;

(f) giving positive reinforcement (praise or reward) for creativity, initiative, problem-solving, helpfulness and other behaviour that shows commitment to the task;

(g) visibly 'championing' the team in the organisation, fighting (if necessary) for the resources it needs and the recognition it deserves.

Assuming that we've now gathered and built a group of people into a close-knit, performing team, we can turn to the normal business of teamworking: the patterns and processes of team behaviour, or dynamics.

NOTES

3   TEAM DYNAMICS

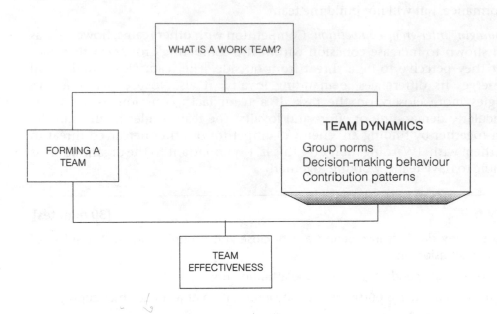

3.1   Group norms

Work groups establish *norms* or common patterns of behaviour, to which all members of the group are expected to conform. Norms develop as the group learns what sorts of behaviour work and don't work, in terms of maintaining the group and protecting its interests. There may be norms of interpersonal behaviour (the way the members speak to each other and so on), dress, timekeeping, attitudes (towards management, for example) and/or work practices and productivity. In other words, group norms are 'the way we do (or don't do) things round here'.

Norms may be reinforced in various ways by the group.

(a) *Identification with the group* may be offered as a reward for compliance, through marks of belonging, prestige and acceptance.

(b) *Sanctions* or *penalties* of various kinds may be imposed as a deterrent to non-conforming behaviour: ostracising or ignoring the member concerned ('sending him to Coventry'), ridicule or reprimand, even physical hostility. The threat of expulsion from the group is the final sanction.

In other words the group's power to influence an individual depends on the degree to which he values his membership of the group and the rewards it may offer, or wishes to avoid the negative sanctions at its disposal.

Activity 7   [20 minutes]

How might group norms:

(a) cause problems for a new manager;

(b) adversely affect performance;

(c) help in the process of management control;

(d) help in the process of change management?

3.2 Decision-making behaviour

As we have noted, empowerment involves groups in decision-making. This can be of benefit where:

(a) pooling skills, information and ideas – perhaps representing different functions, specialisms and levels in the organisation – could increase the quality of the decision; groups have been shown to produce better evaluated (although fewer) decisions than individuals working separately: even the performance of the group's best individual can be improved by having 'missing pieces' added by the group;

(b) participation in the decision-making process makes the decision *acceptable* to the group, whether because it represents a consensus of their views, or simply because they have been consulted. Acceptance of the decision by the group may be important if it affects them, and/or they are responsible for carrying it out.

However, it is worth considering *how* a group arrives at a decision. Depending on the personalities of its members and of its leader, and the nature of the task (for example whether it needs to be completed within a short or long time-frame), a team may arrive at decisions in a number of ways.

Does it allow itself to be persuaded by its leader, or another dominant member?

Does it defer to the member most qualified to make a particular decision?

Does it collect information and views from all its members – but allow the leader/dominant member/qualified member to make the decision?

Does it collect information and views from all its members and try to reach general consensus or agreement, however much discussion that takes?

Does it collect information and views from all its members and take a democratic vote on the decision?

Does it keep any dissenting views or contradictory information quiet, to allow consensus to prevail?

Does it insist on dealing with dissenting views and contradictory information, even if it takes longer to reach a decision?

Depending which behaviour is adopted, there is clearly a trade-off between:

(a) the speed of the decision;

(b) the acceptability of the decision to all group members; and

(c) the quality of the decision from the point of view of results.

Activity 8 [20 minutes]

If you were team leader in the following situations, what kind of decision-making behaviour would you encourage?

(a) The computer expert in your team has suggested that the team should change over to a different, more efficient software package. Some of the team have only just mastered the current software, after quite a struggle. The new software will, however, iron out some very frustrating problems in the work.

(b) The office manager has offered you a choice of yellow or blue, when the offices are redecorated next month, but she needs to do the purchasing almost immediately. What would your team prefer?

There are problems in group decision-making.

(a) *Group decisions take longer to reach than individual decisions* – especially if the group seeks consensus by working through disagreement. (This is the preferred practice in Japan.)

(b) *Group decisions tend to be riskier than individual decisions*. This may be because:

  (i) shared responsibility blurs the individuals' sense of responsibility for the outcome of the decision;

  (ii) contradictory information may be ignored, to protect the group's consensus or pet theories;

  (iii) cohesive groups tend to feel infallible: they get over-confident;

  (iv) group cohesion and motivation may be founded on values like innovation, boldness and flexibility – which support risk-taking.

(c) *Group decisions may partly be based on group norms and interests* – the group's own 'agenda' – rather than organisational interests: group maintenance is itself a powerful *raison d'être*.

3.3   Contribution patterns

One way of analysing the functioning of a team is to assess who (if anybody) is performing each of Belbin's *team roles* (discussed earlier). Who is the team's plant? co-ordinator? monitor-evaluator? and so on.

Another method is to analyse the frequency and type of individual members' contributions to group discussions and interactions. This is a relatively simple framework, which can revolutionise the way you behave in groups – as well as your understanding of the dynamics of a given team.

Who contributes?

The team leader should identify which members of the team habitually make the most contributions, and which the least. You could do this by taking a count of contributions from each member, during a sample 10-15 minutes of group discussion. (Count any spoken remark addressed to the discussion, not asides to other members, or mutters to self.) For example:

Robbie	I
Martha	
Jason	III
Mary	HHT HHT I
Gary	HHT HHT IIII
Paul	II
Mark	HHT II

If the same general pattern of high contribution (Mary, Gary), medium contribution (Mark) and low contribution (Robbie, Martha, Jason, Paul) tends to be *repeated*, irrespective of the matter being discussed, you might suspect that Mary and Gary are 'swamping' the other members, or that the other members have a problem communicating, or are not interested, or have nothing to contribute, or *feel* they have nothing to contribute. This team has a problem that needs to be addressed. Confronting the team with its contribution count may spark off an honest discussion of the problem – if group relationships are strong enough to support the conflict that may be required.

How do they contribute?

Consultants Neil Rackham and Terry Morgan have developed a helpful categorisation of the types of contribution people can make to team discussion and decision-making.

Category	Behaviour	Example
Proposing	Putting forward suggestions, new concepts or courses of action.	'Why don't we look at a flexi-time system?'
Building	Extending or developing someone else's proposal.	'Yes. We could have a daily or weekly hours allowance, apart from a core period in the middle of the day.'
Supporting	Supporting another person or his/her proposal.	'Yes, I agree, flexi-time would be worth looking at.'
Seeking information	Asking for more facts, opinions or clarification.	'What exactly do you mean by "flexi-time"?'
Giving information	Offering facts, opinions or clarification.	'There's a helpful outline of flexi-time in this BPP Study Text.'
Disagreeing	Offering criticism or alternative facts or opinions which contradict a person's proposals or opinions.	'I don't think we can take the risk of not having any staff here at certain periods of the day.'
Attacking	Attempting to undermine another person or their position: more emotive than disagreeing.	'In fact, I don't think you've thought this through at all.'
Defending	Arguing for one's own point of view.	'Actually, I've given this a lot of thought, and I think it makes sense.'
Blocking/difficulty stating	Putting obstacles in the way of a proposal, without offering any alternatives.	'What if the other teams get jealous? It would only cause conflict.'
Open behaviour	Risking ridicule and loss of status by being honest about feelings and opinions.	'I think some of us are afraid that flexi-time will show up how little work they really do in a day.'
Shutting-out behaviour	Interrupting or overriding others; taking over.	'Nonsense. Let's move onto something else – we've had enough of this discussion.'
Bringing-in behaviour	Involving another member; encouraging contribution.	'Actually, I'd like to hear what Fred has to say. Go on, Fred.'
Testing understanding	Checking whether points have been understood.	'So flexi-time could work over a day or a week; have I got that right?'
Summarising	Drawing together or summing up previous discussion.	'We've now heard two sides to the flexi-time issue: on the one hand, flexibility; on the other side, possible risk. Now ...'

Each type of behaviour may be appropriate in the right situation at the right time. A team may be low on some types of contribution – and it may be up to the team leader to encourage, or deliberately adopt, desirable behaviours (such as bringing-in, supporting or seeking information) in order to provide balance.

You might draw up a *contribution profile*, by following the same procedure as a contribution count, but adding behavioural categories (perhaps a few at a time, at first). If you were worried about interpersonal conflict in your team, for example, you might look specifically for attacking, defending, blocking/difficulty stating, shutting-out and disagreeing: are such behaviours common in the team? Are particular individuals mainly at fault? Are attacks aimed at a particular person, who is forced to defend: a purely interpersonal conflict? Or is disagreement constructive and based on real objections – not linked to attacking or shutting-out? (See if you can see a problem in the following example.)

Contribution profile	Mary	Martha	Paul	Gary	Mark	Jason	Robbie
Attacking					ЖҐ	ǀǀǀ	ǀ
Defending	ЖҐ						
Blocking			ǀǀ	ЖҐ	ǀǀ		
Shutting-out	ЖҐ			ЖҐ			
Disagreeing	ǀ			ǀ			

Activity 9 [20 minutes]

'The problem with teamwork is "the other people".' Is teamworking just a management fashion that imposes an unnatural way of working on individuals who would be more effective on their own?

Discuss in groups of 6-10 people, for 10 minutes. Appoint two extra people as observers: one to make a *contribution count,* and another to make a *contribution profile.* When your discussion is finished take another 10 minutes to write down the implications of their findings.

4 TEAM EFFECTIVENESS

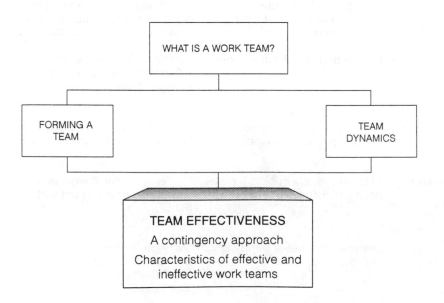

4.1 A contingency approach

An effective team is one which:

- achieves its task objectives *and*

- maintains co-operative working through the satisfaction and interrelationships of its members.

Unfortunately, no two groups of people are the same – and they may also be doing different work in different organisational set-ups. So the team leader will need to take a contingency approach. How much supervision does the team need? Should you let the team make the decisions? Do more team members need to contribute to group discussions? Should you discourage disagreement in the group? Answer: it all depends.

Charles Handy suggested the framework shown in figure 6.1 as a guide to the factors that influence a group's effectiveness. The *intervening factors* are those that the team manager can manipulate in order to alter the *outcomes*, according to the situation (s)he has been *given* to start with.

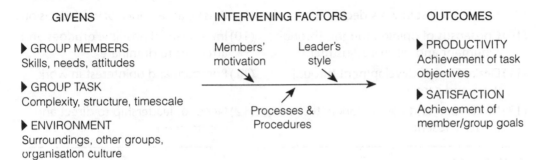

Figure 6.1 Group effectiveness

As an example, if the members have a high need for structure, but the task is very complex and ambiguous, and the organisation culture is intolerant of failure (all givens), the manager may need to adopt a relatively authoritarian management style, motivate team members by rewards for results, and establish 'safe' control procedures (intervening factors) if the team is to succeed without too much stress (outcomes).

If a manager is to improve the effectiveness of the work team (s)he must have some idea of what an effective or ineffective group is like.

4.2 Characteristics of effective and ineffective work teams

Some pointers to group efficiency are *quantifiable* or numerically measurable factors; others are more *qualitative* factors, which can be observed, but are less easily measured. No one factor on its own is significant, but taken collectively they present a picture of how well or badly the group is operating.

Quantifiable factors

Effective work group	*Ineffective work group*
(1) Low rate of labour turnover	(1) High rate of labour turnover
(2) Low accident rate	(2) High accident rate
(3) Low absenteeism	(3) High absenteeism
(4) High output and productivity	(4) Low output and productivity
(5) Good quality of output	(5) Poor quality of output
(6) Individual targets are achieved	(6) Individual targets are not achieved
(7) Few stoppages and interruptions to work	(7) Time is wasted owing to disruption of work flow
	(8) Time is lost owing to disagreements between superior and subordinates

Qualitative factors

Effective work group	*Ineffective work group*
(1) High commitment to the achievement of targets and organisational goals	(1) Little understanding of organisational goals or the role of the group
(2) Clear understanding of the group's work	(2) Low commitment to targets
(3) Clear understanding of the role of each person within the group	(3) Confusion and uncertainty about the role of each person within the group
(4) Trust and open communication between members	(4) Mistrust between group members, and suspicion of leaders
(5) Idea sharing	(5) Little idea sharing
(6) New-idea generation	(6) Few new ideas generated
(7) Mutual help and encouragement, if necessary, through constructive criticism	(7) Competition, self-interest and hostile criticism within the group
(8) Group problem-solving, addressing root causes	(8) Superficial problem-solving, addressing symptoms, not causes
(9) Active interest in work decisions	(9) Passive acceptance of work decisions
(10) Consensus of opinion sought, through argument and mutual adjustment	(10) Interpersonal hostility, grudges and attempts to dominate
(11) Desire for self-development through work and career	(11) Boredom and uninterest in work
(12) Motivation and ability work in the leader's absence	(12) Need for leadership to direct and control work

Activity 10   [20 minutes]

Try to interview somebody who manages a work team, who would be willing to talk to you for just 10 or 15 minutes. Run through the checklist of factors given above, asking your interviewee to give a 'Yes' or 'No' to each of the statements. Put a question mark (?) where it was difficult for the respondent to answer, because the factor was not easy to define or measure. You might want to reconsider some of our factors, or the way they are phrased, in the light of the answers you get. What conclusions can you draw from your survey?

Chapter roundup

● A *group* is a collection of people who *perceive* themselves to be a group. A group with a strong sense of collaborating towards the fulfilment of their collective goals is a *team*.
  An *effective* team is one which achieves its tasks and satisfies its members.

● Collections of individuals *develop* into groups or teams through the stages of forming, storming, norming, performing (and possibly dorming). They can also be built into teams by enhancing their identity and solidarity as a group, and by focusing attention on their task objectives.

● Groups 'behave' differently from individuals. Some of the *dynamics* of groups of which a manager should be aware include:
  — the tendency of groups to develop norms of behaviour;
  — the ways decision-making behaviour affects team performance and satisfaction;
  — the way in which personal, interpersonal and task factors influence the contributions of team members.

Chapter roundup *continued*
- A contingency approach to team effectiveness includes attention to:
  — *the givens*: the group, the task and the environment
  — *intervening factors* which the manager can manipulate: leadership style, motivation, processes and procedures
  — *the outcomes*: group productivity and member satisfaction.

Quick quiz

1 What is (a) brainstorming? and (b) a quality circle?

2 What should a manager look for when selecting team members?

3 What are Belbin's eight roles for a well-rounded team?

4 Outline what happens in the 'storming' stage of team development.

5 What is 'cohesion', and what effect does inter-group competition have on it?

6 Suggest five ways in which a manager can get a team 'behind' task objectives.

7 Why do individuals comply with group norms?

8 Why are groups particularly (a) useful and (b) risky for decision-making?

9 List six of Rackham and Morgan's categories of contribution to group discussion.

10 Suggest five quantifiable characteristics of effective teams and five qualitative characteristics of ineffective teams.

Answers to quick quiz

1 (a) A process by which people produce spontaneous ideas, sparked off by a problem or task.

   (b) Usually 6–10 employees from different levels and disciplines meeting to discuss problems related to quality or quality control in their area of work.

2 Skills, knowledge, experience, political power in the organisation, access to resources, competence.

3 Co-ordinator, shaper, plant, monitor-evaluator, resource-investigator, implementer, team worker, finisher.

4 Storming brings out members' own ideas and attitudes. There may be conflict as well as creativity.

5 Solidarity. Faced with competition it causes a group to close ranks, focuses its energies and makes the group concentrate on objectives.

6 Set clear objectives, get the team to set targets/standards, provide information and resources, give feedback, praise and reward, and champion the team in the organisation.

7 To be accepted and to avoid sanctions or penalties.

8 (a) More ideas, suggestions, and participation usually make the decision more acceptable.

   (b) Decisions take longer and may be based on group norms and interests.

9 Proposing, building, supporting, seeking information, giving information, disagreeing. For other categories refer to page 121.

10 Refer to section 4.2.

Answers to Activities

1 The primary groups are probably your tutor group or class. If at work, it would be the section in which you work. If the groups are large, you may feel reluctant to put forward ideas or ask questions, but even within a large group you should feel there is support and that help is at hand if you need it.

2 For your ideal team, you might have listed: a person with originality and ideas; a 'get up and go' type, with energy and enthusiasm; a quiet logical thinker who can be sensible about the ideas put forward; a plodder who will be happy to do the routine leg-work; and a team player who can organise the others and help them reach agreement on ideas.

3 Categorising the behaviour of group members in the situations described results in the following: (a) storming, (b) dorming, (c) performing, (d) forming, (e) norming.

4 (a) Recreation helps the team to build informal relationships: in this case, the chosen activity also reminds them of their task, and may make them feel special, as part of the motor racing industry, by giving them a taste of what the end user of their product does.

  (b) A team challenge pushes the group to consider its strengths and weaknesses, to find its natural leader, to co-operate and help each other in overcoming obstacles.

  (c) This exercise creates an 'us' and 'them' challenge: perceiving the rival team as the enemy heightens the solidarity of the group.

  (d) This exercise encourages the group to raise problems and conflicts freely, away from the normal environment of work, and also encourages brainstorming and the expression of team members' dreams for what the team can achieve in future.

5 You may have found it easier to work as a team this time. The group has probably generated a number of ideas as to what form the party should take. Activities may have been allocated (drinks, food, music) and decisions made on how to publicise the event. Hopefully, you have not yet reached the 'dorming' stage.

6 Problems may arise in an ultra close-knit group because:

  (a) the group's energies may be focused on its own maintenance and relationships, instead of on the task;

  (b) the group may be suspicious or dismissive of outsiders, and may reject any contradictory information or criticism they supply; the group will be blinkered and stick to its own views, no matter what; cohesive groups thus often get the impression that they are infallible: they can't be wrong – and therefore can't learn from their mistakes;

  (c) the group may squash any dissent or opinions that might rock the boat. Close-knit groups tend to preserve a consensus – falsely if required – and to take risky decisions, because they have suppressed alternative facts and viewpoints.

This phenomenon is called 'groupthink'. In order to limit its effect, the team must be encouraged:

  (a) actively to seek outside ideas and feedback;

  (b) to welcome self-criticism within the group; and

  (c) consciously to evaluate conflicting evidence and opinions.

7 Group norms might have the effect of:

  (a) 'freezing out' a new manager who wants to change group behaviour;

  (b) limiting output to what the group as a whole feels is fair for what they are paid:

over-producing individuals are brought into line with the group output norm, so as not to make the group look bad;

(c) aiding management control by a process of self-regulation, if the group norms can be aligned with task objectives; under-producing individuals, for example, are brought into line by group pressure to pull their weight;

(d) aiding management in changing attitudes: if a manager can involve some individuals in accepting and communicating change, the rest of the group may be brought into line with the adjusted norm.

8 (a) The new software is clearly desirable for the task. You could make a decision yourself, supported by the expert advice of the relevant team member. However, there does not seem to be a time limit on the decision (it is only a suggestion) and there does seem to be a good reason for taking the time to consult the rest of the group. The change is something that will affect them all, and you can anticipate conflict (from the members who find technology a struggle); it should be brought into the open and worked through into consensus if possible. Agreement will make implementing the change much easier later on.

(b) This decision is more about acceptability than about quality: the colour is entirely a matter of taste, and the group will have to live with it, so they should be invited to share the decision. On the other hand time is short, and it is the sort of argument that could go to and fro for ever: you are unlikely to persuade people that one colour or the other is 'better', if they prefer the other one! A quick, democratic vote may show clear support one way or the other: if opinion is tied, the leader should make an authoritative casting vote, without wasting time over it.

9 In analysing the contributions, you may have found that strong characters were inclined to dominate the meeting. Attempts should have been made to draw quiet people into the discussion. There may have been arguments over certain points and perhaps peace restored by another member of the group. The observers may have noticed non-verbal communication taking place.

10 Hopefully, you found the checklist in section 4.2 effective. If not, change the wording. From the answers you received you should be able to judge how effective the team/group is.

Assignment 6 [About 1¹/₂ hours]

You have been asked to give a talk on team forming and building. Write notes for the talk covering the following points.

(a) The difference between a group and a team

(b) What team building involves

(c) The elements of team solidarity

(d) What has to be done to get a team behind its objectives

(e) The quantifiable factors found in an ineffective team.

Chapter 7

MONITORING PERFORMANCE

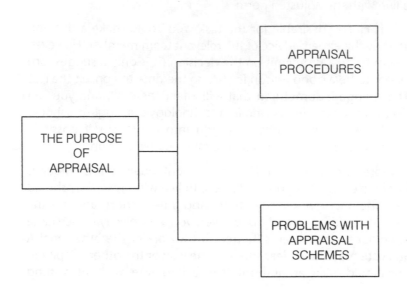

Introduction

Before a manager can set about improving performance, (s)he will need to analyse whether, in what way, and how much it needs to improve! The process of monitoring individual and group performance, and giving helpful feedback for improvement, is generally called *performance appraisal*. The purpose of appraisal was traditionally regarded as constructive criticism of the employee by his or her manager, but nowadays it tends to be more about:

(a) helping the employee to overcome any problems or obstacles to performance;

(b) identifying where an employee's potential for improved performance and greater challenge could be better fulfilled;

(c) setting goals and priorities for further monitoring and development.

Your objectives

After completing this chapter you should:

(a) be able to explain the need for systematic performance monitoring and appraisal;

(b) be able to suggest criteria for performance assessment;

(c) be able to outline a systematic appraisal and reporting procedure, and appreciate some of its human relations problems;

(d) be able to suggest how employee potential can be monitored and assessed.

1 THE PURPOSES OF PERFORMANCE APPRAISAL

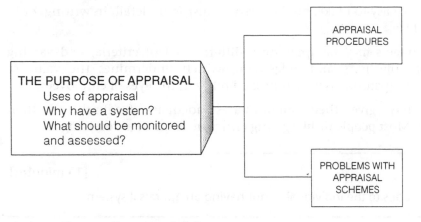

1.1 Uses of appraisal

Jeannie Brownlow has decided to leave Gold and Silver where she has worked for five years as a supervisor. When the personnel manager asked for her reasons she said, 'I'm fed up. You don't know where you are here. No one tells you if you're doing the job well, but they jump on you like a ton of bricks if anything goes wrong. Talk about "no news is good news" – that's the way it is here'.

Monitoring and evaluating the performance of individuals and groups is an essential part of people-management. It has several uses.

(a) Identifying the current level of performance to provide a basis for informing, training and developing team members to a higher level.

(b) Identifying areas where improvement is needed in order to meet acceptable standards of performance.

(c) Identifying people whose performance suggests that they might be suitable for promotion in future.

(d) Measuring the individual's or team's level of performance against specific standards, to provide a basis for reward above the basic pay rate (in other words, individual or group bonuses).

(e) Measuring the performance of new team members against the organisation's (and team's) expectations, as a means of assessing whether selection procedures have been successful.

(f) Improving communication about work tasks between managers and team members, as a result of discussing the assessment.

(g) In the process of defining what performance *should* be, establishing what key results and standards must be reached for the unit to reach its objectives.

It may be argued that a particular, deliberate stock-taking exercise is unnecessary, since managers are constantly monitoring and making judgements about their subordinates and (theoretically) giving their subordinates feedback information from day to day.

1.2 Why have a system?

It must be recognised that, if no system of formal appraisal is in place:

(a) managers may obtain random impressions of subordinates' performance (perhaps from their more noticeable successes and failures), but not a coherent, complete and objective picture;

(b) managers may have a fair idea of their subordinates' shortcomings – but may not have devoted time and attention to the matter of improvement and development;

(c) judgements are easy to make, but less easy to justify in detail, in writing, or to the subject's face;

(d) different managers may be applying a different set of criteria, and varying standards of objectivity and judgement, which undermines the value of appraisal for comparison, as well as its credibility in the eyes of employees;

(e) managers rarely give their subordinates adequate feedback on their performance. Most people dislike giving criticism as much as receiving it.

Activity 1 [15 minutes]

List four disadvantages to the individual of not having an appraisal system.

A typical system would therefore involve:

(a) identification of *criteria* for assessment;

(b) the preparation of an *appraisal report*;

(c) an *appraisal interview*, for an exchange of views about the results of the assessment, targets for improvement, solutions to problems and so on;

(d) the preparation and implementation of *action plans* to achieve improvements and changes agreed; and

(e) *follow-up*: monitoring the progress of the action plan.

Definition

A *criterion* (plural: *criteria*) is a factor or standard by which something can be judged or decided. For example, 'meeting output targets' is one criterion for judging work performance.

We will now look at each stage in turn. First of all, what is the basis of appraisal going to be?

1.3 What should be monitored and assessed?

Managers must broadly monitor and assess the same things, so that comparisons can be made between individuals. On the other hand, they need to take account of the fact that jobs are different, and make different demands on the jobholder. If every individual were rated on 'communication skills' and 'teamworking', for example, you might have a good basis for deciding who needed promoting or training – but what about a data inputter or research scientist who does not have to work in a team or communicate widely in your organisation?

Activity 2 [20 minutes]

Think of some other criteria which you would want to use in assessment of some jobs – but would not be applicable in others.

There is also the important question of whether you assess *personality* or *performance*: in other words, do you assess what the individual is, or what (s)he does? Personal qualities like reliability or outgoingness have often been used as criteria for judging people. However, they are not necessarily relevant to job performance: you can be naturally outgoing, but still not good at communicating with customers, if your product knowledge or attitude is poor. Also, personality judgements are notoriously vague and unreliable: words like 'loyalty' and 'ambition' are full of ambiguity and moral connotations.

In practical terms, this has encouraged the use of competence or results-based appraisals, where performance is measured against specific, job-related performance criteria.

So how does a manager choose what criteria to base the assessment on? Most large organisations have a system in place, with pre-printed assessment forms setting out all the relevant criteria and the range of possible judgements. (We reproduce such a form a bit further on in this chapter). Even so, a team manager should critically evaluate such schemes to ensure that the criteria for assessment are relevant to his or her team and task – and that they remain so over time, as the team and task change.

Relevant criteria for assessment might be based on the following.

(a) *Job analysis*: the process of examining a job, to identify its component tasks and skill requirements, and the circumstances in which it is performed.

Definition

Job analysis is the determination of the essential characteristics of a job.

Analysis may be carried out by observation, if the job is routine and repetitive it will be easy to see what it involves. Irregular jobs, with lots of 'invisible' work (planning, thinking, relationship-building and so on) will require interviews and discussions with superiors and with the job holders themselves, to find out what the job involves.

The product of job analysis is usually a *job specification* which sets out the activities (mental and physical) involved in the job, and other factors in its social and physical environment. Many of the aspects covered – aptitudes and abilities required, duties and responsibilities, ability to work under particular conditions (pressure, noise, hazards), tolerance of teamwork or isolation and so on – will suggest criteria for assessment.

(b) *Job descriptions*: more general descriptions of a job or position at a given time, including its purpose and scope, duties and responsibilities, relationship with other jobs, and perhaps specific objectives and expected results. A job description offers a guide to what competences, responsibilities and results might be monitored and assessed.

(c) *Departmental or team plans, performance standards and targets*. These are the most clear-cut of all. If the plan specifies completion of a certain number of tasks, or production of a certain number of units, to a particular quality standard, assessment can be focused on whether (or how far) those targets have been achieved. (Personality and environmental factors may be relevant when investigating why performance has fallen short – but do not cloud the assessment of performance itself.)

Let us now look at some of the performance monitoring and reporting methods used in organisations.

2 APPRAISAL PROCEDURES

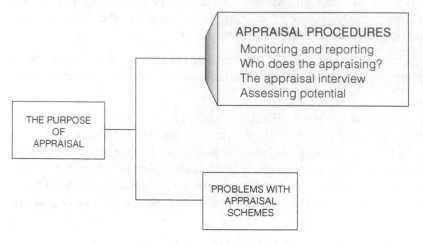

2.1 Monitoring and reporting

Overall assessment

This is much like a school report. The manager simply writes narrative judgements about the appraisee. The method is simple – but not always effective, since there is no guaranteed consistency of the criteria and areas of assessment from manager to manager (or appraisal to appraisal). In addition, managers may not be able to convey clear, precise or effective judgements in writing.

Guided assessment

Assessors are required to comment on a number of specified characteristics and performance elements, with guidelines as to how terms such as 'application', 'integrity' and 'adaptability' are to be interpreted in the work context. This is a more precise, but still rather vague method.

Grading

Grading adds a comparative frame of reference to the general guidelines. Managers are asked to select one of a number of levels or degrees (Grades 1–5 say) which describe the extent to which an individual displays a given characteristic. These are also known as rating scales, and have been much used in standard appraisal forms (for example, see Figure 7.2 on the following page). Their effectiveness depends to a large extent on two things.

(a) *The relevance of the factors chosen for assessment.* These may be nebulous personality traits, for example, or clearly-defined work-related factors such as job knowledge, performance against targets, or decision-making;

(b) *The definition of the agreed standards or grades.* Grades A-D might simply be labelled 'Outstanding – Satisfactory – Fair – Poor', in which case assessments will be rather subjective and inconsistent. They may, on the other hand, be more closely related to work priorities and standards, using definitions such as 'Performance is good overall, and superior to that expected in some important areas', or 'Performance is broadly acceptable, but the employee needs training in several major areas and motivation is lacking'.

Numerical values may be added to gradings to give rating scores. Alternatively a less precise *graphic scale* may be used to indicate general position on a plus/minus scale, as in Figure 7.1.

Factor: job knowledge

High ├────✓────┤ Average ├──────────┤ Low

Figure 7.1 Graphic scale for grading

Personnel Appraisal: Employees in Salary Grades 5–8

Date of Review			Name
Time on Position Yrs Mths	S.G.	Age Yrs	
Period of Review			
Position Title			Area

Important: Read guide notes carefully before proceeding with the following sections

Section One — Performance Factors

| | NA | U | M | SP | E | O | | Section Two | Personal Characteristics |
									1 2 3 4 5
Administrative Skills								Initiative	
Communications – Written								Persistence	
Communications – Oral								Ability to work with others	
Problem Analysis								Adaptability	
Decision Making								Persuasiveness	
Delegation								Self-Confidence	
Quantity of Work								Judgement	
Development of Personnel								Leadership	
Development of Quality Improvements								Creativity	

Section Three — Highlight Performance Factors and particular strengths/weaknesses of employee which significantly affect Job Performance

Overall Performance Rating (taking into account ratings given)

Prepared by: Signature .... Date .... Position Title ....

Section Four — Comments by Reviewing Authority

I R Review Initial

Signature .... Date .... Position Title ....

Section Five — Supervisor's Notes on Counselling Interview

Date

Signature .... Date .... Position Title ....

Section Six — Employees Reactions and Comment

Signature .... Date ....

Performance Classification

Outstanding performance is characterised by high ability which leaves little or nothing to be desired.

Personnel rated as such are those who regularly make significant contributions to the organisation which are above the requirements of their position. Unusual and challenging assignments are consistently well handled.

Excellent performance is marked by above-average ability, with little supervision required.

These employees may display some of the attributes present in 'outstanding' performance, but not on a sufficiently consistent basis to warrant that rating. Unusual and challenging assignments are normally well handled.

Satisfactory Plus performance indicates fully adequate ability, without the need for excessive supervision.

Personnel with this rating are able to give proper consideration to normal assignments, which are generally well handled. They will meet the requirements of the position. 'Satisfactory plus' performers may include those who lack the experience at their current level to demonstrate above-average ability.

Marginal performance is in instances where the ability demonstrated does not fully meet the requirements of the position, with excessive supervision and direction normally required.

Employees rated as such will show specific deficiencies in their performance which prevent them from performing at an acceptable level.

Unsatisfactory performance indicates an ability which falls clearly below the minimum requirements of the position.

'Unsatisfactory' performers will demonstrate marked deficiencies in most of the major aspects of their responsibilities, and considerable improvement is required to permit retention of the employee in his current position.

Personal Characteristics Ratings

1 – Needs considerable improvement – substantial improvement required to meet acceptable standards.

2 – Needs improvement – some improvement required to meet acceptable standards.

3 – Normal – meets acceptable standards.

4 – Above normal – exceeds normally acceptable standards in most instances.

5 – Exceptional – displays rare and unusual personal characteristics.

Figure 7.1 Personnel appraisal form

Results-orientated schemes

All the above techniques may be used with more or less results-orientated criteria. A wholly results-orientated approach sets out to review performance against specific targets and standards of performance, which are agreed – or even set – in advance by a manager and subordinate together. This is known as *performance management*.

Activity 3 [15 minutes]

Give three advantages of a performance management approach to appraisal.

In introducing 'performance management', we have raised the possibility that an employee might be involved in monitoring and evaluating his or her own performance. If targets are clear, and the employee is able to be honest and objective, self-assessment may be both effective and satisfying.

2.2 Who does the appraising?

Organisations have begun to recognise that the employee's immediate boss is not the only (or necessarily the best) person to assess his or her performance. Other 'stakeholders' in the individual's performance might be better, including the people (s)he deals with on a day to day basis:

(a) the current (and perhaps previous) boss (including temporary supervisors);

(b) peers and co-workers;

(c) subordinates; and even

(d) external customers.

360 degree feedback

360-degree feedback is an approach which collects comments and feedback on an individual's performance from *all* these sources (usually anonymously using questionnaires) and adds the individual's own *self*-assessment.

The advantages of 360-degree feedback are said to be as follows.

(a) It highlights every aspect of the individual's performance, and allows comparison of the individual's self-assessment with the views of others. (Rather revealing, in most cases.)

(b) Feedback tends to be balanced, covering strengths in some areas with weaknesses in others, so it is less discouraging.

(c) The assessment is based on real work – not artificial (eg interview) situations. The feedback is thus felt to be fairer and more relevant, making it easier for employees to accept the assessment and the need for change and development.

Activity 4 [20 minutes]

Peter Ward, who introduced 360-degree feedback at Tesco in 1987, gives an example of the kinds of questionnaire that might be used as the instrument of 360-degree feedback. 'A skill area like "communicating", for example, might be defined as "the ability to express oneself clearly and to listen effectively to others". Typical comments would include "Presents ideas or information in a well-organised manner" (followed by rating scale); or: "Allows you to finish what you have to say".'

Rate yourself on the two comments mentioned here, on a scale of 1–10. Get a group of friends, fellow-students, even a tutor or parent, to write down, *anonymously*, on a piece of paper *their* rating for you on the same two comments. Keep them in an envelope, unseen, until you have a few.

Compare them with your self-rating. If you dare... What drawbacks did you (and your respondents) find to such an approach?

Upward appraisal

A notable modern trend, adopted in the UK by companies such as BP, British Airways and Central TV, is *upward* appraisal, whereby employees are rated not by their superiors but by their subordinates. The followers appraise the leader.

The advantages of this method might be as follows.

(a) Subordinates tend to know their (one) superior better than superiors know their (many) subordinates.

(b) Instead of the possible bias of an individual manager's ratings, the various ratings of several employees may reflect a rounded view.

(c) Subordinates' ratings have more impact, because it is less usual to receive feedback from below: a manager's view of good management may be rather different from a team's view of being managed!

(d) Upward appraisal encourages subordinates to give feedback and raise problems they may have with their boss, which otherwise would be too difficult or risky for them.

Activity 5 [15 minutes]

Imagine you had to do an upward appraisal on your boss, parent or teacher. Suggest the two major problems that might be experienced with upward appraisal.

Having reported on an individual's performance – whether in a written narrative comment, or on a prepared appraisal form – a manager must discuss the content of the report with the individual concerned.

2.3 The appraisal interview

There are basically three ways of approaching appraisal interviews.

(a) The *tell and sell* method. The manager tells the subordinate how (s)he has been assessed, and then tries to 'sell' (gain acceptance of) the evaluation and any improvement plans.

(b) The *tell and listen* method. The manager tells the subordinate how (s)he has been assessed, and then invites comments. The manager therefore no longer dominates the interview throughout, and there is greater opportunity for counselling as opposed to pure direction. The employee is encouraged to participate in the assessment and the working out of improvement targets and methods; change in the employee may not be the sole key to improvement, and the manager may receive helpful feedback about job design, methods, environment or supervision.

(c) The *problem-solving* approach. The manager abandons the role of critic altogether, and becomes a counsellor and helper. The discussion is centred not on assessment of past performance, but on future solutions of the employee's work problems. The employee is encouraged to recognise the problems, think solutions through, and commit himself to improvement. This approach is more involving and satisfying to the employee and may also stimulate creative problem-solving.

> **EXAMPLE**
>
> A survey of appraisal interviews given to 252 officers in a UK government department found that:
>
> (a) interviewers have difficulty with negative performance feedback (criticism), and tend to avoid it if possible;
>
> (b) negative performance feedback (criticism) is, however, more likely to bring forth positive post-appraisal action, and is favourably received by appraisees, who feel it is the most useful function of the whole process, if handled frankly and constructively;
>
> (c) the most common fault of interviewers is talking too much.
>
> The survey recorded the preference of appraisees for a 'problem-solving' style of participative interview, over a one-sided 'tell and sell' style.

Many organisations waste the opportunity represented by appraisal for *upward communication*. If an organisation is working towards empowerment, it should harness the aspirations and abilities of its employees by asking positive and thought-provoking questions.

(a) Do you fully understand your job? Are there any aspects you wish to be made clearer?

(b) What parts of your job do you do best?

(c) Could any changes be made in your job which might result in improved performance?

(d) Have you any skills, knowledge, or aptitudes which could be made better use of in the organisation?

(e) What are your career plans? How do you propose achieving your ambitions in terms of further training and broader experience?

Follow-up

After the appraisal interview, the manager may complete his report with an overall assessment and/or the jointly-reached conclusion of the interview, with recommendations for follow-up action. This may take the following forms.

(a) Informing appraisees of the results of the appraisal, if this has not been central to the review interview. (Some people argue that there is no point making appraisals if they are not openly discussed, but unless managers are competent and committed to reveal results in a constructive, frank and objective manner, the negative reactions on all sides may outweigh the advantages.)

(b) Carrying out agreed actions on training, promotion and so on.

(c) Monitoring the appraisee's progress and checking that (s)he has carried out agreed actions or improvements.

(d) Taking necessary steps to help the appraisee to attain improvement objectives, by guidance, providing feedback, upgrading equipment, altering work methods or whatever.

If follow-up action is not taken, employees will feel that appraisal is all talk and just a waste of time, and that improvement action on their side will not be appreciated or worthwhile.

2.4   Assessing potential

Definition

> *Potential review* is the use of appraisal to forecast where and how fast an individual is progressing.

Potential review can be used as feedback to the individual to indicate the opportunities open to him or her in the organisation in the future. It will also be vital to the organisation in determining its management promotion and succession plans.

Information for potential assessment will include:

(a) strengths and weaknesses in the employee's existing skills and qualities;

(b) possibilities and strategies for improvement, correction and development;

(c) the employee's goals, aspirations and attitudes, with regard to career advancement, staying with the organisation and handling responsibility;

(d) the opportunities available in the organisation, including likely management vacancies, job rotation/enrichment plans and promotion policies for the future.

No single review exercise will mark an employee down for life as 'promotable' or otherwise. The process tends to be on-going, with performance at each stage or level in the employee's career indicating whether (s)he might be able to progress to the next step. However, an approach based on performance in the current job is highly fallible. L J Peter pointed out that managers tend to be promoted from positions in which they have proved themselves competent, until one day they reach a level at which they are no longer competent – promoted 'to the level of their own incompetence'!

Moreover, the management succession plan of an organisation needs to be formulated in the long term. It takes a long time to equip a manager with the skills and experience needed at senior levels, and the organisation must develop people continuously if it is to fill the shoes of departing managers without crisis.

Some idea of *potential* must therefore be built into appraisal. It is impossible to predict with any certainty how successful an individual will be in what will, after all, be different circumstances from anything (s)he has experienced so far. However, some attempt can be made to:

(a) determine *key indicators of potential*: in other words, elements believed to be essential to management success; these include past track record, and also administrative, interpersonal and analytical skills; leadership; orientation towards work, and a taste for making money; or a suitable mix of any of these;

(b) *simulate* the conditions of the position to which the individual would be promoted, to assess his performance. This may be achieved using case studies, role plays, presentations or team discussions and so on. An alternative approach might be to offer them *real* experience (under controlled conditions) by appointing them to assistant or deputy positions or to committees or project teams, and assessing their performance. This is still no real predictor of their ability to handle the *whole* job, on a continuous basis and over time, however, and it may be risky, if the appraisee fails to cope with the situation.

In theory, systematic appraisal schemes may seem fair to the individual and worthwhile for the organisation, but in practice the system often goes wrong. Let's see how, and what can be done.

3   PROBLEMS WITH APPRAISAL SCHEMES

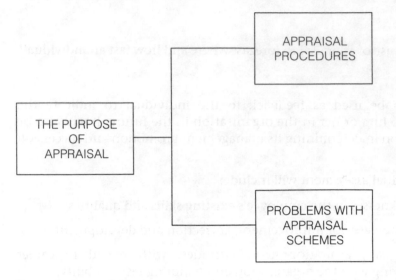

Even the best objective and systematic appraisal scheme is subject to personal and interpersonal problems!

(a) Appraisal is often *defensive on the part of the subordinate*, who believes that criticism may mean a low bonus or pay rise, or lost promotion opportunity.

(b) Appraisal is often *defensive on the part of the superior*, who cannot reconcile the role of judge and critic with the human relations aspect of interviewing and management. (S)he may in any case feel uncomfortable about 'playing God' with the employee's future.

(c) The superior might show *conscious or unconscious bias* in the appraisal or may be influenced by rapport (or lack of it) with the interviewee. Systems without clearly-defined standard criteria will be particularly prone to the subjectivity of the assessor's judgements.

(d) The manager and subordinate may both be *reluctant to devote time and attention to appraisal*. Their experience in the organisation may indicate that the exercise is a waste of time (especially if there is a lot of form-filling) with no relevance to the job, and no reliable follow-up action.

(e) The organisational culture may *simply not take appraisal seriously*: interviewers are not trained or given time to prepare, appraisees are not encouraged to contribute, or the exercise is perceived as a 'nod' to Human Relations with no practical results.

Activity 6   [15 minutes]

What would you anticipate the effects of appraisal on employee motivation to be?

Improving the system

The appraisal scheme should itself be assessed (and regularly re-assessed). Here's a handy checklist.

(a) *Relevance*
   (i)   Does the system have a useful purpose, relevant to the needs of the organisation and the individual?
   (ii) Is the purpose clearly expressed and widely understood by all concerned, both appraisers and appraisees?
   (iii) Are the appraisal criteria relevant to the purposes of the system?

(b) *Fairness*

Is there reasonable standardisation of criteria and objectivity throughout the organisation?

(c) *Serious intent*

(i) Are managers committed to the system – or is it just something the personnel department thrusts upon them?

(ii) Who does the interviewing, and are they properly trained in interviewing and assessment techniques?

(iii) Is reasonable time and attention given to the interviews – or is it a question of 'getting them over with'?

(d) *Co-operation*

(i) Is the appraisal a participative, problem-solving activity – or a tool of management control?

(ii) Is the appraisee given time and encouragement to prepare for the appraisal, so that he can make a constructive contribution?

(iii) Does a jointly-agreed, concrete conclusion emerge from the process?

Chapter roundup

The main points of an appraisal system can be conveyed diagrammatically as follows.

- *Performance appraisal*

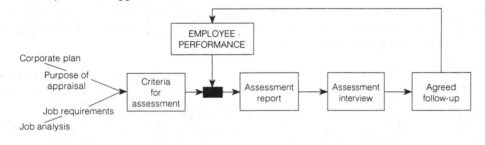

- *Potential appraisal* indicates:
  — the individual's promotability (present and likely future);
  — the individual's training and development needs;
  — the direction and rate of progress of the individual's development;
  — the future (forecast) management resource of the organisation;
  — the management recruitment, training and development needs of the organisation.

Quick quiz

1 What are the purposes of appraisal?

2 What bases or criteria of assessment might an appraisal system use?

3 Outline a results-oriented approach to appraisal, and its advantages.

4 What is 360-degree feedback, and who might be involved?

5 What is upward appraisal?

6 What follow-up should there be after an appraisal?

7 How can appraisal be made more positive and empowering to employees?

8 What kinds of criticism might be levelled at appraisal schemes by a manager who thought they were a waste of time?

9 What is the difference between performance appraisal and performance management?

10 What techniques might be used to measure an employee's potential to become a successful senior manager?

Answers to quick quiz

1 Identifying performance levels, improvements needed and promotion prospects; deciding on rewards; assessing team work and encouraging, communication between manager and employee.

2 Job analysis, job description, plans, targets and standards.

3 Performance against specific, mutually agreed targets and standards.

4 Refer to section 2.2.

5 Subordinates appraise superiors.

6 Appraises should be informed of the results, agreed activities should be taken, progress should be monitored and whatever resources or changes are needed should be provided or implemented.

7 Ensure the scheme is relevant, fair, taken seriously and co-operative.

8 The manager may say that he has better things to do with his time, that appraisals have no relevance to the job and there is no reliable follow-up action, and that they involve too much paperwork.

9 Appraisal is a backward-looking performance review. Performance management is a forward-looking results-orientated scheme.

10 Key indicators of performance should be determined and the employee should be assessed against them. The employee could be placed in positions simulating the responsibilities of senior management.

Answers to Activities

1 Disadvantages to the individual of not having an appraisal system include of the following. The individual is not aware of progress or shortcomings, is unable to judge whether s/he would be considered for promotion, is unable to identify or correct weaknesses by training and there is a lack of communication with the manager.

2 You will have come up with your own examples of criteria to assess some jobs but not others. You might have identified such things as:

(a) numerical ability (applicable to accounts staff, say, more than to customer contact staff or other non-numerical functions);

(b) ability to drive safely (essential for transport workers – not for desk-bound ones);

(c) report-writing (not applicable to manual labour, say);

(d) creativity and initiative (desirable in areas involving design and problem-solving not routine or repetitive jobs in mass production or bureaucratic organisations).

3 Advantages of performance management include the following.

(a) The subordinate is more involved in appraisal of his own performance, because he is able to evaluate his success or progress in achieving specific, jointly-agreed targets. The sense of responsibility and independence may encourage job satisfaction and commitment.

(b) The manager is therefore relieved of his role as judge, to an extent, and becomes a counsellor. A primarily problem-solving approach may be adopted (what does the employee require in order to do his job better?)

(c) Learning and motivation theories suggest, as we have seen, that clear and known targets are important in determining behaviour.

4 Drawbacks to 360-degree appraisal include:

(a) respondents' reluctance to give negative feedback to a boss – or friend;

(b) the suspicion that management is passing the buck for negative feedback, getting people to 'rat' on their friends;

(c) the feeling that the appraisee is being picked on, if positive feedback is not carefully balanced with the negative.

5 Problems with upward appraisal include fear of reprisals or vindictiveness (or extra form-processing). Some bosses in strong positions might feel able to refuse to act on results, even if a consensus of staff suggested that they should change their ways.

6 The effects of appraisal on motivation is a tricky issue.

(a) Feedback on performance is regarded as vital in motivation, because it enables an employee to make calculations about the amount of effort required in future to achieve objectives and rewards. Even negative feedback can have this effect – and is more likely to spur the employee on to post-appraisal action.

(b) Agreement of challenging but attainable targets for performance or improvement also motivates employees by clarifying goals and the value (and 'cost' in terms of effort) of incentives offered.

(c) A positive approach to appraisal allows employees to solve their work problems and apply creative thinking to their jobs.

However, people rarely react well to criticism – especially at work, where they may feel that their reward or even job security is on the line. In addition, much depends on the self-esteem of the appraisee. If s(he) has a high self-image, (s)he may be impervious to criticism. If s(he) has a low self-image, (s)he may be depressed rather than motivated by criticism.

Assignment 7   [About 1¹/₂ hours]

An example of an appraisal report (from the early 1980s) is reproduced as Figure 7.2 in section 2.1. Consider the use of 'rating scales', the use of words like 'weaknesses', the relevance and definition of personal characteristics and the assumption that the employee will 'react' to and 'comment' on the appraisal.

(a) How effective do you think this form is?

(b) Indicate how it could be improved.

(c) What kind of follow-up action might be suggested by the appraisal report?

(d) Why is follow-up important?

Chapter 8

ENHANCING PERFORMANCE

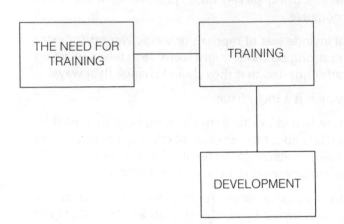

Introduction

You may have anticipated by now that we would take a contingency approach to improving individual and group performance at work. Essentially, 'it all depends' on the situation. We have already discussed factors such as personality, attitudes, intelligence and aptitudes, interpersonal relationships, leadership style, motivation and incentives, stress and conflict, organisational culture and group behaviour. All these things must be 'managed' for improved performance, as we have seen. In the second section of this text, we will see how managers can plan and organise the work, so that it is 'do-able' with greater efficiency and effectiveness.

Two major areas of improvement remain:

- the resolving of personal and interpersonal problems which might hamper performance (discussed in Chapter 9); and

- the training and development of people to perform their tasks better, and to progress at work towards the fulfilment of their potential. That's the topic of this chapter.

Your objectives

After completing this chapter, you should:

(a) be able to analyse training needs and objectives;

(b) be able to evaluate a range of training approaches and methods, taking a contingency approach;

(c) understand how the effectiveness of training might be assessed;

(d) appreciate the importance of personal and career development and how it might be encouraged.

1 THE NEED FOR TRAINING

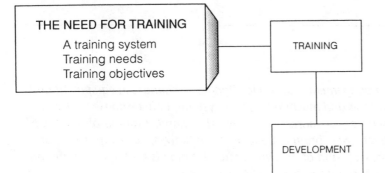

1.1 A training system

Definition

According to the Department of Employment, *training* is 'the systematic development of the attitude/knowledge/skill/behaviour pattern required by an individual in order to perform adequately a given task or job.'

The application of systems theory to the design of training has gained currency in the West in recent years. A *training system*, Figure 8.1, uses rational methods to programme learning, from:

(a) *the identification of training needs*; by comparing the requirements of the job with an assessment of the present capacities and inclinations of the individuals available to do it; (this is called their 'pre-entry' behaviour since they have not yet entered the training system); via

(b) *the design of courses*, selection of methods and media; to

(c) *the measurement of trained performance* – the 'terminal behaviour' resulting from the training system – and its comparison against pre-determined performance targets.

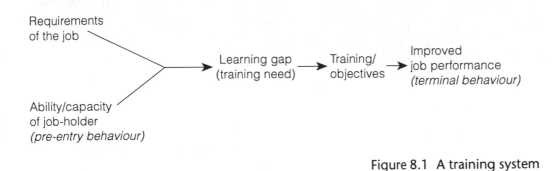

Figure 8.1 A training system

1.2 Training needs

Training should not be a shot in the dark. The training needs of individuals and groups will vary enormously, according to the nature of the job and particular tasks, and the abilities and experience of the employees.

Activity 1 [20 minutes]

Give at least three examples of where a need for training would be obvious and automatic.

For discussion

'Training is to some extent a management reaction to change, eg changes in equipment and design, methods of work, new tools and machines, control systems, or in response to changes dictated by new products, services, or markets. On the other hand, training also induces change. A capable workforce will bring about new initiatives, developments and improvements – in an organic way, and of its own accord. Training is both a cause and an effect of change.' Bryan Livy: Corporate Personnel Management.

Should organisations wait for training needs to be identified – or continuously train people?

Training needs analysis

Training needs may be identified as the gap between what people *should* be achieving and what they actually are achieving. In other words:

Required level of competence *minus* present level of competence *equals* training need.

The *required level of competence* for the job can be determined by:

(a) job analysis, identifying the elements of the task;

(b) skills analysis, identifying the skill elements of the task, such as:
  (i)   what senses are involved (vision, touch, hearing etc)?
  (ii) what left-hand/right-hand/foot operations are required?
  (iii) what interactions with other operatives are required?
  and so on;

(c) role analysis, for managerial and administrative jobs requiring a high degree of co-ordination and interaction with others;

(d) existing records, such as job specifications and descriptions, person specifications, the organisation chart (depicting roles and relationships) and so on.

The *present level of employees' competence* includes not only skill and knowledge, but the employees' inclination or *willingness* to work competently as well. It can be measured by an appropriate pre-test of skills, knowledge, performance, attitude and so on. The ongoing system of performance appraisal (discussed in Chapter 7) may also furnish this information.

1.3   Training objectives

The manager responsible for training will have to make an initial investigation into the problem of the gap between requirements and current performance or competence.

Activity 2 [20 minutes]

Can the manager assume that the gap between requirement and actual performance will be bridged by training? What else might be required?

If it is concluded that the provision of training would improve work performance, training *objectives* can be defined. They should be clear and specific, and related to measurable targets. Ideally they should detail:

(a) behaviour – what the trainee should be able to do;

(b) standard – to what level of performance; and

(c) environment – under what conditions (so that the performance level is realistic).

Objectives are the yardsticks that should allow a manager (and the trainees themselves) to see clearly whether or how far training has been successful. They are usually best expressed in terms of active verbs: at the end of the course the trainee should be able to describe ...., or identify .... or distinguish X from Y .... or calculate .... or assemble .... and so on. It is insufficient to define the objectives of training as 'to give trainees a grounding in ....' or 'to encourage trainees in a better appreciation of ....': this offers no target achievement which can be objectively measured.

Training methods and media must next be evaluated, and a programme designed. There are a variety of options including: (a) formal training and education; and (b) on-the-job training.

2 TRAINING

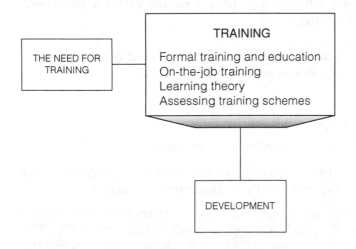

2.1 Formal training and education

Internal courses are sometimes run by the training departments of larger organisations. Skills may be taught at a technical level, related to the organisation's particular product and market, or to aspects such as marketing, teambuilding, interviewing or information technology management. Some organisations also encourage the wider development of staff by offering opportunities to learn languages or other skills.

One convenient and popular method of in-house education is computer-based training (CBT) or Interactive Video (IV), using equipment in offices or even trainees' homes. Training programmes may be developed by the organisation or by outside consultants – or bought 'off the shelf': the software (or 'courseware') can then be distributed, so that large numbers of dispersed staff can learn about new products or procedures quickly and simultaneously.

External courses vary, and may involve:

(a) day-release, which means that the employee attends a local college on one day of the week;

(b) evening classes, or 'distance learning' (a home study or correspondence course, plus limited face-to-face teaching) which make demands on the individual's time outside work;

(c) full-time but brief introductory or revision courses;

(d) a sponsored full-time course at a university for 1 or 2 years.

Formal training tends to have disadvantages in some contexts.

(a) If the subject matter of the training course is not felt to relate directly to the individual's job and organisation culture, the learning will not be applied afterwards, and will quickly be forgotten.

(b) Individuals may feel that courses are, in general, a waste of time. They will not benefit from the training unless they are motivated to learn.

(c) Immediate and relevant *feedback* on performance and progress may not be available from the learning process, especially if knowledge is tested by unrealistic methods (like exams) or at wide intervals. This will lower the learner's incentive and sense of direction.

(d) It does not suit some people, who may not have much experience of (or taste for) classroom learning since school. Some people simply prefer a 'hands-on' type of learning: learning by doing.

 People who learn better from experience than from theory generally progress more through on-the-job training. How do you go about it?

2.2 On-the-job training

Different methods of on-the-job training include the following.

(a) *Induction:* gradually introducing new recruits or transferred employees to their new job, workmates and workplace, and their requirements and norms.

(b) *Coaching:* trainees are put under the guidance of an experienced employee who shows them how to do the job. This is sometimes called 'sitting with Nellie'. The length of the coaching period will depend on the complexity of the job and the previous experience of the trainee. We will discuss coaching further in the Development section of this chapter.

(c) *Job rotation:* the trainee is given several jobs in succession, to gain experience of a wide range of activities. (Even experienced managers may rotate their jobs to gain wider experience; this method is commonly applied in the Civil Service.)

(d) *Temporary promotion:* an individual is promoted into a superior's position whilst the superior is absent. This gives the individual a chance to experience the demands of a more senior position.

(e) *'Assistant to' positions:* an individual with management potential may be appointed as assistant to a manager. In this way, the individual gains experience of management, without a risky level of responsibility.

(f) *Project or committee work:* trainees might be included in the membership of a project team or committee, to obtain an understanding of inter-departmental relationships, problem-solving and particular areas of the organisation's activity.

On-the-job training is very common, especially when the work involved is not complex. It will generally be more successful if:

(a) *assignments have a specific purpose* from which the trainee can learn and gain experience;

(b) *the trainee is a practical type,* who prefers to learn by doing and can tolerate the process of trial and error; (other people might need to get away from the pressures of the workplace to think through issues and understand the underlying principles before applying new techniques);

(c) *the organisation is tolerant of mistakes.* Mistakes are an inevitable part of on-the-job learning, and if they are punished or frowned on, the trainee will be reluctant to take further risks and will be de-motivated to learn.

There may be real risks involved in throwing people in at the deep-end: the cost of mistakes or inefficiencies may be high and the pressure on learners great. (Would you want to learn medical procedures, or air traffic control procedures, on-the-job?)

An important *advantage* of on-the-job training, however, is that it takes place in the environment of the job itself, and in the context of the work group in which the trainee will have to operate. The style of supervision, personal relations with colleagues, working conditions and pressures, the culture of the office/shop floor and so on will be absorbed as part of the training process.

Activity 3 [20 minutes]

If you have had work experience, list the advantages you experienced through on-the-job training. If you have not worked, think about this course and list the disadvantages of the different methods of study you are given.

We discussed learning theory in Chapter 3, but here's a brief 'recap' of the ideas a training manager might find useful.

2.3 Learning theory

(a) The individual should be *motivated* to learn. The advantages of training (to the trainee) should be made clear, and appealing to the individual's own motives – money, opportunity, valued skills or whatever.

(b) Clear *objectives and standards* should be set, so that each task has some meaning. Each stage of learning should present a challenge, without overloading trainees or making them lose confidence. Specific objectives and performance standards for each stage will help trainees in the control process that leads to learning, providing targets against which performance will constantly be measured and adjusted accordingly.

(c) There should be timely, relevant *feedback* on performance and progress. This will usually be provided by the trainer, and should be given during the training process – or certainly not long afterwards.

(d) Positive and negative *reinforcement* should be judiciously used. Recognition and encouragement enhances trainees' confidence in their competence and progress. Punishment for poor performance – especially without explanation or correction – discourages the learner and creates feelings of guilt, failure and hostility, but helpful or constructive criticism is likely to be beneficial.

(e) Active *participation* has more effect than passive reception (because it motivates the individual to learn and enhances concentration and recollection). If a high degree of participation is impossible, practice and repetition can be used to reinforce receptivity, but participation has the added effect of encouraging 'ownership' of the process of learning and changing – committing the individual to it as his or her own goal, not just a process imposed by management.

Implementation of the training scheme is not the end of the story. The scheme should be monitored and assessed to ensure that it is doing its job.

2.4 Assessing training schemes

Validation

Definition

Validation means observing the results of a process (in this case, a training scheme) and measuring whether its objectives have been achieved.

There are various ways of validating a training scheme.

(a) *Trainee reactions to the experience:* asking the trainees whether they thought the training programme was relevant to their work, and whether they found it useful. This form of monitoring is rather inexact, and it does not allow the training manager to measure the results, for comparison against specific training objectives.

(b) *Trainee learning:* measuring what the trainees have learned on the course, perhaps by means of a test or assessment of competence at the end.

(c) *Changes in job behaviour following training:* studying the subsequent behaviour of the trainees in their jobs, to measure how the training scheme has altered the way they do their work. This is possible, for example, where the purpose of the course was to learn a particular skill.

(d) *Impact of training on organisational goals:* seeing whether the training scheme has contributed to the overall objectives of the organisation. This is a form of monitoring reserved for senior management.

Validation is thus the measurement of terminal behaviour (trained work performance) in relation to training objectives.

Evaluation

Definition

Evaluation means comparing the costs of a process (in this case a training scheme) against the benefits which are being obtained.

A training programme should only go ahead in the first place if the likely benefits are expected to exceed the costs of designing and running it. The problem here is not so much in estimating the costs, but in estimating the potential *benefits*.

(a) Costs will be those of the training establishment, training materials, the time (usually with pay) of the staff attending training courses, their travelling expenses, the salaries or fees of training staff, and so on.

(b) Benefits might be measured in terms of:
　　(i)　quicker working and therefore reductions in overtime or staff numbers;
　　(ii)　greater accuracy of work;
　　(iii)　more extensive skills and versatility, offering greater labour flexibility;
　　(iv)　enhanced job satisfaction and reduced labour turnover.

As you will appreciate, the benefits are more easily stated in general terms than quantified in money terms.

Activity 4 [20 minutes]

What technique of training validation is employed in the following cases?

(a) You fill out a Lecturer Assessment Form at the end of term.

(b) You sit an assessment at the end of this module.

(c) You write an essay on 'Motivation'.

(d) You fill out a questionnaire on how you feel about prejudice at work.

(e) A university asks new applicants to state why they chose the particular course and provider: was it by recommendation?

(f) You fill out a report for the Careers Office (in several years' time) on your career progress.

3 DEVELOPMENT

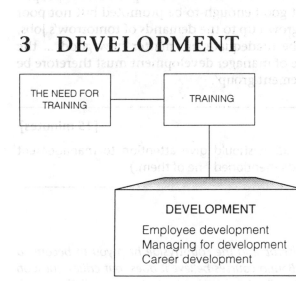

3.1 Employee development

Definitions

Constable and McCormick formulated a useful distinction between education, training and development.

(a) *Education* is that process which results in formal qualifications up to and including post-graduate degrees.

(b) *Training* is the formal learning activity which may not lead to qualifications, and which may be received at any time in a working career; for example, a course in counselling skills;

(c) *Development* is broader again: job experience and learning from other employees, particularly one's immediate superior, are integral parts of the development process.

In every organisation, there should be some arrangement or system whereby:

(a) employees gain *experience*, which will enable them to do another more senior job in time;

(b) employees are given *guidance* and *counselling* by their bosses or more senior members of the team;

(c) employees are given suitable *training* and *education* to develop their skills and knowledge; and

(d) employees are enabled to *plan their future* and the opportunities open to them in the organisation.

This is all part of employee development.

Management development

The development of managers is considered particularly important, because the organisation needs to ensure that it has a supply of suitable people ready to move into management positions when others move upwards, or out of the organisation. This is called *management succession*.

Drucker has suggested that management development should be provided for all managers, not just the ones who are considered promotable material. 'The promotable man concept focuses on one man out of ten – at best one man out of five. It assigns the other nine to limbo. But the men who need management development the most are not the balls of fire who are the ... promotable people. They are those managers who are not good enough to be promoted but not poor enough to be fired. Unless they have grown up to the demands of tomorrow's jobs, the whole management group will be inadequate, no matter how good ... the promotable people. The first principle of manager development must therefore be the development of the entire management group'.

Activity 5 [15 minutes]

Suggest three reasons why an organisation should give attention to management training and development. (We've already mentioned one of them.)

For discussion

'*Does getting wet, cold and generally miserable in the countryside help you to become a better manager? Supporters of Outward Bound courses believe it does, but critics question the value of having highly-paid and specialised executives tramping around the woods honing boy-scout-level skills.*

Is outdoor training not just a way of keeping ageing physical exercise teachers, sadistic ex-corporals and overpaid consultants employed? And is it just an expensive fad in training, no better or worse than classroom teaching?' Financial Times, *January 1993.*

What do you think?

How can a manager contribute to the development of his or her team? We have already discussed the identification of training needs and the provision of training, but what other forms of guidance, support and encouragement might a manager give? We will look at a few aspects.

3.2 Managing for development

Organisations are trying to encourage and empower individuals to take responsibility for their own *self-development*. Personal Development Plans (PDPs) are essentially action plans for individuals' skill and career development. These put the onus on the individuals themselves to seek out and organise training and development opportunities. A 1995 report by the Institute of Employment Studies suggests that the number of large employers looking to introduce PDPs is rapidly increasing.

This puts managers in a new guiding and enabling role. In most organisations, however, the manager will still be the one most responsible for:

(a) guiding or *coaching* work performance – or appointing someone else to do so;

(b) giving advice and support as an individual's *mentor* – or appointing someone else to do so;

(c) *challenging* the individual to greater effort and responsibility; and

(d) *facilitating* the individual's development by providing the authority, information, time and/or resources (s)he requires.

Coaching

Coaching is on-the-job guidance, advice, correction and teaching with a view to improving performance. A coach should:

(a) demonstrate how areas of a job are performed, and guide the trainee's own performance of the same tasks, by advice and correction;

(b) help the trainee to identify problems or development needs in his or her work;

(c) seek out or identify opportunities for the trainee to develop, through doing new things at work;

(d) help the trainee plan the solutions to problems, or approaches to new challenges at work;

(e) be patient and tolerant of the trainee's initial mistakes, seeing them as necessary learning and problem-solving opportunities;

(f) encourage the trainee to assess his or her own progress and performance, and to formulate further plans for improvement.

Essentially, coaching is a *collaboration* between the coach and the trainee, in which the coach's special role is encouragement and guidance as the trainee develops on the job. The coach needs to resist the temptation to control or direct the trainee in specific methods or directions (a role more suited to an 'instructor'), especially if progress is slow and gained through error. A coach therefore requires:

(a) patience;

(b) tolerance (even appreciation) of risk and the absence of clear-cut solutions;

(c) the ability to see and use new challenges and problems as learning opportunities;

(d) skills in communication and personal encouragement;

(e) willingness to adopt a non-directive style; and

(f) commitment to the coaching role over a long period, if necessary.

Mentoring

A mentor is a guide, ideally both more experienced and more powerful in the organisation, whose concern is the trainee's long-term personal development. (S)he may occupy a role as the trainee's teacher/coach, counsellor, role model, protector and/or champion/sponsor in the organisation, spur to action or improvement, critic, encourager and so on, as appropriate to the situation at a given time.

A mentor should:

(a) help the trainee to greater self-awareness, by listening to, questioning and challenging his or her ideas, and feeding back on his or her behaviour;

(b) help the trainee to formulate and clarify his or her needs and ambitions in life, and to identify where events and opportunities at work fit into those plans;

(c) encourage the trainee to take responsibility for his or her development, while offering support – personally and within the organisation – if required;

(d) help the trainee to reconcile his or her non-work needs, interests and circumstances with the demands of work (or vice versa);

(e) help the trainee to plan specific development and career paths or directions, offering opportunities where appropriate and possible.

Mentoring is even more non-directive than coaching, as well as potentially longer in duration, and broader in scope. It clearly requires first-class interpersonal and communication skills, particularly empathy (or 'understanding'), active listening and guidance.

Activity 6 [30 minutes]

Pedler, Burgoyne and Boydell indicated three different styles of helping people to learn. These were the instructor (I), the coach (C) and the mentor (M). For each dimension identify which of the statements refer to the instructor, coach and mentor. (We have done the first one for you).

Dimensions

Focus of help:
(1) Task   I   (Immediate, short term)
(2) Development of person   M   (Ongoing)
     through life
(3) Results of job   C   (Medium to long term)

Timespan:
(1) Career or lifetime
(2) One month to one year
(3) A day or two

Approach to helping:
(1) Act as friend willing to play 'devil's advocate', listen and question to enlarge awareness
(2) 'Show and tell' – give supervised practice
(3) Explore problem together and set up opportunities to try out new skills

Associated activities:
(1) Analyse task; give clear instruction; supervise practice; give feedback on results at once
(2) Link work with other parts of life; clarify broad and long-term aims and purpose in life
(3) Jointly identify the problem; create development opportunity and review

'Ownership' of development:
(1) Learner
(2) Helper
(3) Shared

Attitude to ambiguity:
(1) Eliminate
(2) Use as a challenge, as a puzzle to be solved
(3) Accept as being part of the exciting world

Benefits to the company:
(1) Goal-directed performance, orientated to improving and being creative
(2) Conscious questioning approach to the mission of the company
(3) Standard, accurate performance

Challenging

One last word needs to be said on the subject of challenging individuals to personal development. As we discussed in Chapter 3, change and learning can seem threatening to the individual's security and self-image. Learning new things and taking the risk of trying them out, especially at work, puts the individual's sense of competence on the line. Some people actively resist skill and career development in order to stay within their 'comfort zone'. Managers need to balance the elements of:

(a) *challenge*, which stretches team members to learn and improve, taking them beyond their present level or scope of performance, into an area of risk; and

(b) *support*, which offers a position of security, competence and reassurance from which to move out and experiment with new areas.

If a manager is challenging but not supportive, the team may feel perpetually insecure and not in control: a very stressful position. If (s)he is very supportive but not at all challenging, the team will be cosy but complacent: individuals who want opportunities to stretch themselves may be frustrated. If the manager is neither challenging nor supportive, the team is completely adrift, with no sense of direction or leadership. If the manager is both challenging and supportive, (s)he will foster a flexible team, willing to step out into new areas in the confidence that their manager is behind them.

This can be shown as a challenge-support matrix, as shown in figure 8.2. (We've come up with catchy tags for each style, to help you remember them, but feel free to develop terms to suit yourself!)

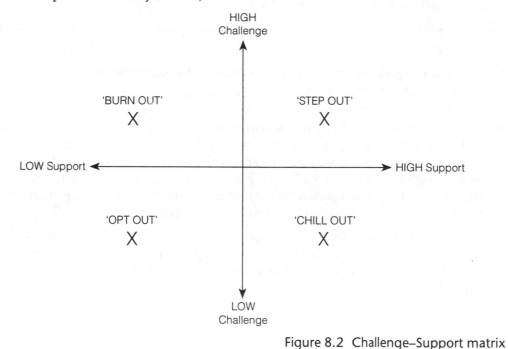

Figure 8.2 Challenge–Support matrix

EXAMPLES

● A National Health Service development programme for unit general managers includes a budget for each individual to spend – as he or she wishes – on personal development. This can be spent on courses, seminars or books, or on 'buying in' a coach or instructor, or visiting other organisations to observe their methods – whatever. This approach empowers would-be learners, and encourages creative thinking about development needs and opportunities.

EXAMPLES *(continued)*

● In 1990, the Rover Car Group launched a multi-million pound 'internal business', dedicated to providing learning and development opportunities to all employees: the Rover Learning Business. Employees are encouraged to formulate individual development plans, with the opportunity to learn management skills.

3.3 Career development

Note that development includes *career development* and succession planning by the organisation. This will require attention to a number of matters outside the scope of education and training courses, including the following.

(a) The types of *experience* a potential manager needs to acquire. It may be desirable for a senior manager, for example, to have experience of:
  (i) both line/operational and staff/specialist management – in order to understand how authority is effectively exercised in both situations, and the potentially conflicting cultures/objectives of the two fields;
  (ii) running a whole business unit (of whatever size) in order to develop a broader perspective; this is likely to be a vital transition in a manager's career, from functional to general management;
  (iii) dealing with head office – in order to understand the dynamics of organisational control and politics.

Activity 7   [15 minutes]

See if you can suggest two more areas of experience that might be useful for a manager to acquire in order to enhance his or her prospects.

(b) The individual's *guides and role models* in the organisation. It is important that individuals with potential should measure themselves against their peers – assessing their relative weaknesses and strengths – and emulate role models, usually superiors who have already 'got what it takes' and proved it. Potential high fliers can be fast-tracked by putting them under the guidance of effective motivators, teachers and power sources in the organisation.

(c) The level of *opportunities and challenges* offered to the developing employee. Too much responsibility too early can be damagingly stressful, but if there is not *some* degree of difficulty, the employee may never explore his full potential and capacity.

Chapter roundup

● A systematic approach to training can be illustrated as follows.

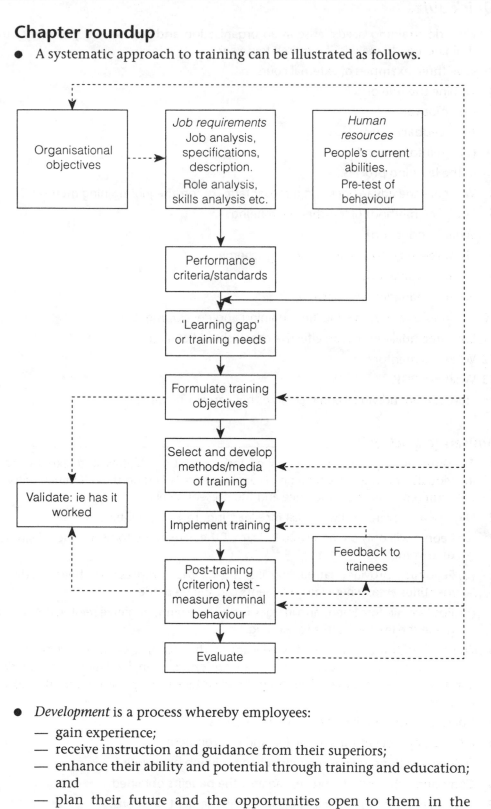

● *Development* is a process whereby employees:

— gain experience;

— receive instruction and guidance from their superiors;

— enhance their ability and potential through training and education; and

— plan their future and the opportunities open to them in the organisation.

This is a collaborative activity of the organisation and the individual.

Quick quiz

1   How do 'training needs' arise in an organisation and how would you carry out a 'training needs analysis' if required to do so?

2   Give three examples of external courses.

3   Outline the role of:

   (a) motivation;

   (b) feedback; and

   (c) 'reinforcement'

   in the learning process.

4   What are the advantages and disadvantages of 'on-the job' training methods?

5   List three methods of 'on-the-job' training.

6   What is induction?

7   List three ways to validate a training scheme.

8   What is evaluation?

9   What is management succession?

10 Distinguish between education, training and development.

11 List three qualities that an effective coach should exhibit.

12 What is a mentor?

13 What are PDPs?

14 How can an individual enhance his or her career prospects?

Answers to quick quiz

1   The answer depends on the job or tasks and the abilities and experience of individuals or groups. Training needs analysis entails finding the difference between the required level of competence and the present level.

2   Day release, evening classes, distance learning, revision, full-time courses.

3   (a) People will only be motivated to learn if they are made to realise the advantages of learning.

   (b) Feedback provides satisfaction if it shows that progress has been made and identifies areas where improvements can still be made.

   (c) Positive reinforcement encourages further learning; negative reinforcement may make the learner hostile to learning.

4   The main advantage is that it is relevant to the job. It takes place within the job environment, so that the style of supervision, personal relations and working conditions are absorbed. The main disadvantages are pressure and the cost of mistakes.

5   Coaching, job rotation, 'assistant to' positions.

6   Introducing new recruits to the job and environment.

7   Trainee reactions, trainee learning, changes in job behaviour.

8   Comparing the cost of a process against the benefits obtained.

9   The movement of suitable people into management positions.

10 Refer to section 3.1.

11 Patience, tolerance, communication skills.

12 An experienced guide within the organisation.

13 Personal Development Plans.

14 Gain experience in all areas and with all levels, accept opportunities and challenges.

Answers to Activities

1 Examples where the need for training is obvious could include any of the following. New regulations or legislation; new technology; if seeking accreditation for training scheme; poor individual or group performance; as a result of problems such as high labour turnover, conflict, crises; or as part of a regular programme of formal training needs analysis.

2 Will training automatically improve performance? It might – indeed it should, all other things being equal – but a training course is not a simple remedy for poor performance. Contingency theory ('It all depends') must be applied to situations where employee performance is below the desired standard. An employee who is adequately trained to perform may still not be able or willing to do so, because of badly designed working methods or environment, faulty equipment, inappropriate supervision, poor motivation, lack of incentive, or non-work factors, such as health, domestic circumstances and so on. In particular, it must be remembered that performance is not just a product of The System, but a product, and manifestation, of human behaviour. Training methods, and their expected results, must take into account human attitudes, values, emotions and relationships.

3 You have probably covered most of the following points.

Advantages include working for a specific purpose, carrying out practical work, the feeling of achievement when a task is completed successfully, knowing you have made a contribution to the organisation's objectives, learning to work with others. If mistakes are made they are rectified and do not affect your overall performance (unless you make too many or keep making the same mistakes).

Disadvantages could include the difficulty of relating exercises or assignments to the 'real work' situation, working mainly on your own and the few practical applications for your studies. Unlike work, you only have one chance to get things right: the marking system means that if you make a mistake there is little you can do once the work is handed in and marked.

4 Techniques of training validation used in the given examples are as follows.

(a) Trainee reaction

(b) Trainee learning

(c) Trainee learning

(d) Change in behaviour (attitude) following training (reading Chapter 5, perhaps!)

(e) Impact of training on the organisation's goals.

(f) Impact of training on your goals.

5 Reasons for management training include the following.

(a) The prime objective of management development is improved performance capacity – both from managers and from those they manage.

(b) Management development secures management succession: a pool of promotable individuals in the organisation.

(c) The organisation's showing an interest in the career development of staff may motivate them and encourage loyalty.

6 Focus of help: (1) I   'Ownership':   (1) M

(2) M   (2) I

(3) C   (3) C

Timespan:	(1)	M	Attitude to ambiguity:	(1)	I
	(2)	C		(2)	C
	(3)	I		(3)	M
Approach to helping:	(1)	M	Benefits to company:	(1)	C
	(2)	I		(2)	M
	(3)	C		(3)	I
Associated activities:	(1)	I			
	(2)	M			
	(3)	C			

7   Here are two further areas of useful experience for managers.

(a)   International operations, if the organisation is in (or moving into) international markets. Understanding of different national cultures and business environments will be crucial.

(b)   Other fields and types of organisation. Some consultancies, for example, offer secondments with businesses; 'human resource' (personnel) managers are encouraged to gain experience in operational departments.

Assignment 8   [About 1¹/₂ hours]

Bruce Collins (who already works for your organisation) is about to join your staff. The following is an extract from his most recent report.

'Bruce is meticulous in all he does. Although he learns thoroughly, he does not learn quickly, preferring to observe others in action before committing himself to any new activity. When he does start, he is very effective.'

The work with which Bruce will be involved is entirely new to him. None of his colleagues does similar work. Off-the-job training is available: a suitable, two-week course will start the week after Bruce joins your staff. The current job-holder, Fiona, from whom Bruce will be taking over, will leave one week after the end of the course; the next opportunity for Bruce to undertake this course will be in six months' time.

Having planned Bruce's induction, you now have to plan his training programme.

(a) What general considerations would you take into account when planning the training programme?

(b) Discuss what other points you would consider in this particular situation.

Chapter 9

PROBLEM-SOLVING

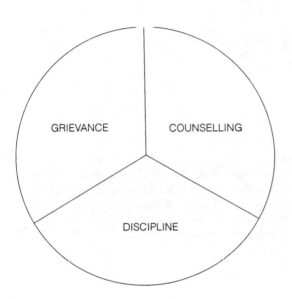

Introduction

In Chapter 8, we discussed how a manager can improve *performance*, by training and developing employees so that more of their potential is fulfilled. However, the more basic responsibility of management is to *maintain performance:* not to let it fall below the level and standard required by the organisation's objectives. This is partly achieved through managing the task effectively (as we will discuss in Section 2 of this text) but there will also be times when performance is adversely affected by personal and interpersonal factors within the team. Some such problems – including conflict, negative attitudes, perceptual distortion, communication barriers, stress and poor motivation – have already been covered. In this chapter, we look at various ways in which the manager can help to resolve such issues in the work team.

Your objectives

After completing this chapter you should:

(a) understand the value of employee counselling and be able to outline an effective framework for counselling;

(b) be able to outline disciplinary procedures and anticipate the interpersonal difficulties in disciplinary situations;

(c) be able to suggest a framework for the resolution of employee grievances.

1   COUNSELLING

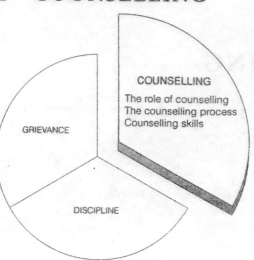

Definition

'*Counselling* can be defined as a purposeful relationship in which one person helps another to help himself. It is a way of relating and responding to another person so that that person is helped to explore his thoughts, feelings and behaviour with the aim of reaching a clearer understanding. The clearer understanding may be of himself or of a problem, or of the one in relation to the other.' (Rees).

1.1   The role of counselling

The Institute of Personnel Development's 1992 *Statement on Counselling in the Workplace* makes it clear that effective counselling is not merely a matter of 'pastoral' care for individuals, but is very much in the organisation's interests.

(a) Appropriate use of counselling can prevent under-performance and reduce labour turnover and absenteeism.

(b) Effective counselling demonstrates an organisation's commitment to and concern for its employees and so is liable to improve loyalty and enthusiasm among the workforce.

(c) The development of employees is of value to the organisation, and counselling can give employees the confidence and encouragement necessary to take responsibility for self development.

(d) Workplace counselling recognises that the organisation may be contributing to its employees' problems and therefore provides an opportunity to reassess organisational policy and practice.

For discussion

'*Staff spend at least half their waking time at work or in getting to it or leaving it. They know they contribute to the organisation when they are reasonably free from worry, and they feel, perhaps inarticulately, that when they are in trouble they are due to get something back from the organisation. People are entitled to be treated as full human beings with personal needs, hopes and anxieties; they are employed as people; they bring themselves to work, not just their hands, and they cannot readily leave their troubles at home.'* (Martin).

Do you agree? Or do you think the non-work interests and affairs of employees are none of their employers' business?

Activity 1 [15 minutes]

The need for workplace counselling can arise in many different situations. Try and think of at least four examples.

> **EXAMPLE**
>
> The Body Shop runs an education and counselling programme on the Human Immuno-deficiency Virus (HIV) and Acquired Immune Deficiency Syndrome (AIDS). Its purpose is to give support to HIV-positive employees and employees with HIV-positive partners, and to prevent fear and discrimination by other employees, while promoting safe practices.

1.2 The counselling process

The counselling process is basically about *empowering* employees: enabling them to recognise, express and take responsibility for their own problem or situation. (This is not the same as giving advice or instruction.) The counsellor may offer *guidance* in identifying the problem and its causes, and *resources* for managing it (information, education, financial and non-financial assistance and so on), but this is still essentially a supportive and enabling role. No solution can be imposed on the individual.

Confidentiality

There will be situations when an employee cannot be completely open unless (s)he is sure that all comments will be treated confidentially. However, certain information, once obtained by the organisation (for example about fraud or sexual harassment) calls for action. In spite of the drawbacks, therefore, employees must be told when their comments will be passed on to the relevant authority, and when they will be treated completely confidentially.

The counselling session

The IPD statement includes a helpful checklist for counsellors, which we reproduce overleaf.

1.3 Counselling skills

Counsellors need to be:

(a) observant enough to note behaviour which may be symptomatic of a problem;

(b) sensitive to beliefs and values which may be different from their own (for example religious beliefs);

(c) empathetic (putting themselves into other people's shoes), to the extent that they appreciate that the problem may seem overwhelming to the individual;

(d) impartial;

(e) non-directive, willing to refrain from giving advice; and

(f) skilled in questioning and active listening.

Counsellors must have the belief that individuals have the resources to solve their *own* problems, albeit with passive or active help.

Counselling checklist

Preparation

- Choose a place to talk which is quiet, free from interruption and not open to view.
- Research as much as you can before the meeting and have any necessary papers readily available.
- Make sure you know whether the need for counselling has been properly identified or whether you will have to carefully probe to establish if a problem exists.
- Allow sufficient time for the session. (If you know you must end at a particular time, inform the individual of this at the beginning of the meeting).
- Decide if it is necessary for the individual's department head to be aware of the counselling and its purpose.
- Give the individual the option of being accompanied by a supportive colleague.
- If you are approaching the individual following information received from a colleague, decide in advance the extent to which you can reveal your source.
- Consider how you are going to introduce and discuss your perceptions of the situation.
- Be prepared for the individual to have different expectations of the discussion, eg the individual may expect you to solve the problem – rather than come to terms with it himself/herself.
- Understand that the individual's view of the facts of the situation will be more important than the facts themselves and that their behaviour may not reflect their true feelings.

Format of discussion

- Welcome the individual and clarify the general purpose of the meeting.
- Assure the individual that matters of confidentiality will be treated as such.
- The individual may be reticent through fear of being considered somewhat of a risk in future and you will need to give appropriate reassurances in this regard.
- Be ready to prompt or encourage the individual to move into areas he/she might be hesitant about.
- Encourage the individual to look more deeply into statements.
- Ask the individual to clarify statements you do not quite understand.
- Try to take the initiative in probing important areas which may be embarrassing/emotional to the individual and which you both might prefer to avoid.
- Recognise that some issues may be so important to the individual that they will have to be discussed over and over again, even though this may seem repetitious to you.
- If you sense that the individual is becoming defensive, try to identify the reason and relax the pressure by changing your approach.
- Occasionally summarise the conversation as it goes along, reflecting back in your own words what you understand the individual to say.
- Sometimes emotions may be more important than the words being spoken, so it may be necessary to reflect back what you see the individual feeling.
- At the close of the meeting, clarify any decisions reached and agree what follow-up support would be helpful.

Overcoming dangers

- If you take notes at an inappropriate moment, you may set up a barrier between yourself and the individual.
- Realise you may not like the individual and be on guard against this.
- Recognise that repeating problems does not solve them.

- Be careful to avoid taking sides.
- Overcome internal and external distractions. Concentrate on the individual and try to understand the situation with him/her.
- The greater the perceived level of listening, the more likely the individual will be to accept comments and contributions from you.
- Resist the temptation to talk about your own problems, even though these may seem similar to those of the individual.

Source: IPD Statement on Counselling in the Workplace

Activity 2   [45 minutes]

This is a role-play exercise, to be done with another person. One of you should take the role of the manager, and the other the role of the team member, Javed, in the following scenario, and actually attempt a counselling session. If possible, get others to observe you, and give you feedback in the specific areas covered by the checklist given above. The person playing Javed should also feed back how the manager's counselling style made him feel.

Javed is a member of the section which you lead. His work is normally well above average and he knows it. You find him mildly arrogant and have difficulty in liking him, although he seems to have a great deal of respect for you. Frankly, you think he is a bit of a crawler.

Of late you have noticed that Javed's work is slipping and he seems to keep himself to himself more than usual. One day he comes to you with a problem that he would normally deal with himself, and he is obviously distressed when you send him away to solve the problem on his own. On your guard, now, you observe that none of the other team members are co-operating with Javed and one or two rather catty remarks are being made behind his back.

You decide to have a counselling session with Javed. Go for it ...

2   DISCIPLINE

GRIEVANCE   COUNSELLING

DISCIPLINE

What is discipline?
Disciplinary action
Managing disciplinary situations
Disciplinary interviews

2.1   What is discipline?

The word discipline brings to mind the use of authority or force, and to many people it primarily carries the disagreeable meaning of punishment. However, there is another way of thinking about discipline.

Definition

Discipline can be considered as: 'a condition in an enterprise in which there is orderliness in which the members of the enterprise behave sensibly and conduct themselves according to the standards of acceptable behaviour as related to the goals of the organisation'.

'Negative' discipline is the threat of sanctions designed to make employees choose to behave in a desirable way, although this need not be a wholly negative matter. Disciplinary action may be *punitive* (punishing an offence), *deterrent* (warning people not to behave in that way) or *reformative* (calling attention to the nature of the offence so that it will not happen again).

The best discipline is *self-discipline*. Most mature people accept that following instructions and fair rules of conduct are part of any job. They believe in performing their work properly, coming to work on time, following their leader's instructions, and so on. If employees know what is expected of them and feel that the rules are reasonable, self-disciplined behaviour becomes a part of group norms.

Types of disciplinary situations

There are many types of disciplinary situations which require attention by the manager. The most frequently occurring are:

(a) excessive absenteeism (not coming to work, perhaps giving the excuse of ill health);

(b) excessive lateness in arriving at work;

(c) defective and/or inadequate work performance;

(d) poor attitudes which influence the work of others or which reflect on the public image of the firm.

Activity 3 [15 minutes]

Suggest five more reasons for management taking disciplinary action. (You might be able to draw on your own experience at work, school or college.)

In addition, managers might be confronted with disciplinary problems stemming from employee behaviour *off* the job: abuse of alcohol or drugs, or involvement in some form of law-breaking activity. If off-the-job conduct has an impact upon performance *on* the job, the manager must be prepared to deal with it.

In order to protect employees from unfair punishments or penalties, there needs to be a clear framework for discipline at work. The Advisory, Conciliation and Arbitration Service (ACAS), which was designed to promote good industrial relations, has laid down voluntary guidelines for disciplinary action. Let's look at what disciplinary procedures might involve.

2.2 Disciplinary action

Any disciplinary action must be undertaken with sensitivity and sound judgement: its purpose is not punishment, or retribution, but improvement of the future behaviour of the employee and other members of the organisation, or the avoidance of similar occurrences in the future.

ACAS guidelines for disciplinary action suggest that an employee should not be dismissed from his or her job for a first offence, except in the case of gross misconduct (such as serious theft, or violence against another employee). Many enterprises have accepted the idea of *progressive discipline*, which provides for increasing severity of the penalty with each repeated offence: a bit like the yellow card (warning), red card (sent off) system used in football. The following are the suggested steps of progressive disciplinary action.

(a) *The informal talk*

If the offence is of a relatively minor nature and if the employee's record shows no previous discipline problems, an informal, friendly talk may clear up the situation. The manager simply discusses with the employee his or her behaviour in relation to the standards expected by the organisation, and tries to get a recognition that such behaviour is unacceptable, with a commitment that it will not be repeated.

(b) *Oral warning or reprimand*

The manager emphasises the undesirability of repeated violations, and warns the offender that it could lead to more serious penalties.

(c) *Written or official warning*

At this stage, the ACAS Code of Practice comes into effect. A written warning is a formal matter, and becomes a permanent part of the employee's record. (It may also serve as evidence in case of protest against the later dismissal of a repeated offender.)

(d) *Disciplinary lay-offs, or suspension*

Disciplinary lay-offs usually extend over several days or weeks. Some employees may not be very impressed with oral or written warnings, but they are likely to find a disciplinary layoff (without pay) a rude awakening.

(c) *Dismissal*

This should be reserved for the most serious offences. For the organisation it involves waste of a labour resource, the expense of training a replacement, and change in the work team. The threat of dismissal may be a sufficient deterrent, but in the last resort, a disruptive, violent or untrustworthy employee may simply have to be expelled from the workplace.

There is a right to *appeal* against disciplinary action; and a right to be accompanied to *disciplinary meetings* by a colleague or trade union representative.

For discussion

How (a) accessible and (b) clear are the rules and policies of your college: do people really know what they are and are not supposed to do? Have a look at the student regulations. How easy is it to see them – or were you referred elsewhere? Are they well-indexed and cross-referenced, and in language that all students will understand?

How (a) accessible and (b) clear are the disciplinary procedures? Who is responsible for discipline?

In addition to formal procedures, discipline raises a number of interpersonal issues.

2.3   Managing disciplinary situations

The following guidelines may help managers reduce the resentment that will be inevitable, to an extent, in all disciplinary actions.

(a) *Immediacy*

The manager should take disciplinary action as speedily as possible. However, (s)he should allow a brief 'cooling off' period in circumstances where on-the-spot emotion might lead to hasty judgements, and the ACAS Code of Practice requires investigation to be made, where possible, before action is taken.

(b) *Advance warning*

In order to encourage self-discipline, and ensure that disciplinary action is (and is seen to be) fair, it is essential that all employees know in advance what is expected of them and what the rules and regulations are. Policy provisions may be included in employee handbooks, recruitment literature or employment contracts.

(c) *Consistency*

Rules and penalties should apply equally to everyone and on every occasion. Inconsistency in application of discipline only creates uncertainty, and loss of respect. (Consistency does not mean imposing a standard penalty every time for a particular offence: there may be mitigating circumstances which partly excuse the offender's behaviour.)

(d) *Impersonality*

'Punishment' should be connected with the 'crime': based on clear rules and standards, *not* personalities. Once disciplinary action has been taken, the manager should not bear grudges or nurse suspicions. Impersonality is sometimes called the 'hot stove' rule (if you touch the stove, you get burnt – nothing personal ...).

(e) *Privacy*

As a general rule (unless the manager's authority is challenged directly and in public) disciplinary action should be taken in private, to avoid the spread of conflict and the humiliation – or martyrdom – of the employee concerned.

The crucial interpersonal event in disciplinary action will be the interview. The following advice takes into account both procedural guidelines and interpersonal issues.

2.4 Disciplinary interviews

Preparation

Preparation for the disciplinary interview will include the following.

(a) Gathering facts about the alleged infringement.

(b) Determination of the organisation's position: how valuable is the employee, potentially? How serious are his offences/lack of progress? How far is the organisation prepared to go to help him improve or discipline him further?

(c) Identification of the aims of the interview: punishment? deterrent to others? problem-solving? Specific standards for future behaviour/performance need to be determined.

Content of the interview

The content of the interview should be as follows.

(a) The manager should explain the purpose of the interview, and state the charges against the employee, clearly and without personal emotion.

(b) The manager should explain the organisation's position: disappointment, concern, need for improvement, impact on others and so on. This should be done frankly – but tactfully, with as positive an emphasis as possible on the employee's capacity and responsibility to improve.

(c) The organisation's expectations with regard to future behaviour/performance should be made clear.

(d) The employee or his/her trade union representative should be given the opportunity to comment, explain, justify or deny. If he is to approach the following stage of the interview in a positive way, he must not be made to feel hounded or hard done by.

(e) The organisation's expectations should be reiterated, or new standards of behaviour set for the employee. It will help him if:
- (i) they are specific, performance-related and realistic: increased output, improved timekeeping, or whatever;
- (ii) they are related to a practical but reasonably short time period. A date should be set to review progress;
- (iii) the manager agrees on appropriate measures to help the employee: mentoring, or counselling, say.

(f) The manager should explain any penalties imposed, and issue a clear warning of the consequences of failure to meet improvement targets.

(g) The manager must inform the employee of his/her right to appeal.

Activity 4   [20 minutes]

Suppose that you, as the personnel manager, have been asked to introduce a new disciplinary procedure.

(a) What points would you have to consider initially?

(b) With whom would you consult before writing it?

(c) How would you communicate it to the workforce?

---

3   GRIEVANCE

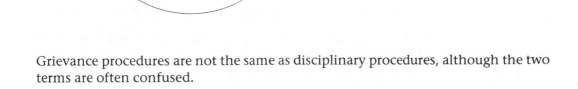

Grievance procedures are not the same as disciplinary procedures, although the two terms are often confused.

Definition

A *grievance* occurs when an individual feels that (s)he is being wrongly treated by a colleague or supervisor: picked on, unfairly appraised or blocked for promotion, or discriminated against on grounds of race or sex.

Some grievances might be resolved informally by the individual's manager. However, there should also be a formal grievance procedure, to which employees at all levels can appeal.

3.1 Grievance policies

Formal grievance policies should be set out in writing and made accessible to all staff. They should accomplish the following.

(a) State the *rights* of the employee for particular types of grievance. For example, if an employee feels that (s)he has been unfairly passed over for promotion, (s)he might be entitled to claim a review of the annual appraisal report, the right to attend a special appeals board – or whatever.

(b) State *time limits* for initiating grievance procedures and the subsequent stages of them. For example, a person who is passed over for promotion should be required to make his or her appeal within a certain time after performance review, and an appeal to higher authority (if any) within a given period after the first grievance interview. There should also be timescales for management to determine and communicate the outcome of the complaint to the employee.

(c) State what the *policies* for pursuing a grievance should be. A typical grievance procedure might be as follows.
   (i) The individual should discuss the grievance with a staff/union representative (or a colleague). If the case seems a good one, (s)he should take the grievance to his or her immediate boss.
   (ii) The first interview will be between the immediate boss (unless (s)he is the subject of the complaint, in which case it will be the next level up) and the employee, who has the right to be accompanied by a colleague or representative as a support and witness.
   (iii) If the immediate boss cannot resolve the matter, or the employee is otherwise dissatisfied with the first interview, the case should be referred higher up.
   (iv) *Written records* of all meetings concerned with the case should be distributed to all the participants.

As with disciplinary action, the main job of conflict resolution will take place in an interview between the manager and the subordinate.

3.2 Grievance interviews

The dynamics of a grievance interview are broadly similar to a disciplinary interview, except that it is the *subordinate* who primarily wants a positive result or improvement in someone else's behaviour.

Prior to the interview, the manager should have some idea of the complaint and its possible source. The meeting itself can then proceed through the following stages.

(a) *Exploration*. What is the problem: the background, the facts, the causes (obvious and hidden)? At this stage the manager should simply try to gather as much information as possible, without attempting to suggest solutions or interpretations: the situation must be seen to be open.

(b) *Consideration*. The manager should:
   (i) check the facts;
   (ii) analyse the causes – the problem of which the complaint may be only a symptom;
   (iii) evaluate options for responding to the complaint, and the implication of any response made.

It may be that information can be given to clear up a misunderstanding, or the employee will withdraw his complaint – having 'got it off his chest'. However, the meeting may have to be adjourned (say, for 48 hours) while the manager gets extra information and considers extra options.

(c) *Reply*. The manager, having reached and reviewed various conclusions, reconvenes the meeting to convey (and justify, if required) his or her decision, hear counter-arguments and appeals. The outcome (agreed or disagreed) should be recorded in writing.

Activity 5 [20 minutes]

Think of a complaint or grievance you have (or have had) at school or college. Have you done anything about it? If so, was it on your own, or through some kind of grievance procedure? If so, what happened: were you satisfied with the process and outcome? If not, why not? How could the procedure have been improved?

Chapter roundup

- Counselling is an interpersonal process by which one person helps another person to help himself or herself. It may be used in a wide range of situations, to do with work and non-work problems and challenges. It may be seen as a part of the empowerment of employees.

- Discipline has the same end as motivation: to secure desired behaviour from members of the organisation. Motivation may even be called a kind of self-discipline – because motivated individuals exercise choice to behave in the way that the organisation wishes. Discipline is more often related to negative motivation, however, an appeal to the individual's need to avoid punishment, sanctions or unpleasantness.

- Grievance procedures embody the employee's right to appeal against unfair or otherwise prejudicial conduct or conditions that affect him and his work.

Quick quiz

1 Give four examples of situations in which counselling might be offered to employees.

2 Should counselling always be completely confidential?

3 List three qualities required by counsellors.

4 Which organisation gives advice on disciplinary matters?

5 What is progressive discipline?

6 What factors should a manager bear in mind in trying to control the disciplinary situation?

7 What should a manager do or consider in preparation for a disciplinary interview?

8 Who may accompany an employee to a disciplinary interview?

9 Outline typical grievance procedures.

10 Name the three stages through which the grievance interview passes.

Answers to quick quiz

1 Disciplinary situations, where there are personal problems and cases of redundancy or harassment.

2 Yes, unless action is required. The employee must be told if confidentiality cannot be kept.

3 They should be observant, sensitive, empathetic and impartial.

4 ACAS

5 Progressive discipline is characterised by increasing severity of penalty with each repeated offence.

6 Immediacy, advance warning, consistency, impersonality, privacy.

7 He or she should gather the facts and consider the organisation's position and the aims of the interview.

8 A fellow worker or trade union representative.

9 Discuss the grievance with a colleague; take the grievance to the immediate boss, and try to resolve it in an interview; refer the matter to a higher authority if it is not yet resolved. Written records of all meetings should be kept.

10 Exploration, consideration, reply.

Answers to Activities

1 Workplace counselling could be needed: during appraisal (for problem solving); in disciplinary situations; following change such as promotion or relocation, redundancy, dismissal or approaching retirement; as a result of personal difficulties such as bereavement, sickness, depression, divorce or similar problems; in cases of sexual harassment or violence at work.

2 There are no right answers to this problem: it depends how each pair decided to play their roles. You should now appreciate how difficult managing people can be.

3 Reasons for disciplinary action might include:

(a) Breaking rules regarding rest periods and other time schedules, such as leaving work to go home early.

(b) Improper personal appearance or dress.

(c) Breaking safety rules, such as failing to observe fire regulations, failing to wear protective clothing and so on.

(d) Other violations of rules, regulations and procedures, such as smoking in a non-smoking office, or abuse of expenses claims.

(e) Open insubordination: refusal to carry out a legitimate order.

(f) Fighting, sexual harassment, racial abuse or other forms of unacceptable conflict.

4 Having introduced a new disciplinary procedure, the following would have to be borne in mind.

(a) You would have to consider employment legislation with regard to warnings and dismissals, limits of authority as to who would be authorised to carry out which steps of the procedure. For example, section leaders may have the authority to issue verbal warnings but all further steps are carried out by managers.

(b) Other managers and trade union officials if a union is recognised within the organisation.

(c) Possibly by a general meeting so that everyone is told at once, but it must also be confirmed in writing to all employees.

5   Assuming you did do something about your grievance, you probably found there were various stages of the procedure. Hopefully the first and second stages were sufficient to solve the problem, but you may have felt that the procedure was too cumbersome or long-winded.

Assignment 9   [About 1¹/₂ hours]

You have been asked to devise a disciplinary procedure. You will have to consider the types of offence and the degree of discipline the offence will incur. Also think about progressive discipline and what action will be taken if the employee repeats the offence or breaches discipline in some other way.

Write a draft procedure.

Part B

MANAGING ACTIVITIES

Chapter 10

PLANNING AND ORGANISING

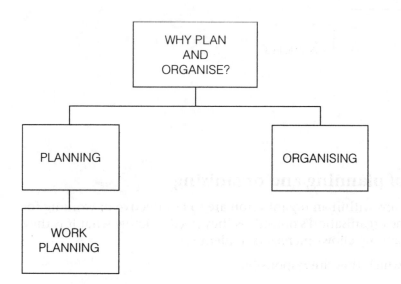

Introduction

As you may remember from our discussion of the functions of management in Chapter 1:

● *Planning* is the process of deciding what the 'ends' of activity should be (objective-setting), and determining the most appropriate 'means' of achieving those ends (plans, policies, procedures and so on).

● *Organising* is the process of establishing a framework within which plans can be carried out: determining structures and systems for co-ordinating the human and other resources required.

In this chapter, we will look briefly at the purpose and context of planning and organising, and propose a very simple framework for planning and organising, which we will be applying in Chapters 11 and 12.

Your objectives

After completing this chapter you should:

(a) appreciate the role of planning and organising in achieving controlled performance;

(b) be able to define efficiency and effectiveness;

(c) be able to outline the cycle of planning and control;

(d) be aware of the different types and levels of planning in an organisation and be able to distinguish the process of 'work planning';

(e) be able to outline a simple framework for work planning;

(f) be aware of the implications of organising for organisational structure, co-ordination and communication, as well as task allocation.

1 WHY PLAN AND ORGANISE?

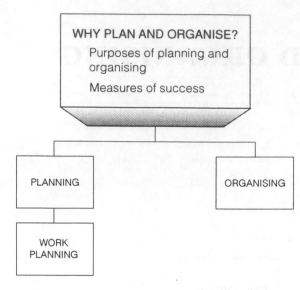

1.1 Purposes of planning and organising

If individuals and groups within an organisation are to be effective in working for the achievement of the organisation's objectives they need to know what it is they are expected to do. Planning allows managers to identify:

(a) the objectives for which they are responsible;

(b) what actions will serve towards achieving those objectives; and

(c) how far they are being successful in achieving those objectives.

Planning and organising are important functions in an organisation for the following reasons.

(a) *Uncertainty.* Organisations cannot deal with things ad hoc, as they occur, without chaos. The future cannot be foreseen with certainty in any case, and even the best-laid plans will go wrong to a greater or lesser degree (which is where 'control' comes in). Nevertheless, plans and structures give some direction and predictability to the work of the organisation: in other words, they are a form of risk management.

(b) *The need for co-ordination.* Organisations are collections of individuals and groups (or sub-systems): each will perceive its own part of the organisation's activity, and work towards its own objectives accordingly. Planning and organising ensures that:
   (i)   sub units of the organisation know what it is they need to achieve, and when;
   (ii) work 'flows' from one process (or department) to another without holdups or clashes, and without idle time or overwork for staff and machinery;
   (iii) the resources required for a task are available where and when they are required;
   (iv) required work is being done by somebody – but not being duplicated by others, with a waste of effort;
   (v)   all of the above are achieved in such a way that products/services of the required quality are available to customers at the right place, at the right price and at the right time.

For discussion

Suggest examples of the planning/organising needed in each of the areas given in (i) to (v) above, and what would happen if planning was not carried out.

(c) *The need for objectives.* Human beings are 'purposive': they like to feel that their actions have a point. If the organisation doesn't set objectives, people will set their own, according to their own interpretation of the situation: chaos ensues. Objectives are also important in learning and motivation, so people can target and adjust their behaviour according to what they want to achieve.

Two key aims of business management, and therefore of planning and organising, are:

- *efficiency and*
- *effectiveness.*

We will be discussing this further in Chapter 15, as we explore how performance can be monitored and measured; but we will explain the terms briefly here, so we know what we are aiming for in planning and organising!

1.2 Measures of success

Efficiency

Efficiency is a term often used loosely to express the idea of 'doing things well'.

Definition

Efficiency is the relationship between inputs used and outputs achieved. The fewer the inputs used to obtain a given output, the greater the efficiency. Efficiency can be expressed as: $\dfrac{\text{output}}{\text{input}}$

If a car does 400 miles on 10 gallons of petrol it does 400 ÷ 10 = 40 miles per gallon. This is a measure of its efficiency at using fuel.

Efficiency is about avoiding *waste* – of effort, time and material resources – in producing desired outputs, or achieving the organisation's goals. Efficient operation might involve:

(a) producing no less, but no more, than the demand for the product;

(b) avoiding spoiled or unacceptable products, according to the organisation's quality standards;

(c) avoiding overmanning (employing more people than the task requires), or improving productivity: output (or profit, say) per employee;

(d) avoiding unnecessary movements, operations and routines (such as paperwork, task duplications, double-checks and so on) which take time, without adding value in the process;

(e) avoiding expense of finance and resources which add no value and earn no return.

Effectiveness

It has been argued that efficiency focuses too much on controlling the 'inputs' to the organisation's activities, and not enough on the 'outputs'. (You can improve efficiency by cutting costs instead of improving sales ...)

Definition

Effectiveness is the measure of how far an organisation (and its managers) achieve their output requirements, as defined by performance objectives and targets.

In other words, *effectiveness* is about 'doing the right things', not just 'doing things right'. Effectiveness-orientated managers are concerned with fulfilling objectives with regard to:

(a) output quantity;

(b) output quality and customer satisfaction;

(c) added value (the value added to inputs, reflected in the sale price of the output);

(d) innovation, or new products/services/improvements implemented.

Activity 1   [10 minutes]

Read through and tick in the relevant columns whether the statements relate to efficiency or effectiveness.

	Efficiency	Effectiveness
(a) A customer is satisfied	☐	☐
(b) The factory produces more cars	☐	☐
(c) Waste has been reduced	☐	☐
(d) Better quality products are produced	☐	☐
(e) Ten employees were given early retirement packages	☐	☐
(f) The company increased its dividend payment to shareholders	☐	☐

Efficiency and effectiveness require:

(a) an idea of what outputs the organisation wants from the production system;

(b) an idea of what inputs will be required; and

(c) a way of monitoring and measuring performance, to ensure that it conforms to the organisation's expectations.

In essence, this is the process of planning and control.

2 PLANNING

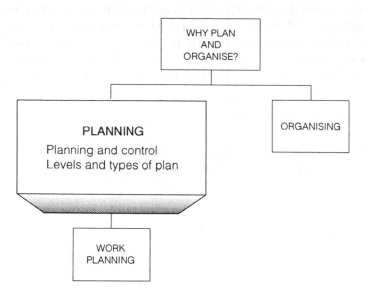

2.1 Planning and control

Planning is the process of deciding what should be done. *Control* is the process of checking whether it *has* been done, and if not, doing something about it. The combined processes of planning and control are known as a *control cycle*, see Figure 10.1.

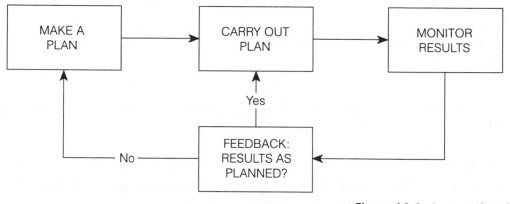

Figure 10.1 A control cycle

In more detail, the control cycle in management has six basic stages.

(a) *Making* a plan: deciding what to do and identifying the desired results. The plan should include:
   (i) *aims*, which dictate;
   (ii) *priorities*, or 'key results' (objectives which must be achieved for the aims to be fulfilled) and 'key tasks' (things that must be done on time and to the required standard if the key results are to be achieved), for which there should be;
   (iii) *performance standards*, the definition of how well key tasks must be performed in order to achieve key results (acceptable quality, cost or amount of output, say); and
   (iv) *specific short-term goals* for key tasks, against which progress can be monitored; so that
   (v) *action plans*, specifying 'what, how, who, when, where and how much' can be formulated.

(b) *Carrying out* the plan, or having it carried out by subordinates.

(c) *Monitoring and measuring* actual results achieved.

(d) *Comparing* feedback on actual results against the plans.

(e) *Evaluating* the comparison, and deciding whether further action is necessary to ensure the plan is achieved. If results are worse than planned (negative feedback), the activity will have to be adjusted to get it back on course. If they are better than planned (positive feedback), it may be desirable to maintain the deviation from the plan, or to adjust the plan itself to take advantage of the situation.

(f) *Implementing corrective action* where necessary.

All *managers plan. Some may do more, or more complex, planning than others, but all do some. Let's look briefly at the levels and types of plan used in organisations.*

2.2   Levels and types of plan

Planning involves decisions about:

- *what* to do in future
- *how* to do it
- *when* to do it and
- *who* should do it (this is also the area covered by 'organising').

Such questions are relevant at all levels of organisational activity:

(a) at a *strategic* level – deciding what business the organisation should be in, and what its overall objectives should be;

(b) at a *tactical* level – deciding how it should go about achieving its overall objectives: what products it should produce, how it will organise work and so on;

(c) at the *operational* level – deciding what needs to be done from day to day and task to task.

There are therefore a number of different types of plan, which can be categorised as follows.

Objectives

Objectives are the end goals, towards which all the organisation's activities will be directed: to earn a profit, say, or provide a certain service.

Strategies

Strategies are long-term plans for the activities and resources which will achieve the organisation's objectives. (A manpower strategy, for example, is a plan for the number and types of staff to be acquired and maintained in the long term.)

Policies

Policies are general statements or 'understandings' which provide guidelines for management decision making. (It might be company policy, for example, to offer five year guarantees on all products, or to promote managers from within the organisation.) Policy guidelines allow managers to exercise their own discretion and freedom of choice, but within certain acceptable limits.

Procedures

Procedures are chronological sequences of actions required to perform a task: they exist at all levels, but become more extensive lower down in an organisation's hierarchy, where the work is more routine. They have three main advantages.

(a) *Efficiency*. Procedures (ideally) prescribe the most efficient way of doing a job.

(b) *Routine*. Procedures remove the need for the exercise of discretion, where fresh decisions are not necessary.

(c) *Standardisation* of work makes output more predictable and more consistent throughout the organisation.

Rules

A rule (or regulation) prescribes a specific, definite action that *must* be taken in a given situation. It allows no discretion – unlike a policy. For example:

(a) 'employees in department X are allowed 10 minutes exactly at the end of their shift for clearing up and cleaning their work-bench';

(b) 'employees with access to a telephone must not use the telephone for personal calls'.

Programmes

Programmes are co-ordinated groups or series of plans which together achieve a particular objective; for instance, a company might undertake a programme of expansion, computerisation or customer care, involving different aspects and stages of planning.

Budgets

A budget is a formal statement of expected results set out in numerical terms, usually summarised in money values. It is a plan for carrying out certain activities with specified resources within a given period of time, in order to achieve certain targets.

Activity 2 [20 minutes]

Dial-a-Video Limited offers home video rental service to subscribers. Subscribers choose a video from a catalogue, phone Dial-a-Video Limited and the video is delivered by a despatch rider. The Chairman, Rajiv Bharat, says to you: 'I hope to expand the business. I've discovered a market for art movie videos. I've had to knock the directors' heads together to develop plans for building a distribution system: they've agreed a number of stages: for a new catalogue, market research and that sort of thing. We'll charge £4 per video per day including delivery. It is a premium price, but people who like that sort of movie will pay for it. We'll tell the despatch riders not to accept tips though.'

What sort of plans has Rajiv Bharat described to you?

Planning horizons

Planning covers the long-term as well as the short-term. A planning period or time *horizon* is the length of time between making and implementing a planning decision. A decision to build new premises may have a time horizon of many years; a programme to develop a new product might take several years; an operating budget might span a one-year period; a production schedule might be produced weekly.

This has two main consequences.

(a) Long-term objectives might conflict with shorter-term plans, and planners should try to reconcile the two. If a company has a short-term problem with limited funds, for example, it might be tempting to cut costs to maintain profitability – but if spending on research or marketing are ignored, the company's long-term profitability might suffer.

In the short-term, a company might consider profitability as the major objective. In the longer-term, considerations such as social responsibility, employee welfare, corporate image, standards of service and reputation might take on added importance.

(b) Plans, once formulated, should not be rigid, because the future is uncertain: plans might need to be changed if unforeseen circumstances arise. A compromise should be found between the need for flexibility (which suggests keeping plans short-term) and the need for commitment to decisions which have been made (which suggests planning over the whole of a long-term period). The best compromise, perhaps, is regular review of plans, and a willingness to adjust them if necessary.

For discussion

How are you at planning? How did you approach exam-revision, for example, or essay-writing? People must have told you how important it is to 'make a proper plan'. If you didn't do so – why not? Do you think managers suffer from the same difficulties?

3 WORK PLANNING

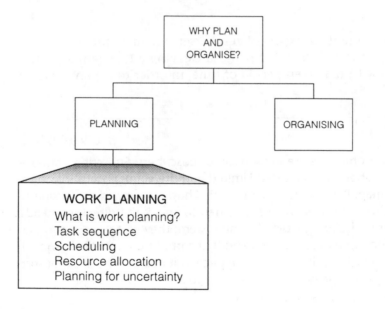

3.1 What is work planning?

Work planning, as the term implies, is the planning of how work should be done: establishing work methods and schedules to ensure that objectives are efficiently met.

There are four basic elements to work planning.

● *Task sequencing or prioritising*: considering tasks in the order in which they must be completed, either
  — because some tasks depend on the completion of other tasks or
  — because some tasks are more important or urgent than other tasks.

● *Task scheduling*: the decision of when tasks should be started and completed.

● *Resource allocation*: the assessment of a task's human, financial and material requirements, and the availability of appropriate resources at the right place and time.

● *Contingency planning*: allowing for changes of plan to cope with unscheduled events.

We will look at each of the stages briefly. They will be used as a simple framework for classifying planning techniques in the following chapters.

3.2 Task sequence

Some jobs are entirely routine, and can simply be performed one step at a time, but for most people, some kind of judgement will be required: a manager, in particular, may have any number of matters calling for his attention at one time, and will have to decide what to do first, what to delegate and so on. Task sequencing basically involves arranging all the tasks which may face an individual (or unit) at the same time in order of 'preference': because of the individual's *responsibility* to the organisation, it will not just be what he would like to get done first, but what will be most valuable to the attainment of immediate or long-term goals.

Priority

A piece of work will be *high priority* in the following circumstances.

(a) *If it has to be completed by a certain time (a deadline)*. The closer the deadline, the more urgent the work will be. A report due the following day will take precedence over an agenda to be circulated in a week's time. Routine work comes lowest on the list, as it can usually be caught up with later if necessary – but if put off too long it may become urgent!

(b) *If other tasks depend on it*. If the preparation of notes for a meeting depends on a particular file, the first task may be to obtain the file: work can't start unless the file is there. Begin at the beginning!

(c) *If other people depend on it*. An item being given low priority by one individual or department – for example, the retrieval or reproduction of a particular document – may hold up the activities of others for whom the processing of the item is high priority.

(d) *If it is important*. There may be a clash of priorities between two urgent tasks, in which case relative consequences should be considered. If an important decision or action rests on a task, that task should take precedence over an urgent, but less important task.

Routine priorities and regular peak times (such as Christmas for retailers, or the beginning of the academic year for BPP) can be planned ahead of time, and other tasks postponed or redistributed around them. Non-routine priorities occur when unexpected demands are made: events crop up, perhaps at short notice, or errors are discovered and require corrective action. Backup plans for likely contingencies should be made (contacts with temporary employment agencies and additional suppliers, for example).

Deadlines

Definition

A *deadline* is the end of the longest span of time which may be allotted to a task: in other words, the last acceptable date for completion.

It is perfectly possible for every activity to have a deadline (at least a pencilled-in one to aid work planning). The deadline for a long-term job – say building a house – will dictate and depend on a series of shorter-term deadlines right back to the laying of foundations and the ordering of bricks. This pyramid of deadlines must be taken into account in scheduling work and allocation of resources, and is the basis of task sequencing.

Activity 3 [10 minutes]

Give three examples of factors that will determine what a task's deadline should be.

Deadlines are important, and we make no apologies for repeating this point. Failure to meet them has a 'knock-on' effect on other parts of the organisation, and on other tasks within an individual's duties. If you are late with one task, you will be late or rushed with the one depending on it. In Chapters 11 and 12 we look at techniques for ensuring that no such slippage occurs.

Once the sequence or order of tasks (or components of a complex activity) has been determined, you can decide when those tasks should be performed: scheduling.

3.3 Scheduling

Definition

Activity scheduling provides a list of activities, in the order in which they must be completed: we have called this task sequencing.

Time scheduling adds to this the timescale or start and end times/dates for each activity.

Time schedules can be determined by different methods.

(a) *Forward scheduling* can be used, starting with a given start time/date and working through estimated times for each stage of the task (allowing for some which may be undertaken simultaneously, by more than one person or machine) to the estimated *completion* time/date. This method can be used, for example, when producing items for stock, or when completing routine tasks.

(b) *Reverse scheduling* is where you start with a *completion* time/date or deadline, and work backwards through estimated times for each stage of the task, determining *start* times for each stage – and for the task as a whole – which will enable you to meet the deadline. This method can be used in 'make to order' production, where a customer specifies a due date when delivery is required. It can also be used to meet deadlines, for example, for a report to be prepared, for office relocation, product launch and many other projects which have a set completion date.

Activity 4 [30 minutes]

You are in charge of organising the annual sales conference of your firm. It will be held in a hotel with a conference room, which will be laid out for your meeting. You will also be the 'secretary' of the meeting, which will involve preparing and circulating the agenda of the meeting to participants, together with briefing information gathered from the sales files, and taking notes for the minutes (written record) of the meeting.

(a) In what order would you sequence your tasks?

(b) What kind of scheduling would you use?

(c) What method would you use to record and to remind yourself of the schedule?

All personnel involved in a task must be given adequate *notice* of work schedules, and the schedules themselves should allow a *realistic* time allocation for each task, if people are to accept the plan without resentment.

3.4 Resource allocation

Resource allocation includes estimates of the task *requirements* with regard to:

(a) 'man hours' (how many people working for how many hours);

(b) machine hours;

(c) raw materials and components (allowing for a certain amount of wastage); and

(d) finance – that is, the cost of all the above.

It also includes estimates of the *availability* of all these resources.

(a) How many people with the required skills or experience are available (inside or outside the organisation)? What is their standard level of productivity, and could it be increased?

(b) What machinery is available, given the demands made on it by the task and by other tasks from other units? What is its standard level of productivity, and could it be increased?

(c) Is there sufficient stock of raw materials or components? If not, can they be bought in or made, and at what cost? Are they of the required specifications and quality? What is the expected usage rate of stock: when will stocks run out and need to be replenished? What is the standard wastage rate in the course of operations, and can this be reduced?

(d) How much money needs to be budgeted or allowed for, to complete the task? Is such an amount available and worth spending, for the expected results?

Activity 5   **[20 minutes]**

Continuing our example of a person organising a sales conference, what kind of resources might (s)he have to plan for?

We have talked about 'estimated' times and resource requirements. Uncertainty is a fact of organisational life. This is where contingency planning comes in.

3.5 Planning for uncertainty

Plans do not give managers control over the future.

(a) The future cannot be forecast with any certainty. You can only anticipate what is *likely* to happen in future, based on what has happened in the past, and any trends or tendencies that you can see in the pattern of past events.

(b) Unexpected, uncontrollable events happen. Computers break down, terrorists blow up buildings, suppliers go bust, transport strikes shut down operations for a day and so on.

Contingencies are unexpected and uncontrollable events which do not feature in the main plan of the organisation. However, some such events can be anticipated: managers do not *expect* them to happen, but acknowledge that they *might* happen, and consider what should be done *if* they do. Contingency plans are those which are prepared in advance to deal with a situation that *may* (or may not) arise.

All plans should be contingency plans to an extent, since planners must make room for:

(a) *margins of error*; time and resource estimates are only estimates;

(b) *changes in the circumstances*;

(c) *slippage* in the schedule which needs to be caught up elsewhere.

Activity 6 [20 minutes]

What kind of contingency plans might you want to make if you were in charge of:

(a) transferring all your transactions onto a new computer system?

(b) accomplishing a project which required all the 'people hours' you have at your disposal?

(c) organising (yet another) sales conference at an external venue?

Remember that planning is part of the control system: plans may constantly have to be adjusted in order to correct or improve performance.

4 ORGANISING

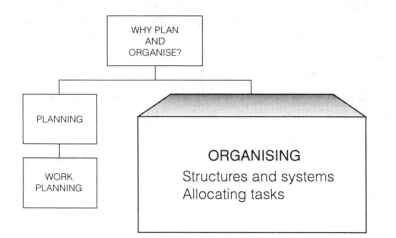

4.1 Structures and systems

As we discussed in Chapter 1, organising – or organisation – implies the establishment of structures, social arrangements, or systems, for the purposes of:

(a) distributing *authority and responsibility* in such a way as to ensure that each task of the organisation is facilitated and controlled: that someone is both authorised to perform it and accountable for performing it;

(b) *communication* of the information needed for the task and for control feedback;

(c) *co-ordination* of resources – including people's time and effort – towards unified objectives, via a hierarchy of objectives and targets for each sub-unit of the organisation; and

(d) the *grouping and allocation* of tasks in logical ways.

The grouping of organisational activities (into teams, departments or larger divisions) can be done in different ways. The most common are as follows.

(a) *By function*, or specialism. Primary functions in a manufacturing company, for example, might be production, sales, finance, and general administration.

(b) *By territory* or geographical area. This method of organisation occurs when similar activities are carried out in different locations. Water and electricity services, for example, operate region by region. Many sales departments are organised territorially, with regional sales areas.

The main advantage of territorial departmentation is better local decision-making at the point of contact between the organisation (eg a salesman) and its customers.

(c) *By product.* Some organisations group activities on the basis of products or product lines. Functional division of responsibility remains, but under the control of a manager with responsibility for a product, product line or brand, with authority over the personnel of different functions involved in its production, marketing and so on.

The main advantages of product departmentation are the development of specialised product knowledge, and the co-ordination of functional activities.

(d) *Matrix organisation.* As we discussed in Chapter 1, the new emphasis on flexibility has created a trend towards task-centred structures, such as multi-disciplinary project teams, which draw people together from different functions. Authority is divided between the members' departmental managers, and the team's product/project manager or co-ordinator.

Having recapped the broader implications of organising for organisation and job design, we will now look briefly at the day-to-day aspects: to whom should a manager allocate or delegate a given task?

4.2 Allocating tasks

Some decisions about division of labour will be pre-programmed by:

(a) *organisational positions and job descriptions,* which dictate who does what (although these are becoming less rigid, in favour of flexibility and empowerment); and

(b) *specialisms.* There may be an obvious expert to whom specialised tasks should be given: a payroll, legal or information technology expert, say.

However, other decisions will require management discretion.

(a) Peak periods in some tasks may necessitate redistribution of staff to cope with the workload: there should be flexibility in who does, and is able to do, non-specialist tasks.

(b) Status and staff attitudes must be considered. Flexibility in reassigning people from one job to another or varying the work they do may be hampered by an employee's perception of his own status: helping out or covering for others may be out of the question: 'I'm a secretary, not a copy typist!' etc. Task allocation must take into account people's experience and seniority – and also the fact that junior employees may want greater challenge and responsibility.

(c) Individual abilities and temperaments differ, and work should be allocated to the best person for the job. Some staff like routine work but crack under pressure, and vice versa; some are good with computers, some with people. Planning should allow for flexibility in the event of an employee proving unfit for a task – or more able than his present tasks indicate.

Chapter roundup

- Planning is the process of deciding what should be done, by whom, when and how. It is essential for co-ordination and control and for the management of risk and uncertainty.

- Planning precedes all other management functions and is carried out at all levels of the organisation. There is a hierarchy of planning from strategic to operational plans.

- Plans are the basis of the control systems of an organisation, through which performance is monitored, measured against the plan and adjusted where necessary.

- Work planning involves:
  - task sequencing or prioritising;
  - time scheduling;
  - resource allocation; and
  - allowance for adjustments and contingencies.

- Organisation is the process of establishing a framework within which plans can be carried out. It is concerned with the division and co-ordination of labour through:
  - organisation structure and
  - the allocation and delegation of tasks.

Quick quiz

1 How does planning contribute to the flow of work?

2 Define efficiency and effectiveness.

3 What are the components of a plan?

4 What are (a) policies, (b) procedures and (c) rules?

5 Why might a task be 'high priority'?

6 What is (a) a deadline and (b) a contingency plan?

7 Distinguish between forward scheduling and reverse scheduling.

8 Give three examples of resources that need to be planned and allocated.

9 Outline three different ways of organising work into departments.

10 Suggest three reasons why a manager might allocate a particular task to a particular individual.

Answers to quick quiz

1 Planning tries to avoid holdups or clashes and idle time or overwork for people or machines.

2 Refer to the definitions in section 1.2.

3 Aims, priorities, performance standards, short-term goals and action plans.

4 Refer to section 2.2.

5 If a deadline is set, if other tasks or people are dependent on it or if it is important.

6 (a) The last acceptable date for completion of a task.

   (b) Planning in advance to deal with a situation which may (or may not) arise.

7 Forward scheduling means starting with a given *start* time/date. Reverse scheduling means working backwards from a given *completion* time/date.

8 People's time, machine time, materials, money.

9 By function, territory, product or matrix organisation.

10 Work might be allocated on the basis of the individual's specialism, abilities, experience or workload.

Answers to Activities

1 The statements fit the following categories.

Efficiency = b, c, e.

Effectiveness = a, d, f.

Statement (e) is an example of increased efficiency because fewer employees (inputs) are needed. Other interpretations are possible however.

2 The plans Dial-a-Video Limited propose are a strategy to exploit the 'art movie' market segment. A programme for the build-up of the distribution. The £4 charge is a tactic or policy. The 'no-tips' plan is a rule or regulation.

3 Factors involved in deciding a deadline include the following.

(a) Customers' requirements, or promises made to them.

(b) Specific events, such as a conference, before which all preparatory tasks must be completed.

(c) Other tasks, which depend on the task's completion by a time which will preserve the smooth flow of work.

4 Sequencing and scheduling a sales conference would involve:

(a)
Book conference centre/hotel	(perhaps months before)
Specify layout of conference room	(two weeks before)
Retrieve relevant files	(two weeks before)
Prepare agenda/info	(one week before)
Circulate agenda/info	(five days before)
Check layout of conference room	(two days before)
Take minutes of meeting	(day of meeting)

(b) Reverse scheduling – work back from the date of the conference.

(c) You might have suggested a diary, or a timetable, or some kind of chart, a checklist – and so on. (We will be looking at a range of such techniques in the following chapters.)

5 Resources for the sales conference will include the conference centre; equipment (overhead projectors etc); staffing of the conference centre; time of speakers; materials such as paper and slides; telephone and fax facilities; refreshments – and so on.

6 Contingency plans for the situations given would include the following.

(a) New systems may have 'bugs', or be unfamiliar to operators. A good contingency plan would be running the old system in parallel with the new one for a trial period.

(b) People get sick, or need holidays, or have problems getting to work during transport strikes, or go on strike themselves. You may have contingency plans to do with pre-notifying holidays, or laid-on transport in the event of transport strikes. A general contingency plan would be a temporary staff agency on standby to provide replacement/overflow staff.

(c) Again, transport may cause unexpected problems, or there could be an upset such as the venue being double-booked, the key speaker falling ill, or overhead projectors not working. Alternative transport/speaker/venue might be preplanned, and back-up visual aids equipment (such as a flip-chart) on hand. You can't anticipate everything ...

Assignment 10 [About 1¹/₂ hours]

You and your fellow students have to carry out a group assignment involving desk research, field research (interviews in the street), oral presentations using visual aids and a full written report on your findings.

(a) Why does the group need to make plans for this assignment?

(b) What elements will the group have to consider when planning?

(c) What would be the most effective way of allocating the tasks?

(d) Which time scheduling method would you employ and why?

Chapter 11

MANAGING TIME

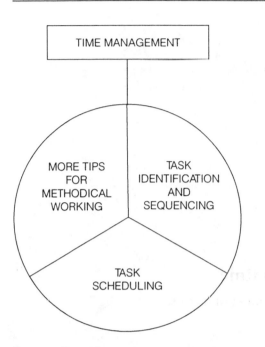

Introduction

Time is a resource, like money and raw materials. You have a finite and fixed amount of it, and various demands in your lifestyle and activities compete for a share of it. It means little in itself, but you can use it - efficiently or otherwise - to accomplish your purposes. Time is an input to every system, with an infinite variety of outputs. If you work in an organisation, your 'time is money': you will be paid for it, or for what you accomplish during it.

Time, like any other resource, needs to be managed, if it is to be used efficiently (without waste) and effectively (productively).

In this chapter, we take a practical look at how planning and organising contribute to efficient time management. We are mainly concerned with issues and techniques you may come across every day in your study or work or the conduct of your personal affairs: coping with a workload or a number of various tasks. (In Chapter 12, we will look at more complex tasks, or projects, involving the co-ordination of other people's time as well as your own.)

Your objectives

After completing this chapter you should:

(a) be aware of the demands on your time and be able to apply the principles of efficient time management and methodical working;

(b) be able to formulate personal goals and plans, and work out priorities;

(c) be able to use lists, action plans, timetables and charts, as appropriate for your activities;

(d) be able to implement follow-up systems to ensure that you have used your time effectively.

1 TIME MANAGEMENT

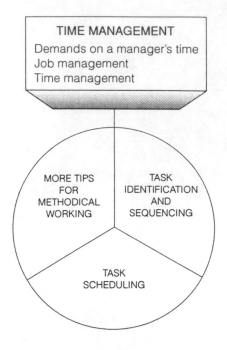

1.1 Demands on a manager's time

A manager's use of time is affected by a number of factors.

The nature of the job

A manager's job involves regular contact with other people in the organisation: it is important to control the inevitable interruptions which this causes. Other typical causes of wasted time include prolonged or unnecessary meetings, and the preparation of unnecessary paperwork (which could be replaced with a brief oral communication).

The personality of the manager

A confident and assertive manager may be better able to resist interruptions and unnecessarily lengthy contacts than one who is diffident, and finds it difficult to 'say no'. A manager may fail to delegate, and end up with a lot of routine work on his own plate. On the other hand, he may simply be disorganised or lacking in self discipline and so be comparatively idle one minute and hectically busy the next.

The influence and demands of colleagues

There will be extra demands on the manager's time if:

(a) subordinates keep referring to the manager for decisions;

(b) subordinates require either close supervision or a consultative style of management;

(c) the culture of the organisation or department requires lots of communication, informal relationship-building, Management by Walking Around, an 'Open Door' availability policy and so on: this takes time.

Activity 1 [10 minutes]

Suggest two ways in which the management style of a superior may make extra demands on a manager's time.

There are two elements to a manager making effective use of time.

(a) Job management – making sure that he or she is knowledgeable about and equipped for his or her job, and that the job, policies and procedures, communication channels and so on are conducive to efficient working.

(b) Time management – allocating time to tasks in the most effective manner.

1.2 Job management

The manager should not waste time wondering what to do next, doing tasks that will not achieve objectives, or doing tasks that might better be done by someone else. He ought to be thoroughly knowledgeable about the policies, systems and procedures of the organisation, and about the structure of authority and responsibility ('proper channels') as well as about his own area of authority or expertise.

Delegation skills will be an important element in job management. Effective use of opportunities for delegation will ensure that the manager is not having unnecessary demands made on him by work inappropriately delegated upwards by subordinates, or downwards by more senior managers.

Communication skills will also be important. Skills in interpersonal relations can be used to get to the purpose of conversations, interviews and meetings with less time wasted. Learning to read faster, write more concise reports and sort out essential from non-essential information will also help efficient management of time.

1.3 Time management

Time management will involve the following.

(a) *Identifying objectives* and the key tasks which are most relevant to achieving them – sorting out what the manager *must* do, from what he *could* do, and from what he would *like* to do.

(b) *Prioritising*: assessing tasks for relative importance, amount of time required, and any deadlines or time-spans.

(c) *Scheduling* – assigning start and end times/dates to tasks (in other words, timetabling).

(d) *Control*: avoiding, where possible, disruption by the unexpected.

Activity 2 [10 minutes]

Think about how effectively you manage time by answering these questions.

1   Do you often miss deadlines for activities you are responsible for?

2   Are you often late for meetings or appointments?

3   Do you have to work late regularly to get things done?

4   Do you feel you are constantly trying to beat the clock?

5   Are you too busy to find time to plan?

6   Do you seem to have more work to do than others?

7   Have you got a good balance between time spent on study or work, with family, on yourself?

We will now look in more detail at some practical techniques for time management. Regard what follows as a 'toolbox': take out of it whatever suits you and the particular task you have in hand. But be warned: if you actually do all these things, it may change your life ...

2 TASK IDENTIFICATION AND SEQUENCING

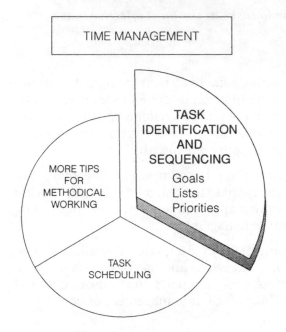

2.1 Goals

If you have no idea what it is you are supposed to accomplish, or only a vague idea, all the time in the world will not be long enough to get it done. You need to set goals for yourself, and to be useful, those goals need to be:

(a) *specific*; and

(b) *measurable*.

So, for example, a daily goal might be: 'to complete all correspondence by 12.00' or 'to interview six people'. A performance goal might be: 'to see that invoices are issued and despatched for all goods sold, on the day of sale'.

On the basis of such goals, you can start making plans.

2.2 Lists

Lists are useful ways of identifying and remembering what needs to be done, and of monitoring how far you've got! You should work from a list of 'Things to do' all the time. If you don't do this already, try it once: you will be hooked, and your daily productivity will shoot up.

(a) Make a list every day before you start work. It is probably best to do this the night before – away from the pressures of work – so long as you don't forget to take your list to work with you the next day!

(b) On the day itself, refuse to do anything that is not on your list. This does not mean that if something more urgent than anything you are currently doing comes up you can ignore it. It means that every new task that arises has to be added to your list.

(c) Every time you finish something on your list, cross it off. This is the really satisfying part of making lists!

(d) At the end of the day take all the items that are still on the list and transfer them to your list for the next day. Don't skip this part and just staple today's unfinished list to tomorrow's unstarted one. The physical act of writing tasks down on paper is an important part of the process.

Do not rely on your memory, even if you think your memory is a fantastically good one. It is highly unlikely to be infallible, and in any case you are not just creating a memory-jogger: the idea is that you should be able to see at a glance *all* the things you have to do so that you can get them into perspective. The items do not need to be in any particular order at this stage: the important thing is that you list down everything that you have to do.

Checklists

A checklist, or 'tick chart', is simply a list which allows for ticking or 'checking' off each task as it is completed (instead of crossing out). Again, it may or may not reflect the order in which you actually perform the tasks. You may simply have a column to put ticks against each task, or you may want to have a space for times/dates on which you started or finished the activity, or even for stages of the activity (for example, where a particular document is at a given date) – or elements of all of these.

As an example, here is a checklist for an advertising manager preparing deadlines for a number of press advertisements.

Ad	Due date	Writer	Designer	Photographer	Film	Print	Proofed	Sent?
Times	3/9	21/8	22/8	24/8	30/8	-	2/9	✓
Standard	3/9	22/8	23/8	26/8	30/8	-	2/9	✓
A5 classified	7/9	29/8	30/8	-	-	-	4/9	✓
Leaflet A	12/9	10/8	12/8	15/8	-	2/9		
Leaflet B	13/9	2/9	3/9		-			

Activity 3 [30 minutes]

Suppose you are the advertising manager's assistant. She has fallen ill on the 5th September, and has asked you to take over the ad and leaflet production. 'I've left you my work checklist,' she says. 'You can work from that.' You find on her desk the checklist given as our example above.

(a) What can you tell from the checklist?

(b) What does this suggest about the usefulness of checklists?

(c) What tasks that you (as a real person, now) have to perform might benefit from the same approach?

2.3 Priorities

Once you have a list or checklist of tasks, you can decide what order to tackle them in.

Task importance

Remember, a job will be *important* (or high priority) if:

(a) it has to be completed by a deadline in order to fulfil its objective (particularly if the deadline is close, so the task is also *urgent*);

(b) other important tasks depend on its completion; or

(c) the potential consequences of *not* doing the task on time are long-term, difficult to reverse, far-reaching and/or costly.

Use your own personal scale to grade activities on your list. For example:

1 – 3   Unimportant
4 – 6   Moderately important
7 – 10 Very important

Another approach that often works well is to imagine that you only have time to do *one* thing on your list: which would it be? That is your first priority. And if you have enough time for one *more* thing? And another? When you have identified your top three or four priorities, tackle them, in order.

Take care to do some important, fairly important *and* routine tasks every day: unimportant, routine tasks (like filing) may become hindrances to doing more important tasks, if they are neglected ...

Task urgency

Note that tasks need not be important just because they are *urgent*. It is possible to be tyrannised by urgent tasks as their deadlines approach, when in fact they could be delegated, or the deadline could simply be moved back because the task is not otherwise a high priority.

However, if an important task is also urgent, do not put it off, *especially* if it is large and unpleasant. Today's routine may become tomorrow's emergency – and, worse, today's emergency may become tomorrow's disaster!

In fact, you should try to treat *all* important tasks *as if* they were urgent. Procrastination, taking your time (or just plain dithering) is a natural tendency – fewer than 2% of people are reckoned to have a true sense of urgency – but time really does slip away if you don't grab hold of it.

For discussion

'Work expands to fill the time available.' Do you ever feel this: that the more time you have, the less you get done? Why might a manager want to take this phenomenon into account?

Task sequence

Some plans, as we have seen, are already set up as *procedures*, or sequences of tasks, in the order in which they must be performed. In other cases, you may have to put your list of things to do in order, if there is a logical sequence to them. A checklist for an employee in charge of receiving supplies into the stores department, for example, might be as follows.

GOODS INWARDS
1 Receive goods
2 Check goods against order
3 Sign goods received note
4 Inspect goods
5 Retrieve stock record card
6 Record stock details
7 Re-file record card
8 Prepare storage labels
9 Affix labels
10 Place goods in store

If you haven't done the particular task before, it may not be immediately obvious what the sequence of actions is. A fairly simple approach to working it out is to 'map' it, using what is called a *precedence network*. We will be discussing network analysis in detail in Chapter 12, as it is particularly useful for planning complex projects. A simple precedence network, however, shows which activities need to be completed before others, Figure 11.1. The squares or 'nodes' denote activities, and the arrows show logical progression and precedence.

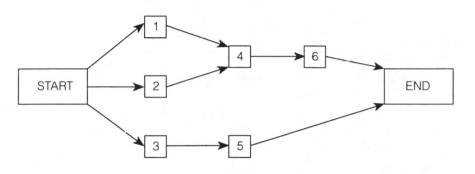

Figure 11.1 Precedence network

Consider Figure 11.1 above as a plan for going away on holiday, say.

Activity 1	=	Reserving your holiday place by phone
Activity 2	=	Booking travel insurance
Activity 3	=	Renewing your passport
Activity 4	=	Sending in a completed booking form. (This *follows* a reservation and requires details of insurance cover.)
Activity 5	=	Obtaining a travel visa. (This can't be done until you have a valid passport.)
Activity 6	=	Collection of tickets (for which you need to have made a written booking).

And you're off! The advantage of such a method is that (unlike a checklist) it allows you to show where a number of activities need to be done at roughly the same time (like activities 1, 2 and 3 above).

Activity 4 [30 minutes]

Choose any task you have to complete in the coming week.

(a) Brainstorm a list of the activities it will require, in no particular order.

(b) Put your list into the order in which you will (roughly) have to do the activities.

(c) Convert your checklist into a precedence network. (You could draw one large enough to write the activity into each node box, instead of numbering and listing the activities.)

Now you have planned and prioritised your activities, the next step is to plan and allocate your time.

3   TASK SCHEDULING

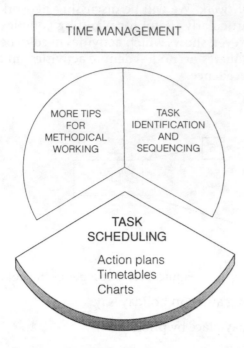

You may remember from Chapter 10 that scheduling can be done in two ways.

(a) *Reverse scheduling* – working backwards from a deadline or target completion date. If you know what your end time/date is, and can estimate how long each task will take, you can *subtract* each task time from the due time/date, to get target start times for each task, and for the activity as a whole.

(b) *Forward scheduling* – working forwards from a start date, and *adding* the estimated time of each task to get a total activity duration, and therefore an estimated completion time/date.

Whichever method is used, bear in mind that task times will only be estimates. You may wish to build in some extra 'slack' time, so that:

(a) you are less likely to fall behind; and

(b) if you *do* fall behind on one task, you will have some catch-up time built into the estimate for the following task, so that it can be completed on time.

There are various ways of setting out schedules. Here are some popular ones.

3.1   Action plans

Action plans set out a programme of work or action, including time scheduling. Our example of a checklist for an advertising manager was a kind of action plan.

The following is another example, for the writing of a report.

Activity	Days before due date	Target date	Date begun	Date completed
1 Request files	6	3/9		
2 Draft report	5	4/9		
3 Type report	3	6/9		
4 Approve report	1	8/9		
5 Signature	1	8/9		
6 Courier	0	9/9		

3.2 Timetables

The same information could be formatted as a timetable or diary entry. You may already be using such methods to timetable your studies – and/or your social life! Timetables and diaries are designed to:

(a) remind you of key times and dates;

(b) remind you to make necessary advance preparations; and

(c) help you allocate your time effectively – no 25-hour days or clashing appointments.

Activity 5 [15 minutes]

Here is a timetable/diary page for the week of the 3rd to 9th September. Enter the schedule given in Section 3.1 as an action plan, as you would do a class timetable or appointments diary. Consider how you would highlight the due date.

SATURDAY 3	WEDNESDAY 7
SUNDAY 4	THURSDAY 8
MONDAY 5	FRIDAY 9
TUESDAY 6	Week commencing 3 SEPTEMBER S S M T W T F 3 4 5 6 7 8 9

3.3 Charts

Longer-term schedules may be more conveniently read using charts, peg-boards or year-planners. These can be used to show:

(a) the length of time to be taken for scheduled events or activities;

(b) the relationship between events or tasks – for example, whether they take place at the same time or in sequence. This can be particularly useful for identifying where excessive or clashing demands are being made: you have scheduled two tasks at once, or scheduled a task over a period when you planned a holiday, say;

(c) the relationship between planned and actual task duration or output.

Bar charts

Figure 11.2 is a simple example, which you may have seen used, of a year planner: in this case, a general plan for a fashion retail outlet.

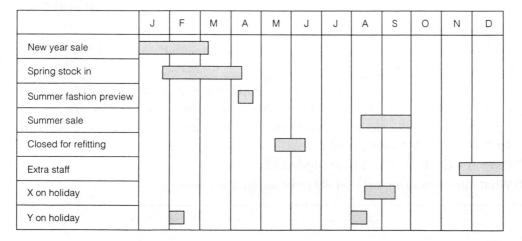

Figure 11.2 A bar chart year planner

Gantt charts

Another widely-used form of chart, which is used to show *progress* as well as schedule, is the Gantt chart, developed by H L Gantt for progressing the building of US Navy ships during the First World War.

A Gantt chart is like the horizontal bar chart used above, but each division of space represents both an amount of *time* and an amount of *work* to be done in that time. Lines or bars drawn across the space indicate how much work is scheduled to be done and/or how much work has actually been done: the more work, the longer the line or bar.

The advantage of such a chart is that you can see the relationship between time spent and amount done or produced. You can compare amounts produced in one week or month, say, with those in another (by the relative lengths of the bar or line). You can, similarly, compare amounts scheduled to be done with those actually done.

The information below, about planned work and actual progress, is set out in a Gantt chart; to show you what it looks like, see Figure 11.3.

Day	Daily schedule (units)	Cumulative schedule (units)	Work done in the day (units)	Cumulative work done (units)
Mon	100	100	75	75
Tues	125	225	100	175
Wed	150	375	150	325
Thu	150	525	180	505
Fri	150	675	75	580

Daily schedule and work actually done

Monday	Tuesday	Wednesday	Thursday	Friday
- - - ➤100	- - - - ➤125	- - - - - ➤150	- - - - - ➤150	- - - - - ➤150
➤ 75	➤ 100	➤150	➤ 180	➤ 75

- - - - ➤ Scheduled work

——➤ Work done

Figure 11.3 A Gantt chart

Activity 6 [30 minutes]

Look at the Gantt chart in Figure 11.3.

(a) What information is clearly shown by the chart? (Is it more obvious how production is doing on the chart than on the tabulated data from which it was drawn?)

(b) What further Gantt chart might be helpful for the manager of this work, which can be drawn from the data given?

(c) Draw the Gantt chart you have suggested.

(d) What information is most usefully provided by this new chart?

4 MORE TIPS FOR METHODICAL WORKING

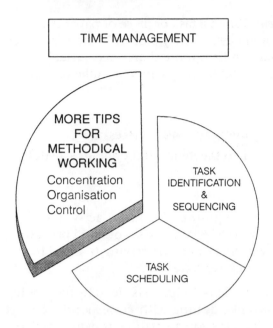

4.1 Concentration

Concentration involves:

● not trying to do two things at the same time;

● avoiding interruptions and distractions;

● attempting to finish tasks once you have started them.

The following tips may be useful.

(a) Make sure that everything that you need is available *before* you start work. If not, one of the things on your *list* will be to order the supplies, obtain the information or do whatever it is that is holding you up.

(b) Before you start a task clear away everything from your desk that you do *not* need for that particular task. Put irrelevant things where you will be able to retrieve them easily when you come to deal with the tasks that you *do* need them for. If they are not needed by *anyone*, throw them away.

(c) The *half open door*. Do not be available to all comers at all times. Ways of avoiding interruptions include the following.
   (i) Being *unavailable*. Use call-diverting facilities on your telephone (and/or ask your secretary, if you have one), or try working somewhere other than your usual desk or office.
   (ii) Setting up *surgery hours* during which – and *only* during which – your door is open to visitors.
   (iii) Operate *management by exception*. Tell your staff to report to you only when there is a problem or deviation from plan, or important new information.

(d) *Appointments with yourself*. If you need to spend time alone, making plans, reviewing progress – or indeed making sure that you get personal time for rest and relaxation – it is a good idea to treat this as if it were a meeting. Make a time for it in your diary, and stick to it: take it seriously, and do not let other activities encroach on it.

4.2 Organisation

Apart from working to plans, checklists or schedules, your work organisation might be improved by the following.

(a) *An ABCD method of in-tray management.* When a task or piece of paper comes in to your in-tray or 'to do' list, you should never merely look at it and put it back for later. This would mean you would handle it more than once – usually over and over again, if it is a trivial or unpleasant item! Resolve to take one of the following approaches.

> **A**ct on the item immediately
>
> **B**in it, if you are sure it is worthless, irrelevant and unnecessary
>
> **C**reate a definite plan for coming back to the item: get it on your schedule or timetable
>
> **D**elegate it to someone else

(b) *Organise your work in batches* of jobs requiring the same activities, files, equipment and so on. Group your filing tasks, copying tasks or word processing tasks, for example, and do them in a session, rather than having to travel to and fro or compete for equipment time for each separate task.

(c) *Take advantage of your natural work patterns.* Self-discipline is aided by developing regular hours or days for certain tasks, like dealing with correspondence first thing or filing at the end of the day. If you are able to plan your own schedules, you might also take into account your personal patterns of energy, concentration, alertness etc. Large or complex tasks might be undertaken in the mornings before you get tired, or perhaps late at night with fewer distractions, while Friday afternoon is not usually a good time to start a demanding task in the office ...

4.3 Control

Control over work must be maintained to ensure that jobs do in fact reach completion, and if those jobs involve various tasks over varying periods, planning will be necessary to keep track of future events, deadlines, results and so on.

Systems which provide for this are called *bring forward* or *bring up* systems. Anything which needs action at a later date (and therefore may get forgotten) should be processed in this way, for example:

(a) checking on progress of an operation;

(b) checking completion when the deadline is reached;

(c) checking payments when they fall due;

(d) retrieving files relevant to future discussions, meetings, correspondence.

Checklists are useful, as we suggested earlier, for monitoring what has been done and what hasn't. Diary systems may also be used. A reminder may be put in the diary or timetable for the relevant day, to check 'task x completed?', 'payment received?', 'response received to letter ref: IO/cw2?', 'one week left for revision' and so on. If you use card index or concertina files, you could slip a card or note into the sequence or appropriate date section, for checking on the day.

For discussion

Examine any timetables, charts or work programmes that relate to your course. How effective are they in communicating information? How useful are they as a plan you can actually work to? What controls or checks do they include, and what other forms of progress monitoring are applied to your work, if any? (You may be able, now, to suggest ways in which your work programme could be improved ...)

Chapter roundup

- Effective time management requires:
  - goals
  - plans
  - priorities
  - schedules
  - concentration
- Tools of time management include:
  - lists and checklists
  - precedence networks
  - action plans
  - timetables
  - charts; and
  - ABCD in-tray management

Quick quiz

1 Distinguish between job management and time management.

2 How can delegation skills improve a manager's use of time?

3 What is a checklist and why might it be useful?

4 When will a task be (a) 'high priority' and (b) 'urgent'?

5 What does a 'precedence network' show? Draw a simple network to illustrate.

6 What kind of help does a diary offer a time manager?

7 What does a Gantt chart show?

8 What does 'concentrated' working involve? Suggest a way of achieving it.

9 What is the 'ABCD' method of in-tray management?

10 What is a 'bring forward' system? Give two examples.

Answers to quick quiz

1 Refer to the Signpost in section 1.1.

2 The manager does not waste time doing jobs which would be more effectively completed if delegated.

3 A checklist lists all the tasks that need to be done. It helps with both planning and control, because it can be ticked off as tasks are completed.

4 (a) When it has to meet a deadline to achieve objective, when other tasks depend on its completion, or when there will be serious problems if it is not completed.

(b) When it is important and the deadline is very close.

5 It depicts the order in which tasks should be completed. See Figure 11.1 for a diagram.

6 It records appointments, deadlines and reminders and can be used for planning and to monitor progress.

7 It shows an amount of time, the amount of work to be done in that time, and the amount actually done.

8 Concentration involves not trying to do more than one thing at a time, avoiding distractions and finishing what you have started. Two ways of achieving this are:

(a) ensuring everything is available for the job;

(b) using the 'half open door' approach.

9 A – act on it; B – bin it; C – create a plan; D – delegate it.

10 A reminder system. Checklists, diary systems.

Answers to Activities

1 A superior may interfere too much in the manager's job and want constant reports: very disruptive. (Tact in warding off such attention can be a valuable attribute.) On the other hand, if the superior delegates too much, the manager's workload may be excessive.

2 If you answered yes to any of 1-6, and no to question 7, then you need to improve your time management. If you answered more than five of them this way, then time management must be a priority, particularly whilst you are trying to find time for your HND/HNC studies.

3 (a) Studying the manager's checklist shows that you don't need to worry about the ads: they are finished and sent off. Leaflet A is at the printers, and has been for 3 days: it still needs to be proofed and sent off before the 12th – a week to go. Leaflet B seems to be at the designers – with just over a week to go: it is clearly falling behind and will need watching: in particular, the photography seems to be held up and will have to be dealt with first.

  (b) Checklists are particularly helpful in the event that you have to hand a task over to someone else for completion.

  (c) You might have suggested shopping lists or things to do in general – or points to be covered in an essay (a very useful planning habit to get into!).

4 The example we have chosen is giving a dinner party.

  (a) Brainstorming suggests the following: menu, date, time, people to invite, cooking, table decorations, contacting people, shopping, wines, setting table, shopping list.

  (b) We now rearrange these ideas into activity order: people to invite, date, time, contact people, menu, wines, shopping list, shopping, table decorations, setting table, cooking.

  (c) This information then converts to the precedence diagram at Figure 11.4.

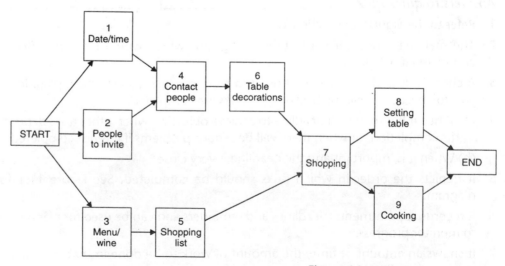

Figure 11.4 Precedence diagram

5 The action plan for dealing with the tasks identified in activity 3 is as shown in Figure 11.5.

SATURDAY 3	WEDNESDAY 7
Request files	
SUNDAY 4	THURSDAY 8
Draft report	Approve report. Signature to report
MONDAY 5	FRIDAY 9
	Courier
TUESDAY 6	Week commencing 3 SEPTEMBER
Type report	S S M T W T F 3 4 5 6 7 8 9

Figure 11.5 Action plan

6 (a) The Gantt chart shows clearly that production is slightly behind schedule on Monday and Tuesday, spot on on Wednesday, better than planned on Thursday, but well short on Friday.

(b) It would be helpful to see how the cumulative production measured against the cumulative schedule, since daily comparisons are up and down.

(c)

Monday	Tuesday	Wednesday	Thursday	Friday
- - - ➤100	- - - - ➤225	- - - - - ➤375	- - - - - ➤525	- - - - - ➤675
➤ 75	➤ 175	➤ 325	➤ 505	➤ 580

(d) It is easy to see that the final weekly total output is well down on schedule.

Assignment 11 [About 1¹/₂ hours]

Biddles have eight consultants who work in different areas of the country. They rarely come into the office and rely mainly on irregular telephone calls and mail being sent to their homes. They usually make at least four visits daily unless they are carrying out consultancy work. As their areas are quite large, it can be difficult for office staff to organise visits as the staff are not familiar with the areas. Jim Biddle spends a lot of time reading reports of visits to keep up with the consultants' progress.

A recent problem arose when Jim received information regarding three companies. The first was having difficulties and Jim thought that Biddles would be able to help. The second company wanted an urgent 'follow-up' meeting; the third was rumoured to be in severe financial difficulties and Jim did not want to become involved with them. When he was unable to contact the relevant consultants by telephone, he sent memos out by first class mail to their homes before he caught his flight to Canada. During the night, the postal workers took industrial action which lasted forty-eight hours. When he returned he found that the first company had not been contacted and the business had gone to a competitor. The second company had telephoned to complain that no-one had been in touch and one of his consultants had agreed to carry out work with the third (financially embarrassed) company.

(a) Identify the major problems related to time management.

(b) How could time be managed more effectively, therefore eliminating problems of this type?

Chapter 12

MANAGING PROJECTS

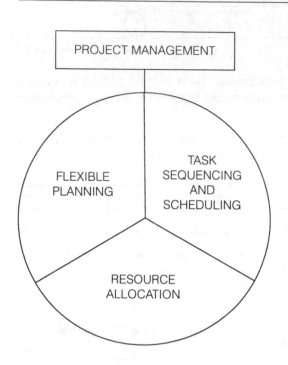

Introduction

In the previous chapter, we discussed how planning and organising could be applied to the collection or sequence of routine and non-routine tasks that confront an individual: the management of one's own 'in-tray' and time.

Managers are also responsible for planning and organising the work of others, however, and for co-ordinating the resources and stages of a given task so that objectives are achieved. In this chapter, we discuss the management of such complex tasks or projects, and look at some of the practical techniques managers use for each of these areas.

Your objectives

After completing this chapter you should:

(a) be aware of the complex nature of project management, and the need for co-ordination of activities and resources

(b) be able to draw up a work breakdown structure and use it to estimate job times

(c) be able to construct a network for a given activity, identify the critical path (using CPA) and recognise its implications for resource allocation and scheduling

(d) be able to construct a Gantt chart for scheduling and resource allocation, and interpret data on such a chart

(e) be aware of how 'slack' can be built into the project plan, including the use of Programme Evaluation and Review Technique (PERT)

1   PROJECT MANAGEMENT

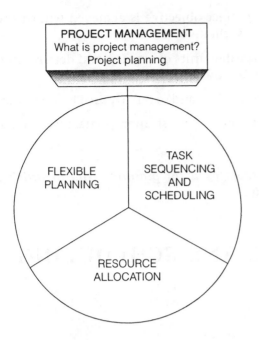

1.1   What is project management?

Definition

A *project* is an undertaking, often cutting across organisational and functional boundaries, and carried out to meet established goals within cost, schedule and quality objectives.

Project management is directed at a particular end: achieving specific objectives within a specific time span. It is not, like general management, directed at maintaining or improving continuous work activities.

Activity 1   [20 minutes]

See if you can think of an example of a project in each of the following areas.

(a) Building and construction.

(b) Manufacturing.

(c) Management.

(d) Research and development.

Project management therefore requires even closer attention to planning, organising and control, with regard to:

(a) *quality* – the end result should conform to specification; in other words, the project should achieve what it was meant to do;

(b) *cost* – the project should be completed without exceeding authorised expenditure (as specified in a budget) of money and other human and material resources;

(c) *time* – each stage of the project's progress must conform to schedule, so that the end result is achieved when requested or required.

1.2 Project planning

A project plan aims to ensure that the project objective is achieved within the requirements of quality, cost and time. This will involve:

(a) breaking the project down into manageable units of activity, and determining the sequence of, or relationships between, those units or tasks;

(b) estimating the resources (materials, money, time and so on) required for each unit;

(c) sequencing and scheduling each unit in the most appropriate way for co-ordinated performance.

We will now look at techniques and tools used for planning and organising interrelated and interdependent activities.

2 TASK SEQUENCING AND SCHEDULING

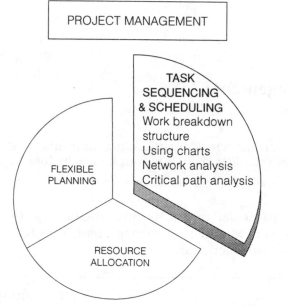

2.1 Work breakdown structure (WBS)

Breaking a project down into its component phases or stages is often the best way of:

(a) discovering exactly what work must be accomplished;

(b) determining the resources required; and

(c) sequencing and co-ordinating the work done.

This is called establishing a *work breakdown structure* (WBS) for the project.

Activity 2 [30 minutes]

Suppose you set yourself the project of cooking a dinner party for yourself and five friends.

(a) Define the objectives of the project: devise a three course meal menu.

(b) Estimate (roughly):
   (i) the cost and
   (ii) the time it will take you to prepare.

(c) Establish a work breakdown structure, in the form of a detailed list of things to do, for preparing your menu.

(d) What does your WBS tell you about your cost and time estimates?

Figure 12.1 is a simple example of a *diagrammatic* work breakdown structure for a house-building project. We have only broken down two of the component stages to the second level (the foundations and the wiring), but you should get the idea. The breakdown process continues until the smallest sub-unit or task is reached, for which man and machine hours can most easily be calculated and scheduled.

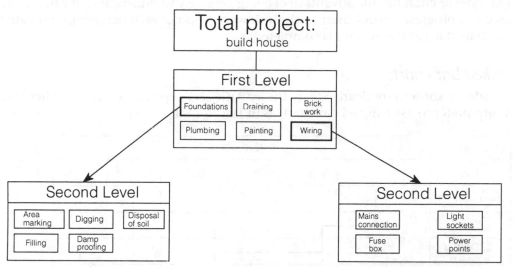

Figure 12.1 Diagrammatic work breakdown structure

Once the component activities of the project have been determined, they can be sequenced and scheduled. We have already covered some basic scheduling techniques in Chapter 11. Here, we will show how some of the simple charts can be applied to more complex project planning.

2.2   Using charts

Bar line charts

A simple project plan can be shown on a *bar line* or *Gantt* chart. Figure 12.2 is an example of a chart for a project to build a garage.

No.	DESCRIPTION OF WORK OR ACTIVITY	TIME (DAYS)													
		1	2	3	4	5	6	7	8	9	10	11	12	13	14
1	Excavate for foundations and services (drainage)	▨													
2	Concrete foundations			▨											
3	Build walls and soakaways for drainage					▨									
4	Construct roof									▨					
5	Fit garage doors									▨					
6	Provide services (electric)											▨			
7	Plaster												▨		
8	Decorate													▨	

Figure 12.2 Gantt chart for building a garage

This chart shows the sequence of activities to be followed, as well as the duration of each activity. You need to excavate before you can put in foundations, before you can build walls: once you've got to that stage, you can do the roof and doors together, if you have the manpower – sheltered from the elements – you can then follow the next sequence.

Activity 3 [15 minutes]

How could you, very simply, turn this chart into a work schedule?

This type of chart has the **advantage** of being very easy to understand. It can also be used as a progress control chart, with the lower section of each bar being completed (eg shaded in) as the activity is completed.

Linked bar charts

In order to show more clearly where the activities are dependent on each other, you might prefer to use a linked bar chart, as in Figure 12.3.

DESCRIPTION OF WORK OR ACTIVITY	TIME (DAYS)													
	1	2	3	4	5	6	7	8	9	10	11	12	13	14
Excavate for foundations and services (drainage)														
Concrete foundations														
Build walls and soakaways for drainage														
Construct roof														
Fit garage doors														
Provide services (electric)														
Plaster														
Decorate														

Figure 12.3 Linked bar chart

This shows the link between activities. In our example, the roofing and door-fitting can be done together, starting on day 9, but the door-fitting only takes one day, while the roofing takes two days – and needs to be finished before electrical wiring can be done, hopefully on day 11. The door-fitting therefore has a certain amount of leeway: it can be started late if necessary, since it does not hold up any other activity until the roofing and electrical installation are finished. This leeway is called float time, and is shown by the dotted line on the chart: the activity can be moved into the dotted area if necessary. Activities that have no float time are called critical activities: they must be completed on time in order to avoid a knock-on effect which will make the project as a whole run over time.

Activity 4 [20 minutes]

You are the site manager of the garage construction project. You have drawn up the linked bar chart above as a guide to all your on-site staff as to the order of activities and the speed of progress required to meet the customer's two-week deadline. You decide to use the chart to monitor progress. Using a different-coloured pen, you draw a line beneath the one on your plan chart to show what your team has actually accomplished.

(a) Everything takes the time it was planned to, except that on the Wednesday (day 3) the weather is too bad to work, so that concreting of the foundations actually takes three days.

(b) The door fitting takes one day, and the door-fitter is also qualified to do roofing work. His help will knock a day off the roofing schedule.

Draw the control line onto figure 12.3. Has your project run over time?

The big advantage of such charts is that they are easily understood by all levels of staff, and without undue calculation. However they can only display a restricted amount of information, and the links between activities are fairly crude. To overcome these limitations, when planning and organising more complex projects, we use a more sophisticated technique called network analysis.

2.3 Network analysis

Network analysis is a term for project planning techniques which aim to 'map' the activities in a particular project, and the relationship between them, including:

(a) what tasks must be done before others can be started;

(b) what tasks could be done at the same time;

(c) what tasks must be completed on schedule if the completion date for the whole project is not to slip: the critical tasks.

These relationships and sequences are represented in a network diagram, which flows from left to right. The most commonly used form of network is called an *activity-on-arrow* diagram, because activities are represented by an arrowed line, which runs between one event (start or completion of the activity) and another. Events are depicted by a node, or circle.

Hence in the following example we map activity A, which starts at a certain point (event 1) and ends at a certain point (event 2).

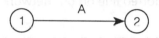

Let us tackle a more complex example. Suppose your work breakdown structure comprises six activities: we will call them activities A–G.

(a) Activities A and B can start together.

(b) You have to have done activity B before you can do activity C.

(c) Once activity A is completed, activities D and E can start, at the same time.

(d) Activity F follows on from activity D.

(e) Activity G will be completed at the same time as activity F, to end the project. However, activities C and E must be completed before G can commence.

Activity 5 [10 minutes]

Do not look at the network diagram below (Figure 12.4). Read (a)–(e) above again. Working from left to right, draw the network diagram showing activities A–G and events 1–6.
Now uncover our solution.

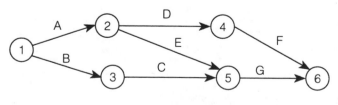

Figure 12.4 Network diagram

One further complication. It is a convention in network analysis that two separate activities should not start and end at the same events. If the real activities *could* start and end at the same event, this is shown on the network by inserting a *dummy activity*, represented by an extra event node with a dotted line joining it to the next event, figure 12.5.

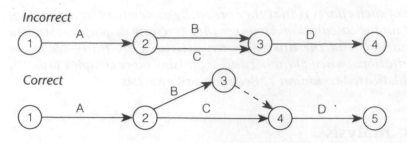

Figure 12.5 Network diagram with dummy activity

The correct version shows that activities B and C *both* have to be completed before D can begin, and the dotted line indicates that no extra activity is actually done and no extra time is taken between event 3 (completion of B) and event 4 (completion of C). The two activities therefore do start and end at the same points in the sequence, but not at the same nodes on the diagram.

Apart from pure convention, dummy activities may be needed to preserve the basic logic of the network.

Activity 6 [10 minutes]

In our network above, at figure 12.4, suppose that activity G depended on the completion of activity D, as well as activities C and E. Activity F still depends on activity D alone. There is no extra time or activity involved; all you need to do is to indicate the link between activities D and G. Draw the 'dummy activity' dotted line on our network diagram, to represent this scenario.

Another use of the dummy activity is to ensure that all activities end up at a single completion event, joining in any loose events.

More information can be added to a network diagram, to describe not just what happens next, but when it should happen, and how long the whole project will take if each activity takes as long as it is supposed to. This technique is called CPA, or critical path analysis.

2.4 Critical path analysis (CPA)

If Activity A takes three days, it is shown like this.

Let us say, building on our original A-G network, that:

Activity   A takes 3 days

B takes 5 days

C takes 2 days

D takes 1 day

E takes 6 days

F takes 3 days

G takes 3 days.

Our network would be as in Figure 12.6.

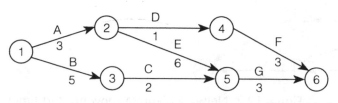

Figure 12.6 Network diagram with timings

Let us assume that you have all the resources you need to carry out the above project as drawn: in other words, you have enough workers to do activities A and B at the same time, and so on. The shortest possible time in which you can complete the project is 12 days. See if you can work out why, before reading on.

Each of the 'routes' of arrows from the first event to the last event is called a *pathway*, or *path*.

Activity 7   [20 minutes]

List all the pathways in Figure 12.6, and add up how many days each path will take to reach event 6.

The shortest possible duration for the project is 12 days. This is the duration of the longest path (AEG), not the shortest! The activities on the longest path determine the deadline for the whole project, because if one of them runs over time, the whole project will run over time. They are therefore *critical* activities, and the path on which they sit is called the critical path. We show the critical path on a network by drawing double or thicker lines between the events on that path.

Activity 8   [30 minutes]

Draw a network for the following project, and identify the critical path.

Activity	Depends on activity	Duration (weeks)
A	–	5
B	–	4
C	A	2
D	B	1
E	B	5
F	B	5
G	C, D	4
H	F	3
J	F	2

Hint: all your activities should 'tie up' at event 7.

Scheduling using the critical path

Once you have estimated activity durations and worked out the total project time, you can start scheduling. First of all, you work forwards from event 1, working out the *earliest start date* of each activity. We show the earliest start date of an activity as follows.

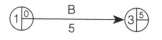

Obviously, event 1 starts at 0 (on day one): the earliest possible time for C to start, given that B takes 5 days, is at the end of day 5. If we do the same exercise with all the activities in our A-G example, we get Figure 12.7.

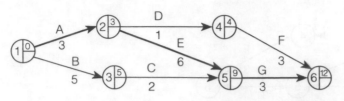

Figure 12.7 Network diagram showing start times

Note that the earliest start date for G (which has to follow A and E) is 9 days. But B and C only take 7 days: they can take two extra days, if necessary, without affecting the start of G.

We make this clear by next working *backwards* from event 6 to event 1, identifying the *latest start dates* when activities can start and still keep up with the timing set by the critical path. The earliest deadline of event 6 is 12 days: this is also its *latest* deadline, because it is the end of the critical path, which must not run late. Activity G takes 3 days, so its latest start date is 12 – 3 = 9 days: again, this is the same as its earliest start date, because G is on the critical path. Activity C takes 2 days, so its latest start date (if G is to start on time) is 9 – 2 = 7 days. However, its earliest start date (if B was on time) was 5 days: it has two days' leeway, or *float*. (Remember: activities on the critical path have no float.)

We insert the *latest* start date in the bottom quarter of the circle, as follows.

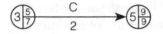

You can see just from this that Activity C can be started any time between days five and seven, giving the project manager a degree of flexibility, but that event 5 is on the critical path and must not run late!

Activity 9 [20 minutes]

Starting from event 6 and working backwards, fill in the latest start dates in Figure 12.7. Which activities can afford to start late, and by how much?

Attach actual dates to your days currently numbered 1-12, and you have a detailed and effective schedule.

3 RESOURCE ALLOCATION

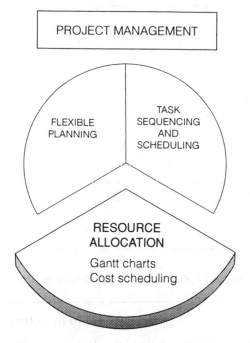

3.1 Gantt charts

As well as plotting time to be taken (and actually taken), Gantt charts can be used to estimate the amounts of resources required for a project.

Let us take the example we have been using so far in this section. We will be starting with our final network showing earliest and latest start times for A–G, so you may like to make a clean copy of the solution to activity 9 and keep it by you for reference.

Suppose that, in addition to the information contained on our network, we know the number of workers required to do each job, as follows.

Activity			
A requires	6 workers		
B	"	3	"
C	"	4	"
D	"	4	"
E	"	5	"
F	"	6	"
G	"	3	"

Suppose that we have a team of *nine* workers, each of whom is paid a fixed wage, regardless of hours worked in a week (so we want to avoid idle time if possible). Each worker is capable of working on any of the seven activities involved in the project (so we can swap them round freely if required).

Figure 12.8 shows a Gantt chart, simply plotting the various paths against the 12-day timescale. We have assumed that activities will be started at the *earliest* start times, adding *floats* (where available) as a dotted line.

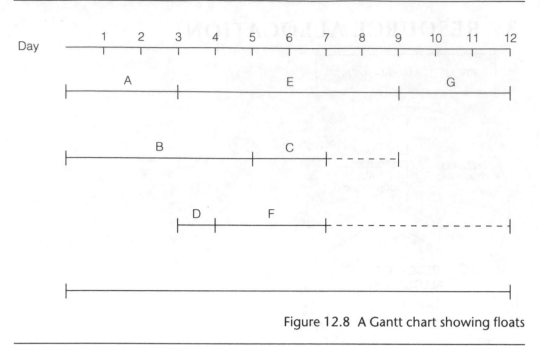

Figure 12.8 A Gantt chart showing floats

Activity 10   [30 minutes]

1 On Figure 17.8 add the *number* of workers *required*, below the line under the relevant activity letter: ___A___   and so on.
   6

2 Now, label the line at the bottom of the chart '*Workers required*'.

3 Draw a line vertically through the *start and end of each activity*, from the 'Time' line (days) to the 'Workers required' line. With each activity beginning or ending, the number of workers required will change.

4 In your first section of the 'Workers required' line, which extends from day 0-3, A and B are going on simultaneously. Mark 'AB' above this section of the line.

5 Activities A and B require 6 and 3 workers respectively: that is, 9 workers. Mark '9' below the 'AB' on the 'Workers required' line.

6 Keep going until you have completed all segments of the 'Workers required' line.

From the answer to the above activity, you may note that on days 6 and 7 you need as many as 15 workers though you only have nine. On days 8–12, you would have most of your team sitting about twiddling their thumbs. What are you going to do?

Let's look at the really busy period of days 4–7. Can you see any activities that *need* not be done during that period? We know that the path DF is *not* on the critical path. It takes four days, and need not finish until day 12: we have a full 5-day float. If we leave DF until its last possible start time (day 9), we are taking pressure off the busy period. Our Gantt chart would be redrawn as in Figure 12.9.

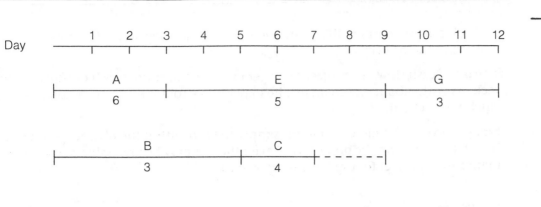

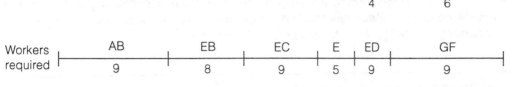

Figure 12.9 The final Gantt chart

The project can be completed without hiring any additional labour, and without running late. Good job! You can keep shuffling non-critical activities and re-calculating worker requirements like this until you are satisfied you have found the best solution. If there is too little float time at convenient stages to allow you do this, you may have to:

(a) reschedule the project to find the *minimum excess demand for labour*, and hire in extra labour for those times; *or*

(b) move critical activities as well as non-critical ones (thereby lengthening the project) to avoid excess demand for labour. The same method should be used to find the *minimum extension of the project's duration* required.

3.2 Cost scheduling

Cost estimating

It is usually not possible to say with certainty what the costs of a project will be, but some idea will be required in advance so that costs can be monitored and controlled. Estimates of costs can be based on rough guesswork (a 'ballpark' estimate), comparison with similar projects in the past, or the initial plans for the project (a 'feasibility' estimate).

The work breakdown structure will clearly be useful in devising estimates because it enables the project manager to compile a complete list of items that will attract expenditure. *Estimation forms* can be designed, based on the WBS, with columns for labour, materials, components and so on for each of the work units or tasks. This ensures that no items are forgotten, and speeds up the process of estimating, where jobs are routine or similar in type.

Cost scheduling

Costs can be scheduled, in exactly the same way as labour requirements.

(a) Draw a bar chart for the project.

(b) Estimate the cost of each activity.

(c) Divide by the duration of the activity to get the cost of the activity per week (or other appropriate time unit).

217

(d) Work out the cost of all activities going on in a given week: ie a total cost per week of the project.

For ease of cash flow, the project manager may need to restrict cash outflows in any week. As with labour requirements, he may be able to do this by rescheduling tasks which have a float.

It may, however, be more important simply to keep within the planned amount for the total expense on the project. And even then, it may be preferable to spend *extra* finance on a project to stop it running over time.

For discussion

In what kinds of project would you consider the time deadlines more important than the expenditure budget? And vice versa? (What projects do you know of which have gone way over budget, or late? Look out for examples in the press.)

Activity 11
[20 minutes]

Find your answer to Activity 2 – your WBS for a dinner party menu.

(a) Make up a cost estimate, based on your WBS. Draw a column marked B for budget, down the right hand side of your list, and enter your estimated amounts for each task.

(b) Go out and find out what it would *actually* cost, and write down each amount in a column marked A for actual, next to your Budget column.

How was your estimating? If you gave your dinner party, you might have written down what you really *paid* for your ingredients in the Actual column. You could monitor how you were doing, compared to your budget. This is called *budgetary control*: another useful management technique!

It should be clear from our discussion of 'estimates' that project planning is inexact and uncertain: the project manager does not have a crystal ball to tell him how long an activity will take, how much it will cost or how successful it will be. Finally, in this chapter, we look briefly at this problem of uncertainty, and how it can be planned for.

4 FLEXIBLE PLANNING

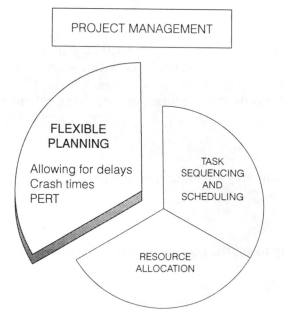

4.1 Allowing for delays

As we have already discussed, activities which are not on the critical path are non-critical, and can, within limits, *start later* and/or *take longer*, without holding up the completion time of the project as a whole. This slack time is called the activity's *float*. It allows unexpected delays to be absorbed and resources to be diverted, to avoid the late start of critical activities.

What happens if your critical activities are threatened with delays, though, and the final deadline simply cannot be extended?

4.2 Crash times

The crash time is the *minimum* time an activity can take to be completed. Crashing often involves the use of extra resources.

Job X takes one worker 1½ days – say, 12 working hours. The worker gets paid £10 per hour, so the cost of the job is £120. If the project manager needs Job X completed at the end of a single day, (s)he might ask the worker to do four hours' overtime to complete the 12 hours work in a single working day. However, the overtime rate of pay is £15 per hour. So the *crash cost* is (8 hours @ £10) + (4 hours @ £15) = £140.

There would be no point crashing non-critical jobs, because you would not shorten the overall project duration or affect the critical path by doing so. However, crashing can be used to shorten the critical path itself, if necessary, to:

(a) catch up with delays; or

(b) shorten the project duration for any reason.

You may have noted that, in most cases, we are still only talking about estimated job times or durations. What happens if you get those wrong in the first place? One answer is to take account of uncertainty and contingencies at the estimating stage. A well-known technique for doing this is PERT.

4.3 PERT

Programme Evaluation and Review Technique (PERT) recognises that the activity durations in the network are in fact uncertain. Instead of one estimate of each activity time, three estimates are used.

- The *most likely* duration of the activity, given what is known about it (which we will call m)

- The *most optimistic* (shortest) estimate, assuming that all goes well (o)

- The *most pessimistic* (longest) estimate, assuming that things that are likely to go wrong will go wrong (p)

These can be converted into a 'mean' (or middle) estimate, which takes into account the small chance that things will go entirely well or entirely badly. The mean time is calculated using the formula:

$$\frac{o + 4m + p}{6}$$

As an example, here are some more data!

Activity	Must be preceded by activity	Optimistic (o) days	Most likely (m) days	Pessimistic (p) days
A	-	5	10	15
B	A	16	18	26
C	-	15	20	31
D	-	8	18	28

The mean times for each activity are as follows.

Activity	$(o + 4m + p)$	$\div 6 =$	Mean time
A	5 + 40 + 15 = 60		10 days
B	16 + 72 + 26 = 114		19 days
C	15 + 80 + 31 = 126		21 days
D	8 + 72 + 28 = 108		18 days

Activity 12 [20 minutes]

Draw the network for A-D, using the mean times. Include earliest start and latest start times, and show where the critical path is.

Other calculations can be made using PERT, including the probability that a job will overrun by a given time. Because of their complexity, PERT systems are often run on computers, which generate the planning and control data required.

PERT is frequently used where there are a number of possible contingencies which would affect the project duration. Construction projects, for example, need to allow for delays due to unfavourable weather.

The issue of uncertainty will be discussed further in Chapter 16.

Chapter roundup

● Project management is directed at a particular end: achieving specific objectives within a limited time span.

● Project planning and organisation involves:
— breaking the project into units (work breakdown structure)
— determining the sequence and/or relationships between those units
— estimating the resources required for each unit
— scheduling time and allocating resources for each unit.

● Popular techniques for project planning include:
— network analysis (including critical path analysis) and
— Gantt charts.

● Network analysis aims to 'map' the relationships and dependencies of tasks in a project. The critical path is the longest path on the network, representing the shortest possible completion time of the project: if any activity on the critical path runs late, the project will run late. Non-critical activities may have some 'slack' time within which they can be extended without having a knock-on effect on the project duration: this is called a float.

Chapter roundup *continued*

- Estimating costs and job times is not an accurate science. One technique for taking uncertainty into account is Programme Evaluation and Review Technique (PERT) which calculates a mean time for each activity using most likely, optimistic and pessimistic estimates.

Quick quiz

1 What is a work breakdown structure, and what can it be used for?

2 What are (a) a critical activity and (b) a float?

3 What are the advantages and disadvantages of using bar charts for project planning and control?

4 What is depicted by (a) nodes, (b) arrowed lines and (c) thick arrowed lines, in a network diagram?

5 In what circumstances might you add a 'dummy activity' to a network diagram?

6 Is the critical path the shortest or longest line from start to end of the project network?

7 What do the numbers represent in the following segment of a network diagram?

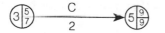

8 If you know how many workers are required for each job, and all team members can do all jobs, how might you go about scheduling your manpower in an efficient manner?

9 What is a 'crash time' and why might you not want to 'crash' a non-critical activity?

10 What is the mathematical formula for calculating a mean time for a job whose duration is uncertain?

Answers to quick quiz

1 It breaks a project down into its component phases or stages. It can be used to discover what work is needed and what resources are required and for sequencing and co-ordinating.

2 (a) One that must be completed on time.

(b) The amount of leeway there is for completion of the activity.

3 Advantages are that they are easily understood and do not require undue calculation. Disadvantages are that they give restricted information and links between activities are fairly crude.

4 (a) Events

(b) Activities

(c) Critical activities

5 When two activities could start and end at the same event.

6 Longest.

7 In the first node, 3 = event; 5 = earliest start; 7 = latest start; C2 means that activity C takes two days. In the second node 5 = event; 9/9 are the earliest and latest start day, so the activity must not run late.

8 Using a Gantt chart.

9 It is the minimum time to complete an activity. Crashing a non-critical activity would not affect the critical path or shorten the overall project time.

10   $\dfrac{o + 4m + p}{6}$

Answers to Activities

1   You will have come up with your own ideas for different projects: here are some suggestions.

(a) Construction of a motorway extension, say, or the Channel Tunnel.

(b) Limited-edition production of a car, for example, or one-off tailor-made products.

(c) Implementation of a computer system, say, or mounting a trade exhibition or conference.

(d) Ironing out bugs in a system or product, completing a market research survey and so on.

Check that your own examples have a beginning, an end, and goals.

2   The answer will depend on your menu, but your WBS may include stages such as: the purchasing of the various ingredients; washing, peeling and chopping vegetables (if any); mixing ingredients; cooking and/or preparing each dish; laying the table and preparing plates and utensils and so on. Your WBS should give you a fairly clear idea of what ingredients, in what quantities, you will need to buy: a more accurate cost estimate than trying to judge the cost of the meal as a whole. The same is true of the timetable, with the added advantage that it provides the basis for an action checklist and schedule for preparation.

3   To turn figure 12.2 into a work schedule, you could put the days of the week across the top instead of the number of days given. So the excavations should take up Monday and Tuesday, the foundations start on Wednesday and so on.

4   The control line added to figure 12.3 yields the result shown here.

DESCRIPTION OF WORK OR ACTIVITY	TIME (DAYS)													
	1	2	3	4	5	6	7	8	9	10	11	12	13	14
Excavate for foundations and services (drainage)														
Concrete foundations														
Build walls and soakaways for drainage														
Construct roof														
Fit garage doors														
Provide services (electric)														
Plaster														
Decorate														

You've made up your lost day of concreting because you had the float time on the door-fitting and were able to divert the door person to the roofing.

5   The solution is given in the text.

6   You should draw a dotted line from event 4 to 5.

7 There are three paths, as follows.

ADF	= 3 + 1 + 3 days	= 7 days
AEG	= 3 + 6 + 3 days	= 12 days
BCG	= 5 + 2 + 3 days	= 10 days

8

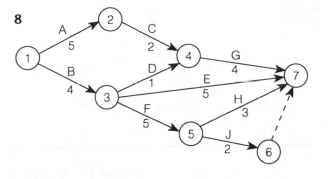

The paths are

ACG	= 5 + 2 + 4	= 11 weeks
BDG	= 4 + 1 + 4	= 9 weeks
BE	= 4 + 5	= 9 weeks
BFH	= 4 + 5 + 3	= 12 weeks
BFJ Dummy	= 4 + 5 + 2 + 0	= 11 weeks

BFH is the longest (and therefore the critical) path: the shortest time in which the project can be completed.

9

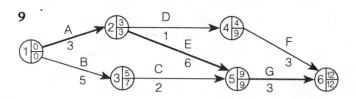

Activity C: anytime between days 5 and 7 (a 2-day float)

Activity F: anytime between days 4 and 9 (a 5-day float)

10

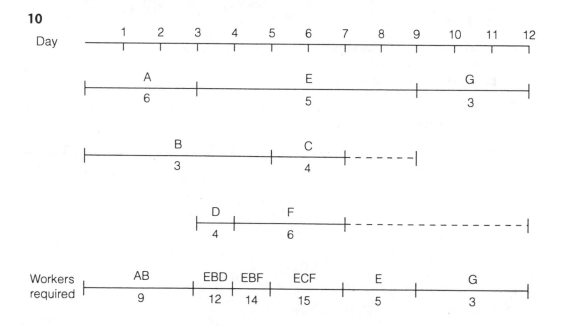

11 Did you totally underestimate your budget, and have to spend your food allowance for the next three weeks? If you did, it might be a good idea to go back to section 3.2 and read up on cost estimating.

12

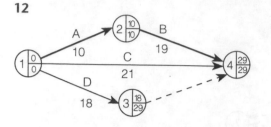

Assignment 12

[About 1¹/₂ hours]

Read the following case examples.

1 A recent military project was the attempted conversion of the Nimrod maritime reconnaissance aircraft into an airborne early warning radar systems platform. This was a sorry tale of continually changing specifications, an aircraft too small for the task and technology not yet developed. The project was cancelled after a few hundred million had been spent and a proven Boeing system was purchased.

2 The *Evening Standard* (11/8/95) reported on Britain's plans to stage a festival to celebrate the next Millennium. 'According to today's reports, however, many companies involved in such events feel there is not enough time to produce a successful Millennium Festival ... Such an event, involving a site of at least 100 acres and 15 million potential investors, would normally take 7-10 years to build ... Prospective operators are also unhappy with the lack of direction. The Millennium Commission has not specified exactly what kind of event it has in mind, except to say that it should rival historical predecessors like the Great Exhibition and Festival of Britain .. "The problem with defining the event is that it is not our place to say what people will want in five or six years."'

Required

(a) What problems of project planning are raised by these case examples? (Think about what factors might make it difficult to come up with accurate breakdowns and cost estimates, for example.)

(b) Suggest ways in which the Millenium project might be organised to make project management possible.

Chapter 13

COMMUNICATION

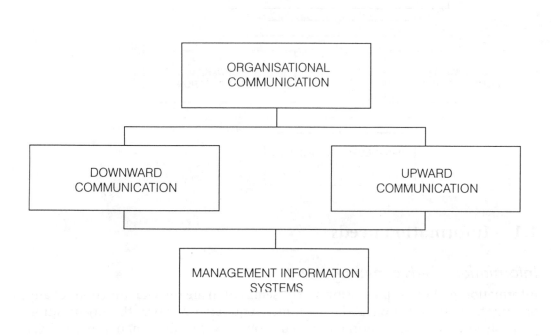

Introduction

Communication in the context of managing *people* was covered in Chapter 5, an important aspect of interpersonal behaviour. If you need to refresh your memory of the process and potential problems of communication, you might like to skim through Section 5.2 before studying this chapter.

Communication in the context of managing *tasks* raises wider organisational issues. It is about how a manager communicates goals and instructions to his or her team; how the information required for tasks and decisions can be gathered and shared; how the team can feed back information on performance for the purposes of control, and so on.

In this chapter we will be looking less at interpersonal communication processes, and more at the purpose, direction and mechanisms of organisational communication.

Your objectives

After completing this chapter you should:

- be able to identify the importance of information and communications in the effective management of activities;
- be able to outline the purposes and media of downward and upward communication in organisations;
- be able to perform basic managerial communication tasks;
- be able to describe the purposes and design of different types of Management Information System.

1 ORGANISATIONAL COMMUNICATION

1.1 Information needs

Information needs of management

Information-gathering, processing and dissemination are the vital functions of any organisation. Information about customer requirements gives the organisation purpose and objectives. Information about objectives enables managers to direct and co-ordinate the activities of others. Information is the basis of planning and decision-making. Feedback information is necessary for control.

Activity 1 [30 minutes]

First, practise your information-gathering skills by locating the section on Mintzberg's classification of management roles. (Don't just flick back through the text: devise an efficient information search strategy!) List the managerial roles.

For each role, give an example of how communication might be used in that role.

We suggest some further examples of management uses of information in the table on the following page.

Information needs of employees

Employees require information from the organisation for a variety of purposes.

(a) *In order to perform their tasks effectively and efficiently.* They need to know about work schedules, resource availability, how to use tools and machinery efficiently and safely, what procedures have been laid down – or where to find out – and so on. This kind of information may be provided through briefings, schedules, job descriptions, procedures manuals, or specific memos, notices or meetings.

(b) *For motivation, learning and development.* Employees need to know what is required from them: performance criteria and standards, targets, budgets, rules and expectations. They need feedback on how their performance measures up to the criteria on which they are judged: without it, they cannot be motivated or enabled to correct sub-standard performance, or to take satisfaction in good performance.

Management function	Some of the purposes of information	Type and sources of information
Planning	● To establish objectives, or end goals towards which all plans must contribute ● To establish strategies for achieving objectives and policies, procedures, rules, budgets etc to guide day to day decision-making towards fulfilment of strategies	● Attitudes/expectations of owners, customers and other stakeholders ● Information from the environment on foreseeable opportunities and threats, past events indicating trends and future probabilities ● Information from within the organisation on identifiable strengths and weaknesses. ● Creative thinking within the organisation, on opportunities and solutions to problems
Control	● To indicate whether and how far a plan has been carried out, whether and how far it has been successful in achieving its objective ● To suggest the adjustment of performance, or the plan itself, to correct any deviation	● Feedback from results of plan ● Feedback from subordinates charged with carrying out plan on how it went ● Information from the environment about changes, requiring adjustment of plans ● Information from within the organisation: suggestions for improvements, identification of problems
Decision-making/ problem-solving	● To identify and analyse a problem or opportunity ● To appraise available resources ● To compare alternative solutions and select optimum solution	● Internal and external information of a wide variety, relevant to situation ● Investigation of internal resources and potential external sources ● Information on likely outcomes of a number of different solutions
Co-ordinating	● To guide planning, so as to avoid duplication of effort – or gaps in effort – between individuals, teams or functions	● Overall objectives of the department/ organisation ● Feedback on results of overall activity ● Plans, deadlines etc of other teams and departments ● Reports on co-ordination problems
Organising	● To indicate how tasks relate to each other, and who should do what	● Information about task requirements, methods and resources required ● Information on staff skills, abilities, motivation ● Information on needs of employees to work in particular conditions, methods, teams etc
Commanding	● To indicate employees' needs and wants, so that they can be offered appropriate motivators ● To ensure that all rights of employees are being fulfilled ● To supply the information required for outside agencies and internal systems: manpower planning, employee appraisal and reward, training etc	● Information about employees' needs, wants and expectations ● External information about employment rights: legal and customary ● Internal information about individual employees and the workforce as a whole

(c) *For job satisfaction.* Employees may feel more trusted if information is freely given about areas relevant to their work. If the information helps them to see how their work relates to that of others, and how it contributes to the organisation, it gives their work additional meaning and satisfaction.

1.2   Information outputs by the organisation

Communication by the organisation to the outside world is far wider than advertising, promotion and press releases. Some organisations (banks, consultancies, research organisations, travel agencies and suchlike) are in effect offering and/or selling information itself as their main product or service.

Activity 2   [20 minutes]

See if you can think of some of the matters about which an organisation may need to give out information (other than information requested by customers as part of the organisation's service) and to whom they would need to give it.

Good business information will be suited to its purpose and to its audience. As you can see from your solution to activity 2 (or ours), this covers a huge variety, and requires a great deal of flexibility from the business communicator.

Since information is the lifeblood of the organisation, the process of communication cannot just be left to chance or individual discretion. Information, like other resources, must be co-ordinated. The organisation's subsystems therefore include a formal communication system.

1.3   Formal communication

The formal structure of an organisation implies a formal structure or system for communication.

(a) The delegation of authority down the chain of command implies communication from superior to subordinate in the form of instructions, orders, job-related information, encouragement, incentive and so on.

(b) Accountability back up the line of command implies communication from subordinate to superior, accounting for the use of delegated authority, reporting results, appealing to the superior with problems or decisions which are not within the area of the subordinate's delegated authority and so on.

(c) Co-ordination links individuals, teams and departments in co-operative systems of working. These links are reflected by the horizontal lines at each 'tier' of the organisation chart: they imply the sharing of information by different units in order to harmonise their efforts, and to fulfil the requirements of their joint superiors (at the next level up).

You can see why people talk about the direction of information flow: downwards, upwards and horizontally/sideways. We will be discussing vertical communication in more detail below.

Communication routes

You have probably come across the phrase 'going through channels'. Because of the need for co-ordination and control, and to preserve the formal organisation structure, the normal channel of communication will follow the line of command: superiors will deal only with their own immediate subordinates, and vice versa. Communication *diagonally* – with someone both at a different level of the hierarchy and in a different section or department – is generally discouraged: individuals are expected to pass the message vertically and horizontally through appropriate linking individuals. See Figure 13.1.

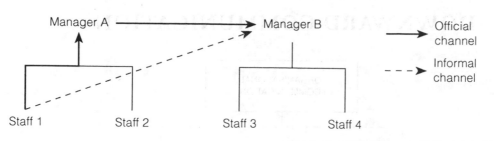

Figure 13.1 Formal and informal communication routes

In a matter of particular urgency the formal channels may be by-passed by simply leaving out the linking individuals. For example, the managing director might wish to declare an important decision directly to all staff. This route should be used only in emergencies, however, since regularly ignoring one link in the communication chain (usually middle-level managers) can cause resentment: 'Why am I always the last one to know?'

It has to be accepted that in some circumstances, 'going through channels' will be time-consuming and frustrating. The use of empowered teams in organisations is a radical way of cutting out the levels and channels through which information has to pass.

Formal communication will usually fulfil the need to know, but the organisation may not necessarily satisfy the 'want' to know. This will result in the informal network, which will sometimes spread irregular and unreliable information.

1.4 Informal communication

The *formal* system of communication in an organisation is always supplemented by an *informal* one: casual talks in the canteen, at the pub, on the way home and so on.

The *grapevine*, the network for rumours and gossip, works very fast – 'word gets around' often before the formal structure has conveyed news. The problem is that it tends to distort information on organisational issues, through rumour and speculation – especially on sensitive issues like pay, redundancy or change.

Formal communication systems do, however, need the support of a good – accurate – informal system. This might be encouraged by:

(a) setting up official communications to feed information into the informal system, eg house journals or briefings; and

(b) encouraging and offering opportunities for 'networking'. A network is a collection of people, usually with a shared interest, who tend to keep in touch to exchange informal information. Ordinary social exchanges should not be stifled at work (unless they start interfering with performance, eg by distracting or delaying an employee in the middle of seeing a customer).

Activity 3 [20 minutes]

How might you, as a manager, *use* the grapevine to help you manage your team?

2 DOWNWARD COMMUNICATION

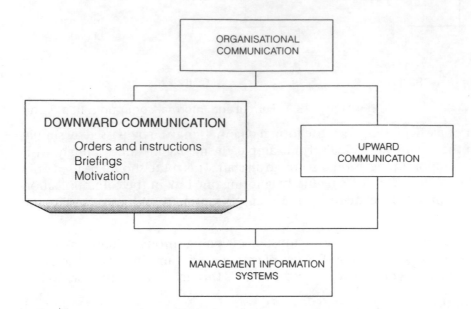

2.1 Orders and instructions

The most basic form of downward communication is giving subordinates orders and instructions to get work done: the management function of commanding. This can be done using a number of communication media.

An organisation manual or handbook

An organisation (or office) manual is often used to draw together information about the structure and products of the organisation, conditions of employment and so on. In a bureaucratic organisation, where work is routine in nature, it may also be used to give guidance or instruction on:

(a) rules and regulations;

(b) standards and procedures for health and safety, grievance, discipline and so on;

(c) procedures and standards for routine tasks.

Oral communication

Oral (spoken) communication can be achieved face-to-face or remotely, by telephone. The advantage of oral communication for giving orders and instructions is that it allows for immediate feedback to be sought and given: the team member(s) can ask for clarification of points which are not clear, or for more information, and can signal clearly to the manager that the orders have been understood and accepted. The advantage of using the *telephone* is that it cuts down on the time and physical movement required for a face-to-face exchange (the manager going to the team member or vice versa). However, *face-to-face communication* allows:

(a) more people to be reached in one go, for example in a team meeting;

(b) even clearer feedback, since both parties can also use non-verbal signals (perplexed expression or confident nod of the head) to reinforce their messages;

(c) greater responsiveness to personal factors, and greater persuasiveness, which may be important if the task is difficult, unpleasant or somehow sensitive.

With continued advances in technology, it is now possible to use conference facilities and videophones, enabling contact with more than one person at a time.

Written direct communication

If you want to give an instruction to your bank manager, say, what method would you use? You might telephone initially, but you would probably want, or be asked, to put your instructions in writing as well. Written communication has major advantages in business, as it provides concrete evidence and confirmation of the message. Details cannot be forgotten – or misremembered – as easily as with a spoken message; nor is understanding subject to the interpretation of tone of voice, or mishearing. Instructions, especially if they are lengthy or complicated, may be best provided (at least, as backup confirmation) in writing: alternatively, team members should be encouraged to take notes themselves, in any oral briefing.

A *memorandum* (or memo) is an often-used format for internal written communication in organisations. It is a bit like a letter, sent through the internal mail system of the organisation, but designed for greater efficiency of communication. A standard memo format is as follows. (It may be written or typed from scratch, but many organisations have memo pads with appropriate headings already printed.)

Organisation's name (optional)
'MEMORANDUM' heading

'To:' (recipient's name or designation)
'From:' (author's name or designation)
'Subject:' (main theme of message)

'Reference:' (for filing)
'Date:' (in full)

The message of the memorandum is set out simply in good English and spaced paragraphs.

'Copies to:' (recipient(s) of copies)
'Enc:' (= enclosure: to indicate accompanying material)

'Signed:' (optional)
author signs/initials

Here is an example of an order (which you will see is put courteously as a request) in memorandum form.

MEMORANDUM

To: Administrative Staff, SE region
From: I M Bossere, Office Manager
Subject: Staff meeting, January 19XX

Ref: JW/nn SE 22
Date: 4th January19XX

The Managing Director intends to hold an informal general meeting with administrative staff at some point during January, to discuss any matters that may be of concern.

Tentative dates for the meeting are Wednesday 23rd or Friday 25th: it will in either case be held in Meeting Room 3 at 6.00pm. Refreshments will be provided by the canteen afterwards, should staff wish to stay.

Please let me know as soon as possible (no later than Wednesday 16th):

1. which date you would find most convenient;
2. whether you are likely to stay for refreshments;
3. any topics which you would like to see on the agenda for the meeting.

Copies to: Managing Director.

IMB

Activity 4

[30 minutes]

Write a memo to Mr Bossere, answering the above invitation and request for information. Use the company's 'house style' for memos.

The content of orders and instructions

Orders and instructions will obviously vary widely, from 'Take that package down to the post room, please' to the plan for a complete work process or project.

The main point about orders and instructions is that they should be:

- clear and
- sufficient

for the recipient to be able to proceed to fulfil the instructions to your satisfaction.

Complete and detailed instructions for a complex task may include the following elements.

(a) *Desired outcomes or results*, including:
    (i)   the standard to which they should be achieved;
    (ii) the criteria on which successful performance will be judged;
    (iii) the time-scale within which the task or project must be completed; and
    (iv) resources available; financial targets and budgets set; payments agreed and so on.

(b) *Definition of all relevant terms*, to minimise misunderstanding.

(c) *A breakdown of the task or project into logical components*, and their:
    (i)   context;
    (ii) requirements;
    (iii) resource budgets (if any);
    (iv) methods (if required) – don't try to teach the experts their job; and
    (v) relevant background.

(d) *Information required to understand and carry out the task.*

For discussion

How helpful are the following common phrases, when it comes to giving clear, sufficient orders and instructions?

- *'As soon as possible' (or even 'ASAP')*
- *'Whenever it's convenient'*
- *'Use your own judgement'*
- *'Let's see how far we get'*
- *'Either type will do'*

The term 'briefing' (or 'brief') is often used for the giving of instructions: the content of such a briefing will be as described above. However, you might prefer to distinguish briefings as being more concerned with stage (d) above: the giving of information necessary to do the job.

2.2 Briefings

Briefings on specific tasks or topics will be much like the giving of instructions, as outlined above. However, briefings can also be used as a wider communication medium, as part of the empowerment of work teams. An organisation, or individual manager, may wish to have a scheme of regular short meetings in order to communicate and explain, on an on-going basis, such issues as:

(a) organisational policy and any changes to it;

(b) plans;

(c) progress in comparison to plan;

(d) results: 'good news swapping' from around the organisation.

As in any form of communication, the important considerations will be:

- *The purpose of the communication*
  - What information is necessary and helpful?
  - What information is relevant and what is irrelevant – and will therefore simply overload the recipient(s)?
  - What will the information be used for – and can it be provided in a way that it will make it easier to use (diagrams, say, or tables of data)?

- *The needs and abilities of the audience*
  - What information is relevant to the audience's needs – or can be made to seem relevant to them?
  - How much information will they be able to take in at one go?
  - What words and styles of communication will they be able – or unable – to understand easily?
  - Will the audience be receptive to the message, or might there be reasons why they will be resistant to it (in which case how can this resistance be overcome – perhaps, by persuasion)?

Team briefings can be seen as a way of motivating *employees by communicating more freely with them the kind of information that used to be held only at the top of the hierarchy. We will look briefly at other types of downward communication used in this way.*

2.3 Motivation

You should be aware that downward communication is not just about directly 'getting things done'. It is also about maintaining the *ability* and *willingness* of team members to carry out your orders and instructions.

(a) *Positive and negative reinforcement.* Downward communication plays a role in motivation in the form of:
  (i) praise for good work or effort;
  (ii) encouragement;
  (iii) discipline: expression of dissatisfaction with poor performance, re-emphasising required standards and so on;
  (iv) constructive criticism.

(b) *Culture.* Leaders communicate the organisation's values and beliefs to their teams.

(c) *Performance feedback.* In Chapter 7, we saw the importance of systematic appraisal of employee performance. In fact, team leaders should constantly provide feedback to members on:
  (i) how they are doing in their tasks and in the team; and
  (ii) how results are progressing in comparison to the plans and standards set for them.

Feedback is essential both for motivation and for learning and development – for the adjustment of performance to bring it (where necessary) back in line with the original plan.

3 UPWARD COMMUNICATION

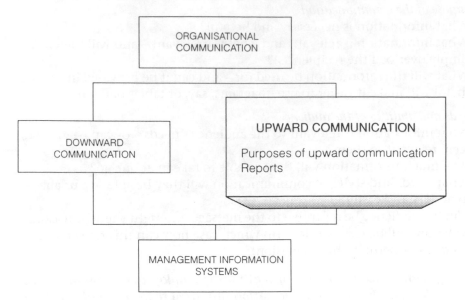

3.1 Purposes of upward communication

The main purposes of upward communication are as follows.

To give feedback on performance

Subordinates *report to* superiors in the organisation hierarchy: if you have been given orders or delegated authority to make a decision or perform a task, you are accountable for the results of that decision or task to your superior. Managers may not be as close to the nitty gritty of daily work as their team members, so they require the team to report on how things are going, progress and problems (if any).

A useful principle to bear in mind here is *management by exception*. If a manager has made a detailed plan, (s)he does not need regular reports about things going according to plan: (s)he already knows what to expect in that case. However, if performance *deviates* from plan, the manager needs to know, in order to take control action to put things right. 'Reporting by exception' means that only deviations from the plan or norm need be reported. This saves a lot of irrelevant communication!

To give information

Managers monitor information which is relevant to the task and team, and which may affect decisions made even higher up the organisation. Information provided by team members includes performance feedback, but may also cover other maters. A manager may, for example, require information for a meeting or report, which subordinates possess or have access to; a team member may have closer knowledge of the production technology involved in her work; a subordinate may be given the task of researching a new product, technology or idea to give the manager a summary or digest of the information that will be relevant.

To give suggestions

Being in possession of practical knowledge and information about the work, team members may be in a position to offer helpful insights for problem-solving or new methods of working, which managers may not have thought of. This is one of the important principles behind the empowerment of teams. Upward communication of suggestions is not always easy, (like any form of 'sticking your neck out') and suggestions are not always taken seriously: genuine empowerment allows suggestions a forum where they can be properly considered by the team.

For discussion

Can you see ways in which your course, for example, could be improved?

(a) What enables you to have an insight into the problem or opportunity, that your course designers/leaders may not have?

(b) What holds you back (if anything) from suggesting the improvements to your course designers/leaders? What would encourage you to do so?

To give feedback about oneself and one's experience of work

Upward communication *should* be a major feature of employee appraisal schemes, although, as we saw in Chapter 7, many organisations fail to take advantage of this opportunity. If team members can be encouraged to discuss their work problems, frustrations and ambitions with their leaders, more relevant training, development and reward systems can be designed.

Like downward communication, upward communication can be done face-to-face, on the telephone, or in writing, with the same advantages and disadvantages discussed in section 2.1 of this chapter. We will look briefly at one particular format, which is much used in business: the written report.

3.2   Reports

Planning a report

Unless you have an *extremely* orderly mind, compiling a report takes *planning*.

If you know who the user is, what information (s)he wants and why, and if you are aware of any requirements of size and time, you will have a good framework for planning the structure and content of your report. Ask yourself the following questions.

(a) What information do I need to provide? What is relevant to the user's requirements?

(b) What is the information for: explanation? description? recommendation? instruction?

(c) Do I need to follow a line of reasoning? If so, what is the most logical way in which data can be organised, to make my reasoning clear? (For/against? Advantage/disadvantage? Chronological order?)

(d) Do I need to include my own personal views? What form should these take: recommendations or suggestions? interpretation? opinion?

(e) What can I do to make the report easier to read? (Headers, numbered points, spacing, non-technical vocabulary, diagrams, clear and precise language and so on.)

Jot down a skeleton of the headings and sub-headings you have decided to use (with notes of any particular points that occur to you as you go along) and you will be ready to write. The formal headings of standard business reports (discussed below) may be useful to help you to organise your thoughts – but may not be necessary or even advisable, if they simply act as a constraint on what you actually want to say, and how you want to shape your argument.

Report structure and style

When a *formal* request is made by a superior for a report to be prepared, such as in a formally worded memorandum or letter, the format and style of the report will obviously have to be formal as well: it will be highly organised in structure and layout, and impersonal in tone. ('It was found that ...' instead of 'I found that...' 'do not' instead of 'don't'; 'showed considerable irritation' instead of 'got cheesed off'.)

An *informal* request for a report – 'Can you jot down a few ideas for me about...?' or 'Let me know what happens, will you?' – will result in an informal report, in which the structure will be less rigid, and the style slightly more personal (depending on the relationship between the writer and user). An informal report is often presented in memorandum format (see section 2.1 above).

If in doubt, it is better (more courteous and effective) to be too formal than over familiar.

The following are standard structures for formal and informal reports.

SHORT FORMAL REPORT

TITLE
At the top of every report (or on a title page, for lengthy ones) should be the title of the report (its subject), who has prepared it, for whom it is intended, the date of completion, and the status of the report ('Confidential' or 'Urgent').

I) TERMS OF REFERENCE
Here is laid out the scope and purpose of the report: what is to be investigated, what kind of information is required, whether recommendations are to be made etc. (This section may more simply be called 'Introduction', and may include the details set above under 'Title'. The title itself would then give only the subject of the report.)

II) PROCEDURE or METHOD
This outlines the steps taken to make an investigation, collect data, put events in motion etc. Telephone calls or visits made, documents or computer files consulted, computations or analyses made etc. should be briefly described, with the names of other people involved.

III) FINDINGS
In this section the information itself is set out, with appropriate headings and sub-headings, if the report covers more than one topic.

IV) CONCLUSIONS
This section allows for a summary of main findings (if the report is complex and lengthy). For a simpler report it may include action taken or decisions reached (if any) as a result of the investigation, or an expression of the overall 'message' of the report.

V) RECOMMENDATIONS
Here, if asked to do so in the terms of reference, the writer of the report may suggest the solution to the problem investigated so that the recipient will be able to make a decision if necessary.

VI) APPENDICES
When additional information is required which does not appear in the body of the report, it should be provided as an appendix, and should be referred to in the main text of the report.

SHORT INFORMAL REPORT

TITLE

Again, the subject title, 'to', 'from', 'date' and 'reference' (if necessary) should be provided, perhaps in the same style as memorandum headings.

1   *Background or Introduction or Situation*
This sets the context of the report. Include anything that will help the reader to understand the rest of the report: the reason why it was requested, the current situation, and any other background information on people and things that will be mentioned in the following detailed section.

2   *Findings or Analysis of the situation or Information*
Here is set out the detailed information gathered, narrative of events or other substance of the report as required by the user. This section may or may not require subheadings: concise prose paragraphs may be sufficient.

3   *Action or Solution or Conclusion or Recommendations*
The main thrust of the findings may be summarised in this section and conclusions drawn, together with a note of the outcome of events, or action required, or recommendations as to how a problem might be solved.

Activity 5

[45 minutes]

You mentioned in conversation with your manager that you considered facilities for staff recreation and refreshment were either non-existent or inadequate. 'Is that really important?', she asked, 'and is it really that bad?' She thinks for a moment, then says: 'OK, why don't you put something in writing for me – and make some recommendations. I might want to show it to the others at the management meeting, though, so put it into some sort of order for me. Thanks.'

This is your brief. Write the report.

The following is an example of a short formal report.

REPORT ON FLOPPY DISK STORAGE, SAFETY AND SECURITY

I INTRODUCTION

This report details the findings of an investigation into methods of computer disk storage currently employed at Head Office. The report, to include recommendations for the improvement of current procedure, was requested by Mr M Ployer, Personnel Department Manager. It was prepared by M Ployee, Supervisor, and submitted to Mr Ployer on 3 October 19—.

II METHOD

In order to evaluate the present procedures and to identify specific shortcomings, the following investigatory procedures were adopted:
1 interview of all staff using floppy disks;
2 storage and indexing system inspected;
3 computer accessory firm consulted by telephone and catalogues obtained (see Appendix I).

III FINDINGS
1 *Current system.*
   (a) Floppy disks are 'backed up' or duplicated irregularly and infrequently.
   (b) Back-up disks if they exist are stored in plastic containers in the personnel office, the same room as the disks currently in use.
   (c) Disks are frequently left on desk tops during the day and even overnight.

2 *Safety and security risks.*
   (a) There is no systematic provision for making copies, in the event of loss or damage of disks in use.
   (b) There is no provision for separate storage of copies in the event of fire in the personnel office, and no adequate security against fire or damage in the containers used.
   (c) There appears to be no awareness of the confidential nature of information on disk, nor of the ease with which disks may be damaged by handling, the spilling of beverages, dust etc.

IV CONCLUSIONS

The principal conclusions drawn from the investigation were that there was insufficient awareness of safety and security among non-specialist staff, that there was insufficient formal provision for safety and security procedure, and that there was serious cause for concern.

V RECOMMENDATIONS

In order to rectify the unsatisfactory situation summarised above, the author of the report recommends that consideration be given as a matter of urgency to the following measures.
1 Immediate backing up of all existing disks.
2 Drafting of procedures for backing up disks at the end of each day.
3 Acquisition of a fire-proof safe to be kept in separate office accommodation.
4 Communication to all staff of the serious risk of loss, theft and damage arising from careless handling of computer disks.

4 MANAGEMENT INFORMATION SYSTEMS

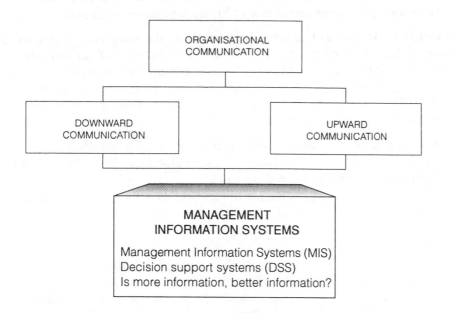

4.1 Management Information Systems (MIS)

We discussed in section 1 of this chapter some of the many types of information managers require to make decisions. It should be fairly obvious that if the information gathering process is not carefully planned:

(a) managers may 'miss' important items of information, while being overloaded with less relevant items;

(b) managers may receive information too late – or too early – for it to be helpful in making a given decision;

(c) the right information, at the right time, may go to the wrong managers;

(d) managers may receive data in a user-unfriendly format, so that its underlying value and 'point' (trends, deviations from plan and so on) are not easily seen.

Definitions

Data are the raw materials of information: facts and figures in an unprocessed state.

Information is data which have been processed (selected, sorted, analysed, formatted) so as to:

- have meaning for the person who receives it; and
- be suitable for a particular purpose.

A *Management Information System* (MIS) is a system designed to collect data from all available sources and to convert it into information relevant to managers at all levels, for the purposes of planning and control of the activities for which they are responsible.

Nowadays, Management Information Systems (MIS) are almost inevitably seen as computerised systems. Computers are able to process, format, store and retrieve certain types of information in far greater volume and at far greater speeds than is possible with manual, paper-based systems.

As an example, consider the point-of-sale system at a supermarket checkout desk. The cashier has input basic data like the items you have bought and their prices (perhaps all contained on their bar codes). What type of 'management information' is made available?

(a) You get a receipt, listing all the items and prices, with subtotals, VAT calculations, totals and so on. This is information which will help you balance your bank statement, plan your finances and future purchases and so on.

(b) The supermarket assistant has the same information, allowing him or her to take the immediate action of asking for the required amount of money: the system may even convert the data into printed details on your cheque. At the end of the day, the takings (cash, cheques and so on) can be reconciled with the totals from the tills, for the purposes of financial control. Details, including VAT totals, will be entered in the accounts.

(c) The supermarket's managers may need different types of information from the system. A computerised point-of-sale system may be able to process the simple sales data gathered over time, to show things like:

  (i)   what stock needs to be replenished on the shelves as a result of sales; what stock needs to be replenished in the storerooms or warehouses, as a result of waning supplies and fast usage rates; (this is called stock or inventory control);

  (ii) which product lines are selling well, and which badly; earnings (and therefore profit margins) of particular product lines;

  (iii) buying patterns of customers: which are the busiest days, or times of day; which products people tend to buy in multiples or large quantities; whether people buy a high proportion of goods on special offer and so on;

  (iv) whether customers pay most by cash, cheque or debit card.

Activity 6 [20 minutes]

What kind of decisions might be based on the information given in (c)? Give an example relating to each of (c)(i) – (iv) above.

You may have noticed that an MIS can process data to provide information for all levels of decision-making and planning.

Operational level MIS

Operational decisions are essentially every-day, small-scale and largely routine. They are sometimes called *programmed* decisions, because they do not have to be made fresh each time, but are dictated by the procedures of which they are a part, and can usually be worked out by a computer: the variables are quantifiable and the rules for making the decision are clear cut.

An MIS at this level is usually used for processing transactions and updating files.

Tactical level MIS

Tactical decision-making is concerned with how the organisation goes about achieving its objectives, and particularly with its control systems.

An MIS at this level will tend to:

(a) gather information from a wider range of sources than an operational-level MIS, taking into account information from the external environment as well as the organisation's own processes;

(b) filter out much of the detail, which may not be required at this level: in other words, make more use of reporting by exception;

(c) investigate, analyse and otherwise process data acquired at the operational level, in order to apply it to tactical decisions. So, for example, basic sales information can be formulated for use in marketing decisions, stock supply decisions, product development decisions and so on.

Three types of formal MIS are often used at the tactical level.

(a) *Control systems* monitor and report on the organisation's activities.

(b) *Database systems* store information which can be drawn upon as and when a manager needs it. The database may consist of the organisation's own files, or information from outside the organisation (like the Internet).

(c) *Decision support systems* store and process information for the analysis of problems and the testing of possible solutions. (We will discuss this in more detail below.)

Strategic level MIS

Strategic decisions are the long-term decisions which define the organisation's purpose and direction, goals and practices. These tend to be non-repetitive, non-routine decisions, which involve a number of variables, not all of which will be clear-cut or quantifiable (values, consumer behaviour patterns and so on). Human judgement is therefore required to a much greater extent: such decisions can rarely be programmed.

An MIS at this level tends to:

(a) draw information from an even wider range of sources outside the organisation;

(b) include more informal information-gathering by managers;

(c) provide more subjective and less detailed information.

In other words different levels of MIS can be shown as follows in Figure 13.2.

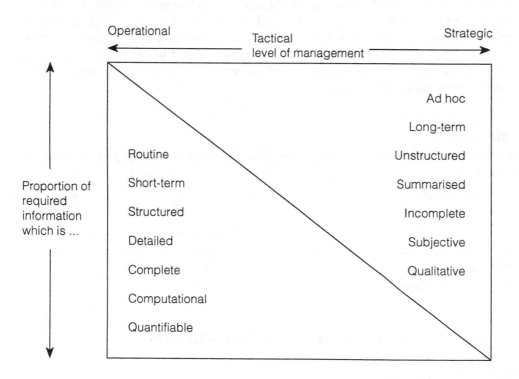

Figure 13.2 Levels of MIS

You can see that while at an operational level, the MIS may be able to make decisions which are highly structured and computational, at tactical and strategic levels this is not possible. All an MIS can do is to give managers information, and insight, into the nature and impact of their decisions.

4.2 Decision support systems (DSS)

Definition

> A *decision support system* is a (usually computerised) MIS designed to produce information in such a way as to help managers make better decisions.

When management decisions are unstructured, there may be uncertainty about the nature of the problem, the range of possible solutions and the possible impact of each of those solutions, under a variety of potential conditions. Decision support systems are designed to offer highly flexible, high interactive, information-processing capabilities, allowing such matters to be analysed. For example:

(a) *Modelling* is the term given to the techniques which represent a real situation, by depicting the interrelationships between relevant factors in the situation in a simplified and structured way. Models can be used to increase a manager's understanding of the situation in which a decision has to be made, and to help him or her evaluate alternative decisions. In effect, models allow managers to try out decisions and see what happens – without incurring any real risks.

(b) *Sensitivity analysis* is a technique which basically asks 'What if ...?': what if a particular piece of data in a decision model were changed? A manager can see what the alternative outcome of a decision would be if different assumptions were adopted. What would be the difference in profit if a higher than planned pay rise were awarded to staff, or if market share fell (or rose) by a given percentage?

(c) *Spreadsheets* are simple models which allow a manager to input a range of interrelated variables into a matrix, and to see the effect of changing one or more of them on the others. You could instantly gauge, for example, how changing the price of your raw materials would affect your cost forecasts and profit margins; how a day's slippage in the schedule for a process might affect your overall plans, and so on.

For discussion

Why should managers get paid so much, when it is the computer that makes all the tough decisions?

What do you think?

Computerised MIS have made it possible for managers to access more information than ever before. (Database software packages and the Internet are making the same kind of information 'memory bank' available to non-business users.) Is this a Good Thing?

4.3 Is more information, better information?

Information overload

It should be clear that managers can undertake no decision-making or communicating task before first *receiving* appropriate information upon which to base it. However, responsibility for the outcome of decisions can make managers seek *too much* information, rather than too little. 'Analysis paralysis' is a catchy term for the inertia that sets in when people attempt to get *all* the information they think they might need for a decision.

Most decisions are in fact based on incomplete information, because:

(a) *all* the information relevant to the decision is not available; or

(b) beyond a certain point, the gathering of *more* information would not be worth the extra time and cost of obtaining and analysing it; or

(c) beyond a certain point, the manager will be unable effectively to take in or take into account more information: (s)he will become unable to see the wood for the trees. This is sometimes called information *overload*.

Providers of management information need to bear in mind that information overload is counter-productive and a waste of resources. Managers (especially at the strategic level) rarely want or need to know as much *detail* as the people lower down the hierarchy, for whom detailed, short-term information is the staple diet of their jobs. The marketing assistant in charge of handling customer queries will need to take in all details of customers' experience with the product, retail outlet or whatever: the marketing director, however, might require only a summary of the number and nature of complaints, or whether they were getting more or less serious/frequent, in order to devise better customer care policies, or to reward staff for improvements.

Management information should therefore be:

(a) *summarised*, or otherwise processed in order to be easily digestible and relevant to its purpose;

(b) provided *by exception*: sparing managers routine, expected, repetitive and irrelevant information, but initiating feedback and reporting in the event of relevant new inputs of information or variance from the routine or plan.

So what is 'good' information?

Here is a brief checklist of ten qualities of good information.

QUALITIES OF GOOD INFORMATION

1 It should be *relevant* for its purpose.

2 It should be *complete* for its purpose.

3 It should *sufficiently accurate* for its purpose. (Information should always be as correct as possible, however it need not always be completely *accurate*, in the sense that an approximation – 'about 100 labour hours' – may be all that is required, rather than figures to the last decimal place ...)

4 It should be *clear* to the user.

5 The user should be able to have *confidence* in it. (It should appear logical, well-researched and supported and so on.)

6 It should be communicated to the *right person*. (The one who needs and can use it to do a job.)

7 There should be no *more* than the user can take in and use.

8 It should be *timely* (ie provided at the right time to be used for its intended purpose).

9 It should be communicated by *appropriate media and channels*.

10 It should be provided at a cost which is less than the value of its benefits to the user/organisation.

> ## Chapter roundup
>
> - Information is the lifeblood of organisations, and the basis for management planning, control, co-ordinating, organising and commanding.
> - Organisations have formal communication systems and channels to ensure that required information exchange takes place. There is also an informal communication system or network(s) in every organisation.
> - Organisational communication can be:
>   - downward (orders, instructions, briefings, motivation, appraisal etc)
>   - upward (reporting, briefings, suggestions, upward appraisal etc)
>   - horizontal (teambuilding, co-ordination, informal etc)
> - Managers need to master basic communication formats such as memos and reports.
> - Management Information Systems (MIS) collect data and convert them into information relevant to managers at all levels, to help them carry out the tasks for which they are responsible. Decision support systems (DSS) are specifically designed to help managers analyse and evaluate their decisions.

Quick quiz

1 Give four examples of (a) managers' and (b) team members' information needs.

2 What is meant by communication which is:

(a) upward;

(b) downward;

(c) horizontal?

3 What is the 'grapevine', and what is it like?

4 What are the advantages and disadvantages of giving orders or briefings by telephone?

5 What two qualities must instructions have in order to be fulfilled satisfactorily?

6 What should be included in instructions for a complex task?

7 What might be covered in regular 'team briefings'?

8 Name the two important considerations when team briefing.

9 Give three examples of positive reinforcement in downward communication.

10 What are the main purposes of upward communication in organisations?

11 List the headings you might use in a typical (a) formal and (b) informal report.

12 Why is there a need for a formal management information system?

13 By what other name can an 'operational decision' be called?

14 What is the difference between data and information?

15 List the ten qualities of good information.

Answers to quick quiz

1 (a) Information is needed to establish objectives, suggest adjustment of performance, appraise available resources and guide planning.

(b) Information is needed to perform tasks effectively, and for motivation, learning, development and job satisfaction.

2 (a) From subordinate to superior.

(b) From superior to subordinate.

(c) Between individuals, teams, departments on the same level of the organisation chart.

3 It is an informal network of gossip and rumours.

4 Advantages are that it cuts down on time and physical movement. Disadvantages are that only one person is reached at a time, there are no non-verbal signals and it is more difficult to persuade and to respond to physical factors.

5 They must be clear and sufficient.

6 Desired results, definition of all relevant terms, a breakdown of the task into logical components, all the information needed to understand and carry out the task.

7 Organisational policy and changes, plans, progress, results.

8 The purpose of communication and the needs and abilities of the audience.

9 Praise, encouragement and constructive criticism.

10 To give feedback, to inform and to make suggestions.

11 (a) Title, Terms of Reference, Procedure or Method, Findings, Conclusions, Recommendations.

(b) Title, Background or Introduction, Findings or Analysis, Action or Solution or Conclusion or Recommendations.

12 The right managers get the right information at the right time in the right format.

13 A programmed decision.

14 Refer to the definition in section 4.1.

15 Refer to section 4.3, page 243.

Answers to Activities

By using the book's index you would come up with the following.

1 *Figurehead*: Giving a speech at a trade conference.

Leader: Walking around the office giving praise and encouragement.

Liaison: Maintaining contact with suppliers and customers.

Monitor: Gathering feedback and reports from team members.

Disseminator: Handing out information on objectives and results.

Spokesman: Representing the team at committee or management meetings; reporting on its performance.

Entrepreneur: Listening to suggestions for opportunities, negotiating for resources, communicating ideas.

Disturbance-handler: Counselling and conflict-resolution interviews/meetings.

Resource-allocator: Gathering information on objectives and feedback on progress.

Negotiator: 'Bargaining' meetings with senior management over budget, or staff representatives over productivity.

2 Amongst other information, an organisation would need to give out the following.

1 Products/services: to customers and potential customers in the market place.

2 Needs and expectations (specifications, orders, requests for estimates and so on): to suppliers, potential suppliers, sub-contractors etc.

3 Terms and conditions of payment for products/services (eg invoices and statements): to customers.

4   Labour requirements, and what the organisation can offer as an employer: to potential employees in the labour pool.

5   Financial performance and plans: to the owners (shareholders), creditors (those to whom it owes money) and other stakeholders.

6   Records and digests of financial transactions – reports and returns: to auditors, the Inland Revenue, Customs and Excise etc as required by law and regulation.

7   The workforce and employment practices: to agencies such as the Health and Safety Executive, Training Commission or trade unions. Also a highly regulated area.

8   The organisation's mission and culture: to the world in general.

3   Since the grapevine exists, and cannot be got rid of, management should learn both to accept it and to use it: to harness it towards achieving the objectives of the organisation. It is important for managers themselves to 'hook into' the grapevine, to be aware of what is going on – and what their subordinates think is going on. The grapevine may also be a useful way of 'feeding' information to staff, where the formal system would be mistrusted, or too slow.

4   You will have put in your own details in your memo answering Mr Bossere, but check that you have the same headings that he used, and that you have answered all three of his questions.

5   Your report to the manager could be on the following lines.

REPORT
RECREATION AND REFRESHMENT FACILITIES

I   INTRODUCTION
This report was compiled by [Your Name] at the request of [Manager's Name], and submitted on the [Date].

II   ANALYSIS OF THE SITUATION
(a) *Importance of facilities*
   (i)   Although it has not been conclusively proven that 'happy' staff are invariably more productive, there is a relationship between job satisfaction and effectiveness. Dissatisfaction can impair performance, engendering a range of negative responses and high labour turnover.
   (ii) The provision of recreation/refreshment facilities would not necessarily be an issue if it were not perceived to be so by staff. [Your Name] has reason to believe that staff do feel disadvantaged by the lack of facilities, and that morale is suffering.
   (iii) Moreover, such facilities impact on staff health: refreshment and recreation are important in the control of fatigue and stress.
   (iv) The matter is therefore worthy of the company's consideration, not only for 'humane' but for practical reasons.

(b) *Present inadequacy: refreshment*
   (i)   Provision for hot drinks is inadequate: the kitchen area is cramped and equipped only with one kettle and insufficient crockery; supplies are ill-organised. Facilities for preparing and/or storing foodstuffs are non-existent.
   (ii) There are few congenial eating-places or food-providers in the surrounding area. Take-away food is expensive, and Luncheon Vouchers not widely accepted.
   (iii) There is insufficient space for staff to take refreshments comfortably, which is less than satisfactory with potentially messy or highly aromatic foods.

(c) *Present inadequacy: recreation*
   (i)   There is no venue for informal communication between staff – except the office, where it is discouraged. The company is frustrating a potential team-building and co-ordinating activity.

Continued ...

REPORT *(continued)*

RECREATION AND REFRESHMENT FACILITIES

(ii) There is no organised encouragement of constructive recreation or relationship-building outside work.

(iii) No effort is made to encourage health and fitness through sports, nor to broaden employees' other interests.

III CONCLUSION AND RECOMMENDATIONS

(a) Without wishing to incur unnecessary expenditure, or concentrating unduly on non-work activities, the company should be concerned to review its provisions, in view of II above.

(b) A Committee should be formed to investigate measures including:

(i) food provision. An independent caterer might be engaged to offer a daily selection of sandwiches and snacks, subsidised via the Luncheon Voucher scheme;

(ii) the setting aside of a rest area, with seating, pleasant décor and extended facilities for the preparation of drinks and simple foods;

(iii) access to sports facilities and/or tickets to artistic/sporting events, which could be made cheaply available to staff.

(c) A 'Social Club' should be instituted to co-ordinate independent activities and encourage wider socialising among employees.

Signed: *Your name*

Date:

6 The supermarket might act on point-of-sale information by taking these decisions:

(i) Ordering more stock from suppliers, or increasing the standard order frequency or size.

(ii) Dropping underperforming products (or promoting them harder, with special offers etc), cutting costs on products with unacceptably low profit margins.

(iii) Encouraging shopping at 'off-peak' periods (with offers etc), designing bulk-packs of popular bulk-bought items, adjusting the terms and advertising of special offers.

(iv) Accepting more credit cards, introducing pre-printed cheques etc.

Assignment 13

[About 1¹/₂ hours]

You have been asked to give a talk to fellow students on communication in organisations. Write full notes for your talk covering the following points.

(a) The different types of communication methods generally used in an organisation and for what purposes formal communication is used.

(b) The motivational benefits gained from effective downward communication.

(c) The benefits of using MIS at the tactical level.

Chapter 14

CO-ORDINATION

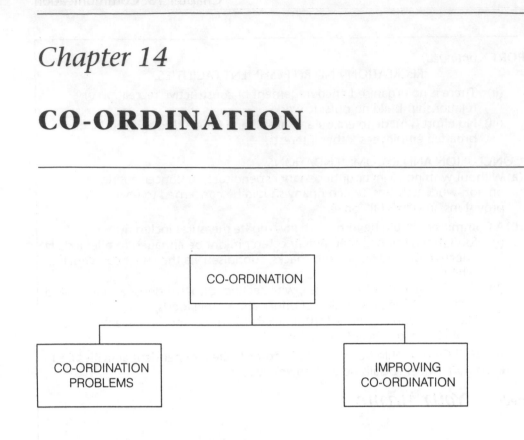

Introduction

We identified co-ordination as one of the functions of management, in Chapter 1, defining it broadly as harmonising the activities of individuals and groups toward their common objectives.

You may have noticed that the term 'co-ordination' has also cropped up throughout this section on Managing Activities. Planning, organisation and communication are three of the key factors in maintaining co-ordinated effort and resources.

In this short chapter, we will draw together these threads, by summarising why co-ordination is difficult, and what can be done to improve it.

Your objectives

After completing this chapter you should:

- understand the nature and importance of co-ordination and why it is difficult to achieve;
- be able to identify signs of poor co-ordination;
- be able to outline strategies for improving co-ordination and for co-ordinating human, physical and financial resources in carrying out activities.

1 CO-ORDINATION

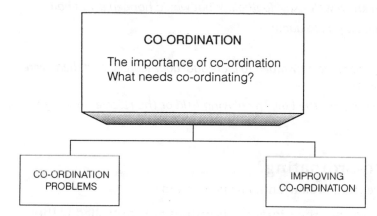

Definition

To *co-ordinate* is 'to plan, or take action to improve, the inter-relationships (especially of timing and methods of communication) between a number of various activities, which contribute to the achievement of a single objective, so that they do not conflict and the objective is achieved with a minimal expenditure of time and effort.' *(Dictionary of Management)*

1.1 The importance of co-ordination

Remember that we defined the purpose of organisations as 'the controlled performance to achieve collective goals'. This is, in essence, what co-ordination involves. Co-ordination is important because:

(a) the organisation is a collection of individuals and groups, each with their own interests and goals; these must be given a unified, common direction if the organisation as a whole is to achieve its objectives;

(b) the organisation's activities involve a variety of:
   (i) people;
   (ii) tasks;
   (iii) resources; and
   (iv) technologies

   all of these will have to be at the right place, at the right time, working in the right way, if smooth operations are to be maintained;

(c) some activities of the organisation will be dependent on the successful and timely completion of other activities (as we saw in network analysis): someone needs to ensure that such interrelationships are taken into account in the overall activity of the organisation;

(d) some activities of the organisation will be higher priority than others (as we discussed in Chapter 10): someone needs to ensure that there is an overall *balance* between urgent/high-priority activities and routine activities, on which the organisation nevertheless depends;

(e) resources (human, material and financial) are limited, and possibly scarce. Different units in the organisation are, in effect, in competition for their 'slice' of the resources available. Someone has to balance their demands and the organisation's priorities to ensure that overall, resources are used efficiently and effectively in pursuit of the organisation's goals.

For discussion

Think about a team sport you know well – say, football. What would happen if you had:

(a) no positions for each of the players to adopt?

(b) no team strategy?

(c) no team purpose – if, say, prizes were awarded to individual goal scorers, and there were no such thing as a team win?

(d) nobody in charge of providing kit, the ball, the playing field or the referee on a regular basis?

1.2   What needs co-ordinating?

From the above, we can see that, broadly, managers co-ordinate:

(a) the *timing* of activities, so that their inter-relationships are controlled without wasted time or bottlenecks;

(b) the *direction* or *purpose* of activities, so that sub-units of the organisation pull together towards common objectives, and the relative priority of activities are balanced;

(c) the *resources* (human, financial and material) required for activities, so that each sub-unit of the organisation is able to do what it should, when it should.

Activity 1   [20 minutes]

(a) Can you immediately think of some techniques we have already discussed which might help a business in each of these areas?

(b) Give an example of a problem arising from failure to co-ordinate in each of these areas.

---

2   CO-ORDINATION PROBLEMS

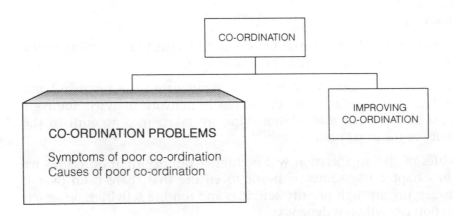

2.1   Symptoms of poor co-ordination

A manager might be alerted to problems of co-ordination by the following tell-tale signs.

(a) Complaints from clients, customers and other external parties, indicating that products are not being supplied on time, or that they have been given different information by different departments of the organisation.

(b) Production problems, with alternating overloads and idle time, and associated problems with labour resourcing and production costs. (The equivalent for service organisations might be missed deadlines or commitments to customers, internal paperwork failing to reach the right people at the right time and so on.)

(c) Persistent conflict within and between departments, especially the placing of blame for problems, and empire-building and power games in place of co-operation.

(d) Lack of communication between units of the organisation.

(e) Appeals to rules and red tape in an attempt to give the appearance of integrated activity.

2.2 Causes of poor co-ordination

Some of the major causes of poor co-ordination are as follows.

(a) *Poor communication* – both vertically and horizontally – so that units do not know what they are supposed to be doing, or what other units are doing, or how the two are meant to be related.

(b) *Inadequate planning and control*, so that the objectives of each unit are not clearly understood, or integrated with those of other units, within overall objectives.

(c) *Weak organisation structure*, which does not make the inter-relationships between units clear, or link them via the chain of command. This problem will be particularly acute where the organisation's task requires interdependent input across the boundaries of departments and functions.

(d) *Interpersonal and/or interdepartmental conflict*. Power and resources are limited in organisations, and there is frequently competition, rivalry, jealousies, the guarding of 'territory' and information and so on, to protect the interests of individuals and groups. This kind of activity is known as organisational politics.

(e) *Differences* between the cultures and tasks of different units. These may be differences in:
 (i) the time pressures a unit works under;
 (ii) the leadership style of the units' managers;
 (iii) the technology used by the units;
 (iv) the methods of working adopted by the units;
 (v) the culture or values of the units;

 and so on.

Activity 2 [20 minutes]

Give an example of each of the types of difference between cultures and tasks of different units suggested above, which might cause problems of co-ordination.

---

3 IMPROVING CO-ORDINATION

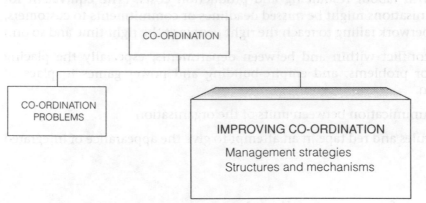

3.1 Management strategies

The role of the manager in co-ordinating the efforts of his or her team – and in co-ordinating them with other teams in the organisation – will be much along the lines we have already discussed in this section on Managing Activities.

Maintaining and improving communication

Communication is essential for co-ordination, ensuring that:

(a) the inter-relationship of activities and plans is understood;

(b) variations from plan in one activity are notified to, and taken into account by, other units;

(c) conflict and organisational politics are not allowed to develop, to obstruct the common goals of the organisation.

Managers should give attention to horizontal, as well as vertical, communication.

Activity 3   [20 minutes]

Suggest three ways in which a manager might encourage *horizontal* communication.

If you need to refresh your memory on organisational communication, briefly review Chapter 13, Section 1.

Planning

Systematic planning and control is essential for co-ordination. Tasks need to be sequenced and scheduled in a way that:

(a) balances their relative urgency and priority;

(b) takes into account their inter-relationships and the dependency of one task on another;

(c) allows resources to be rationally allocated on the basis of priorities and overall objectives; and

(d) allows the plans and schedules of each unit to be integrated with those of other units, towards the organisation's overall objectives.

If you need to refresh your memory on planning and associated techniques, briefly review Chapters 10–12.

Controlling conflict

Managers should try to create conditions in which individuals and departments are able to co-operate instead of conflict.

If you need to refresh your memory on conflict and conflict control, briefly review Chapter 5, section 3.

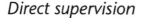

Direct supervision

The manager occupies a co-ordinating role within his or her own section, as the central person responsible for all the work of the group: issuing instructions, monitoring performance and so on.

3.2 Structures and mechanisms

As well as using the co-ordinating function of managers, an organisation can aid co-ordination through its structures and various formal mechanisms.

Organisation structure

The organisation structure may be designed to provide:

(a) *a co-ordinating level of management.* Just as the individual manager acts as the 'lynchpin' of co-ordination for his own unit, so he has a superior who is responsible for co-ordinating his work with that of other units, see Figure 14.1;

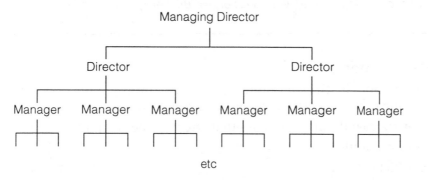

Figure 14.1 Co-ordinating levels of management

(b) *liaison or integration officers* – for example, project co-ordinators, client liaison managers and so on. These posts essentially encourage communication;

(c) *multi-disciplinary teams*, committees, project groups and so on. These are matrix structures, including representation from all departments involved in a given task or activity, with a co-ordinating authority (a project manager, say) crossing functional boundaries.

Standardisation

Standardisation is an important mechanism for co-ordinating work at the operational level: it involves getting people to do things the same way, or with the same results. This adds reliability, or predictability, to work processes, allowing them to be more closely co-ordinated and controlled.

(a) *Standardisation of work processes* is possible for routine tasks, where the actual content of the task is specified or programmed. For example, think about the assembly instructions for a model or piece of furniture, or the operation of a video recorder: the task is designed to be done in the same way, regardless of who is doing it. Standardisation of forms and documents is another important aid to consistency and co-ordination.

(b) *Standardisation of output* is possible for more complex tasks, where discretion is needed in performing the work. The organisation may set standards for design, quality, cost and so on, so that its product or service is consistent, regardless of who does the work and how.

(c) *Standardisation by skill and knowledge* is possible for complex and varied work, which nevertheless requires a certain standard of performance. So, for example, a hospital sets standard requirements for the qualifications of its doctors, as an accountancy firm does for its accountants and so on.

EXAMPLE

McDonald's fast food restaurants are highly standardised in terms of work processes and outputs. This helps them to control consistency of food quality and specification in their outlets spread worldwide. You don't get lettuce in a McDonald's hamburger in the UK, because it is not possible for every hamburger made worldwide to contain lettuce, due to local variations in supply.

For discussion

How well co-ordinated is the course you are on? (Consider how 'smooth' your timetable is: clashes? bottlenecks? idle time? How consistent is the teaching and course material? Is there a course leader or co-ordinator, and what is his or her function?)

Chapter roundup

- Co-ordination is the harmonising of the timing, direction and resourcing of various activities towards a common objective.
- Improving co-ordination requires that attention be given to:
  — communication
  — conflict control
  — integrated planning
  — integrating organisation structures and
  — standardisation

Quick quiz

1 Give three reasons why co-ordination is necessary.
2 Give three examples of the symptoms of poor co-ordination.
3 Why is conflict detrimental to co-ordination, and why does it arise?
4 Why is (a) communication and (b) planning helpful to co-ordination?
5 What can be 'standardised' in order to co-ordinate activities at an operational level?

Answers to quick quiz

1 There must be a common direction for the organisation to achieve its goals; co-ordination also helps to maintain smooth operations and to balance high priority work with routine tasks.
2 Complaints, production problems, persistent conflict.

3 Conflict destroys co-operation. It can arise from blaming others for problems, from empire building and from power games.

4 (a) Communication ensures that the inter-relationship of activities and plans is understood, that variations are notified and that conflict is not allowed to develop.

(b) Planning prioritises, understands the dependency of one task on another, allows resources to be rationally allocated and integrates, plans and schedules.

5 Work processes, output, design, quality cost, skill and knowledge.

Answers to Activities

1 Co-ordination techniques, and problems that might arise if an organisation does not co-ordinate, include the following

(a) *Timing*: scheduling, network analysis, Gantt charts.

Direction: planning and goal-setting, priority-setting, work breakdown, network analysis.

Resources: network analysis, resource allocation charts, budgets.

(b) *Timing*: the costing department is 'behind' in its analysis of production employees' time sheets, leaving the payroll department without the information required to prepare and pay the wages.

Direction: the marketing department is trying to sell an 'upmarket' image of the product, while the production department is trying to increase profits by cutting down on 'frills' and packaging.

Resources: the organisation does not have enough trained staff to cope with a peak work period; there are insufficient components in store to complete a given production order on time.

2 Differences between culture and tasks might cause co-ordination problems for the reasons below.

(i) The implementation of a computer system (devised over a period of months or years) by a project group, in an operational department with tight time schedules for ongoing work.

(ii) The manager of one unit may inform his team of decisions, while the manager of the other consults her team, resulting in different approaches. The clash of style may also prevent effective communication between the two managers.

(iii) Incompatible computer systems in two departments, preventing them from sharing information easily.

(iv) Two departments using different forms for the same purpose, making it difficult to share data, and encouraging different approaches (eg different criteria in staff assessment forms), which may become sources of conflict.

(v) One unit dedicated to serving the customer at all costs, another dedicated to saving costs, and never mind the customer!

3 Horizontal communication might be beneficial if a manager encouraged in the following ways.

(a) Not discouraging *informal* communication at work – even encouraging it, by providing an environment where people can talk during breaks and so on.

(b) Teambuilding and empowerment, so that people do not see themselves as individuals in competition with other individuals, but as teams who must communicate freely in order to do their jobs.

(c) Appointing team members to interdisciplinary or joint team meetings, so that they can exchange information with people at the same level but in different areas of the organisation.

Assignment 14 [About 1¹/₂ hours]

Pence & Sons Ltd. have received a number of complaints from customers about poor delivery and conflicting information from different departments.

They are already aware of internal problems where parts have not been available on time, resulting in machines and operatives standing idle. The sales team have been carrying out a sales drive and the number of orders has increased significantly. This has meant that, because of the holdups waiting for parts, overtime has been increased.

(a) What are the likely results of the present situation?

(b) What should management do in order to improve efficiency and effectiveness?

Chapter 15

REVIEW AND MONITORING

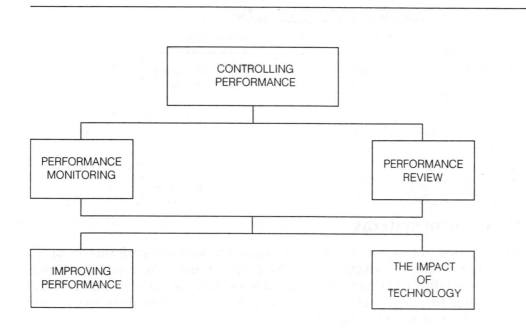

Introduction

In Chapter 10 we saw that planning and organising are closely linked with control: the process whereby performance and results are monitored, compared with plans, schedules and budgets, and adjusted if necessary.

In this chapter, we discuss aspects of the organisation's control systems, and then, specifically, some of the techniques managers use to *review* the effectiveness of procedures, projects and tasks and to continuously *monitor* their progress and efficiency. This is obviously linked to employee appraisal and individual/team performance monitoring, which we discussed in Chapter 7, but the emphasis here is on methods of working and managing tasks, rather than on the performance of the people involved. We do not attempt to tackle the appraisal of the *economic* performance of the organisation, as it lies beyond the scope of this module.

Your objectives

After completing this chapter you should:

- be able to define a control system, and suggest organisational examples;
- be aware of performance standards and indicators that you might use to evaluate your own effectiveness and that of others;
- be able to describe techniques of performance review, including method study, systems analysis and value analysis;
- be able to suggest how performance can be continuously monitored;
- be aware of the impact of technology on the review and monitoring of performance;
- be able to suggest how performance might be improved as a result of monitoring and review.

1 CONTROLLING PERFORMANCE

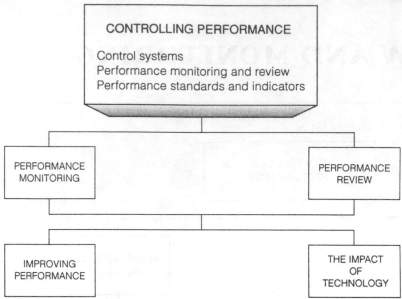

CONTROLLING PERFORMANCE

Control systems
Performance monitoring and review
Performance standards and indicators

PERFORMANCE MONITORING

PERFORMANCE REVIEW

IMPROVING PERFORMANCE

THE IMPACT OF TECHNOLOGY

1.1 Control systems

As we discussed in Chapter 10, *control* is required to keep the performance of the organisation steady. Unpredictable disturbances continually affect the organisation system, so that its actual results deviate from its expected results or goals. A control system is used to ensure that the organisation is aware of these disturbances, and deals with them in an appropriate manner.

Activity 1   [20 minutes]

Give four examples of 'disturbances' to the smooth, planned operation of a business.

Control is achieved by setting standards and plans, monitoring actual performance, comparing actual performance with the standards or plans, and making any necessary adjustments to bring the two back into line.

A simple model of a control system may be drawn as in figure 15.1.

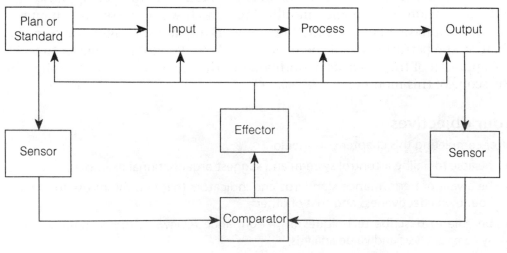

Figure 15.1 Control system

(a) The basis of any control system is the *standard* or *plan*; control will be exercised to ensure that this is adhered to.

(b) A *sensor* is the device by which information about performance is collected and measured, or the person who does the collection and measuring.

(c) A *comparator* is the means by which the actual results of the system are measured against the pre-determined plans or standards. In a business organisation, comparative information might be provided by computers in the form of management reports. Managers, however, will also be comparators: they are expected to make decisions on the results of the comparison.

(d) An *effector* initiates control action. In a production department, an effector may be a component in some automatic equipment which regulates the functioning of the equipment (for example, a thermostat). An effector may also be a manager's instruction and a subordinate's action.

Types of control

Most organisations have formal control systems in place to control performance in the following areas.

(a) *Budgetary control*

Definition

A *budget* is a statement of desired performance, usually expressed in financial terms (expenditure, revenue, profit and so on).

An organisation will have budgets for each area of operation (production, sales, research and so on) as well as for each department: all these are drawn up into the master budget of the organisation. Budgetary control is the process whereby actual figures are entered against budgeted figures for each item and period, so that variances can be identified and dealt with.

(b) *Inventory or stock control*. This system monitors the usage of the organisation's stock of raw materials, components and other temporarily 'idle' resources, in order to determine how much new stock will need to be ordered or made, and how frequently, or when. A typical stock control system triggers reordering when stock falls to a certain level, taking into account the time required to get new stock in: stock is therefore kept between a maximum desirable level (since it costs money to hold idle stock) and a safe minimum level (to meet demand without delay).

(c) *Production control* is concerned with ensuring that production programmes are satisfying demand with efficient use of resources. It involves scheduling, resource allocation and the monitoring of progress so that corrective action can be taken in the event of unexpected delays, shortages or bottlenecks.

(d) *Quality control* is the system concerned with ensuring that output (products and/or services) meet the standards set by the organisation. This is usually done by sampling output: if a certain proportion of sub-standard items is found, control action is triggered.

There may not be systems in place to offer feedback on performance in every situation. This is where performance monitoring and review come in.

1.2   Performance monitoring and review

As 'sensor' in a control system, the manager needs to gather information about his or her unit's performance, for comparison with the unit's plans and budgets. This may be done in two basic ways.

(a) Performance monitoring: 'keeping an eye' on progress, on an ongoing basis. Managers should constantly gather formal and informal control information. Progress may be monitored through observation, reports from team members or control systems, progress meetings, sampling of output quality and so on.

(b) Performance review: taking a look at results and/or methods used in a given period. This may be a major exercise, carried out only every few years: for example a method study reviewing the systems and procedures of the organisation. It may be a regular procedure carried out at six monthly or annual intervals: for example employee appraisals, or the preparation of the annual report and accounts. Or it may be a kind of 'post mortem' examination of the success of a particular project or task, on its completion.

Activity 2 [20 minutes]

Think about your work for this course. Identify three methods by which it is monitored.

We will be discussing some techniques of performance monitoring and reviewing in the following sections of this chapter, but first, we will look briefly at performance standards and indicators. What is a manager actually looking for when (s)he monitors and reviews performance? How does (s)he know whether and how far the unit has in fact been successful?

1.3 Performance standards and indicators

What is a manager looking for that would indicate that successful performance has been achieved? As usual, 'it all depends'.

In *general* terms, there are certain attributes of successful performance which can be measured. (Rather neatly, they all begin with the letter 'e', as you will see below.) In *specific* terms, the manager should be measuring performance against clearly-defined goals and standards set out (hopefully) in the organisation's, and various units', plans and budgets.

The desirable 'E' factors of organisational performance are as follows.

(a) *Effectiveness*. Generally, objectives in this area relate to the firm's ability to serve the needs of its owners and its chosen market. For example:
   (i) market share of a specified market
   (ii) quality of product or service
   (iii) financial performance.

(b) *Efficiency*. Objectives in this area are to do with how resources should be used to achieve the goals of the firm. For example:
   (i) materials and energy usage and wastage rates
   (ii) speed of response to customer enquiries and orders
   (iii) completion of projects on time
   (iv) productivity per person/hour, or per machine/hour.

(c) *Economy* concerns the financial aspects of the firm's operations and flows from the earlier objectives. For example:
   (i) cost per unit
   (ii) contribution per unit.

(d) *Elegance*. Doing things the 'right way'. For example:
   (i) appearance of business premises and staff
   (ii) punctuality and professionalism of service
   (iii) appearance of corporate literature and communications.

(e) *Ethicality* concerns the firm's adherence to its social responsibilities and to business ethics. For example:
   (i) impact of operations on the natural environment
   (ii) hiring and promotion of staff from minority groups
   (iii) non-reliance on contracts with military or political connotations.

The organisation as a whole will have specific *financial* performance indicators, including:

(a) profitability (and value added);

(b) return on capital employed (ROCE) or return on investment (ROI);

(c) survival, and/or growth; and

(d) growth in earnings per share (EPS) or dividend payments to shareholders.

In addition, there may be *non-financial* performance indicators, to do with:

(a) the maintenance of product or service quality;

(b) the image and 'position' of the organisation and its products in the market-place;

(c) innovation – new ideas and products;

(d) the organisation's ability to attract and retain highly-skilled labour;

(e) the efficiency and effectiveness of the organisation's systems and management;

(f) the social responsibility of the organisation.

Activity 3 [30 minutes]

Give an example of a specific goal in (a) to (f) immediately above, which a manager might use as a yardstick for monitoring and review.

Clearly, *goal-setting* is essential to performance monitoring and review. If sub-units of the organisation have coherent and specific goals and targets, the extent to which those goals and targets are reached will be a helpful indicator of successful performance.

EXAMPLE

In 1989, British Airways publicity indicated the following corporate goals.

(a) Safety and security.

(b) Strong and consistent financial performance.

(c) Global reach.

(d) Superior services.

(e) Good value for money.

(f) Healthy working environment.

(g) Good neighbourliness.

'Overall, our aim is to be the best and most successful company in the airline industry.'

We will now look at some of the techniques organisations use for the monitoring and review of performance.

2 PERFORMANCE MONITORING

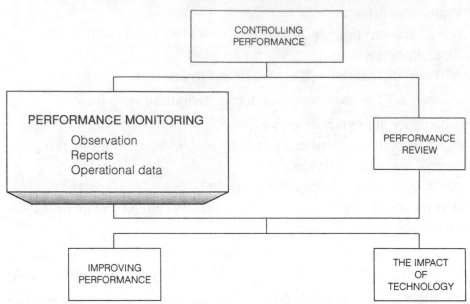

2.1 Observation

Managers may monitor performance by watching operations as they are carried out, or delegating such monitoring to a trained observer.

Task inspection

If the work is repetitive and directly observable, the observer may:

(a) time particular tasks, logging when work is handed out and when it is returned completed; or

(b) record levels of output.

These figures can be compared with standard times or levels (determined by previous study or published standards).

This is obviously time-consuming for the manager or supervisor doing the monitoring. It may also be impractical where:

(a) there is a wide variety of work being done;

(b) large numbers of people are involved in the work;

(c) a long time period is required to study a single 'cycle' of the work;

(d) the work is infrequent;

(e) the work is not readily observable – such as planning.

Activity 4   **[20 minutes]**

Can you think of reasons why staff may not welcome task inspection as a method of performance monitoring?

Activity sampling

Activity sampling means taking a number of observations during the work cycle at random predetermined intervals. In this way, activity can be monitored with reasonable accuracy (since, statistically, the sample should reflect the whole) – without having to stand at the work-place for long hours taking observations. This technique (also known as 'work sampling'), has proved particularly useful for varied work such as that in offices, canteens, warehouses and supermarkets.

2.2 Reports

Instead of attempting direct observation, the manager may monitor performance via reports from operators, and others involved in the task.

As we have discussed elsewhere, reporting *by exception* should be the norm in any control system, so that the monitoring process only brings to the manager's attention *variances* from what (s)he expected and planned to happen. However, a manager may wish to monitor specific aspects of the work, such as time spent on particular tasks, or fluctuations in output, and may request reports on such matters at any time, or on a regular basis.

Time sheets

Staff or supervisors may simply be asked to estimate how things are going, how long a task is taking and so on, from their experience.

Time and diary sheets are a more precise way of keeping track of the allocation and duration of tasks, provided that they are conscientiously maintained and truthful. Sheets are filled in on a daily or weekly basis and summarised for each individual or group to show amounts of time actually spent on various activities. This is particularly useful for activities which cannot be measured in output terms, only in time spent – eg answering phones, talking to supervisors, taking dictation, dealing with visitors, or running errands.

Similar monitoring can be carried out electronically, using computers. A clock-in, clock-out system may be used to log how long an individual spends at work, or on a particular task. Computers can also produce reports of who spent how long doing what. They can even, for example, count the number of keystrokes per minute made by a wordprocessor operator on the keyboard, and print out a report for the supervisor if the keying-in rate falls below a standard level!

Surveys

If performance criteria relate to service, such as staff attitude and friendliness, responsiveness, clarity of information, professionalism and so on, the monitoring mechanism may need to be a *customer survey*. Although management inspection may indicate some areas for approval or improvement, ultimately it is the impression given to the customer that matters.

Performance criteria related to being a responsible and desirable employer might likewise be monitored using *staff attitude surveys*, or staff feedback meetings.

2.3 Operational data

Operations will already have produced a number of records and documents, such as production and sales charts, accounts, order forms, customer complaint forms, stock requisitions and records and so on. These are not the same as management reports: they are designed primarily to provide and record data which are used in transactions and operations. However, a manager can also use them as management information about the level of output, materials usage, performance to schedule, quality problems and so on.

Activity 5 [40 minutes]

The British Airports Authority includes the following service quality factors in its performance monitoring programme. For each, what mechanism of measurement do you think they use?

Service quality factor	Measure	Mechanism
(a) Access	Ease of finding way round	
(b) Aesthetics	Staff appearance	
	Airport appearance	
	Quality/appearance of food	
(c) Comfort	Crowdedness of airport	
(d) Communication	Information clarity	
	Clarity of labelling and pricing	
(e) Friendliness	Staff attitude and helpfulness	
(f) Reliability	Number of equipment faults	
(g) Security	Efficiency of security checks	
	Number of urgent safety reports	

3 PERFORMANCE REVIEW

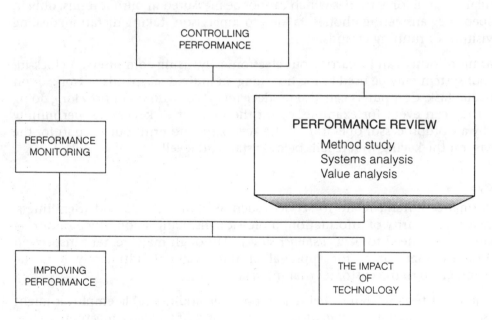

3.1 Method study

Definition

Method study is the systematic recording and critical examination of existing and proposed ways of doing work, as a means of developing and applying easier and more effective methods and reducing costs.

Method study is concerned with how work could and should be done more efficiently. This may include concerns such as organisation structure, work environment, the co-ordination and economical use of resources, the streamlining of systems and procedures and so on.

In America, method study (also called 'organisation and method' study, or 'O & M') is known as *work simplification*.

The approach to a full-scale method study is as follows.

(a) Establish an area for investigation.

(b) Establish terms of reference (say to improve productivity by 10%, or to find how the work force in a department can take on certain extra work without increasing staff numbers).

(c) Investigate the existing methods by:
  (i)   observation of procedures, forms and so on in action;
  (ii) discussion with people involved;
  (iii) studying existing records, such as procedure manuals, job specifications and so on.

(d) Record the existing methods, by narrative, or using charts and diagrams (as discussed below).

(e) Analyse the existing methods, identify weaknesses and strengths, develop alternative methods and discuss these with the operations staff and management affected.

(f) Develop an alternative method, and recommend it for implementation.

(g) If accepted, install and later review and develop the new method as necessary.

There are a number of ways of recording data on existing methods.

Narrative notes

Narrative notes (that is, an ordinary written description) have the advantage of being simple to record but are awkward to change. The purpose of the notes is to describe and explain the system, at the same time making any comments or criticisms which will help to deepen your understanding how it works. Notes need to cover:

(a) what functions are performed when, how and by whom;

(b) what documents and records are used and where they 'go' at each stage;

(c) what resources are required by the system, and where they travel in the course of the operation.

Flow charts

Flow process charts record the sequence of events and movements using certain common symbols. Five symbols have been internationally agreed and are in general use, see figure 15.2.

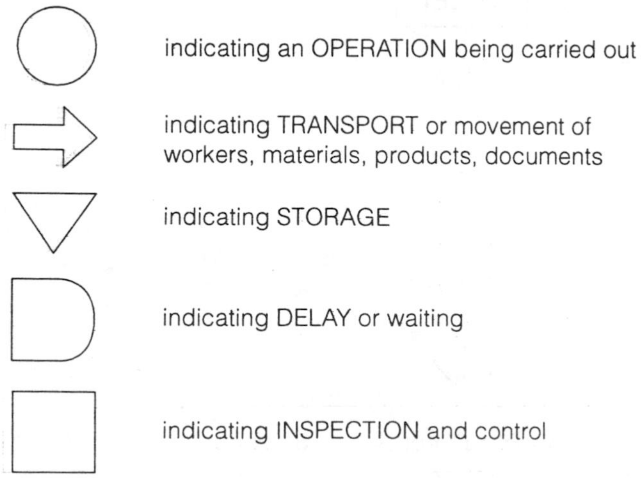

○ indicating an OPERATION being carried out

⇨ indicating TRANSPORT or movement of workers, materials, products, documents

▽ indicating STORAGE

D indicating DELAY or waiting

▢ indicating INSPECTION and control

Figure 15.2 Flow chart symbols

Flow charts can be:

(a) *man* type, recording what an operator does;

(b) *machine* type, recording how equipment is used;

265

(c) *material* type, recording what happens to materials; or

(d) *document* type, showing how documents or other information are moved around within a system.

The symbols are linked, usually vertically, to show the chronological sequence of events (see Figure 15.3). You could also have columns: for each type of event, say, or each department of the organisation (to show physical movements between them), or destinations of various copies of documents (to show who gets them).

Each symbol is numbered, for ease of reference. This also helps the analyst to see at a glance if there are too many delays, too much moving about, too many different operations or insufficient inspection involved in a system.

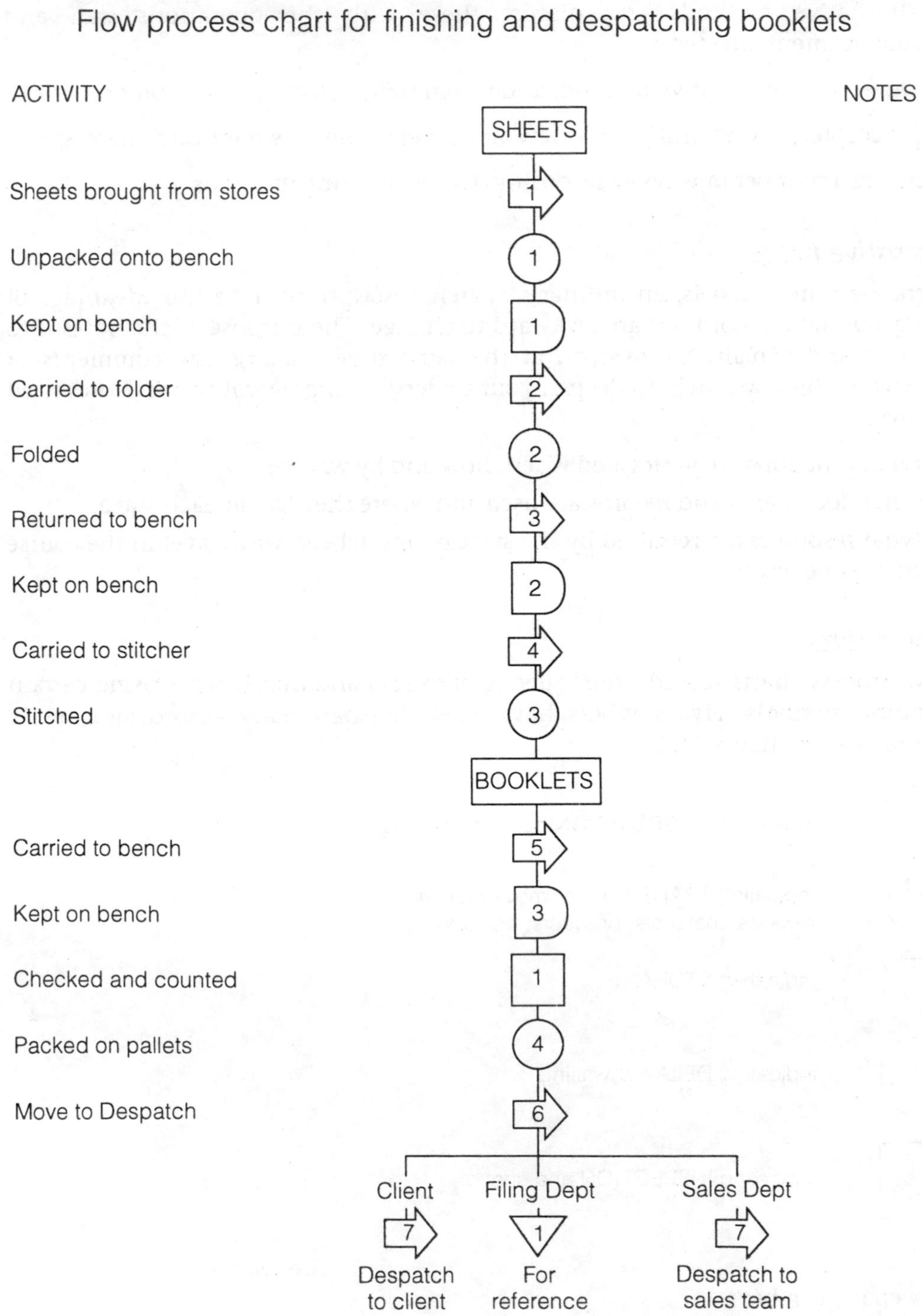

Flow process chart for finishing and despatching booklets

Figure 15.3 Chronological flow chart

Activity 6

Can you suggest any areas where efficiency could be improved, judging by figure 15.3?

Movement charts

Movements charts record physical movements or work flows.

String diagrams, for example, use a plan of the workplace, drawn to scale, with pins at certain terminal points: the routes of movement are shown by string stretched between the pins. This type of diagram will display faults in a layout which cause bottlenecks, back- or cross-tracking or other wasted movements. Below is an example: the diagram is for the preparation of a sales invoice (Figure 15.4).

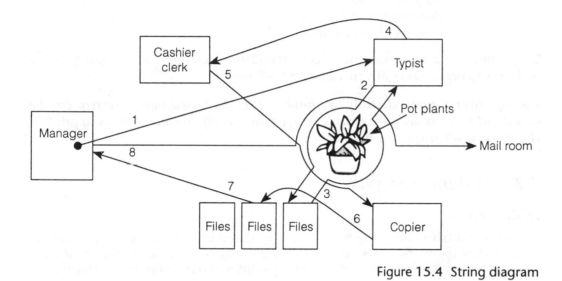

Figure 15.4 String diagram

Activity 7   [20 minutes]

Suggest *three* things that could be relocated which would make a huge difference to the efficiency of the procedure shown in Figure 15.4. (Whatever solution you suggest, redraw the chart and see how it looks!)

Analysing the existing system

Data will be analysed to evaluate:

(a) how *efficiently* the system creates, moves and stores documents and utilises available personnel and resources of time, space, equipment, materials and services;

(b) how *effective* the system is: for example, whether budgets, quality standards and deadlines are adhered to;

(c) whether the organisational structure as a whole is an effective framework for operations.

The activities in a process can be tested by asking five sets of questions:

(a) *Purpose*   What is being done?
                   Why is it being done?
                   What *else* can be done?
                   What *should* be done?

(b) *Place*   Where is it being done?
Why there?
Where *else* could it be done?
Where *should* it be done?

(c) *Person*   Who does it?
Why that person?
Who *else* might do it?
Who *should* do it?

(d) *Control*   When should it be done?
Is it within budget?
Is it of the correct quality?

(e) *Means*   How is it done?
Why that way?
How *else* could it be done?
How *should* it be done?

Once faults have been examined, recommendations can be drawn up, suggesting revisions to organisational structure or procedures.

Having covered method study, we have in fact discussed how a system can be investigated, recorded and analysed. We now, briefly, see how this is applied in the process called systems analysis.

3.2 Systems analysis

Definition

'*Systems analysis* is the process of analysing methods, procedures, sequences of activities, paperwork flows and the inputs required and outputs expected in operational or informational processing systems *which are based on computers*'.

The purpose of systems analysis is to improve existing systems or to design new systems for processing data. It is, in particular, the basis for:

(a) the selection or design of computer systems;

(b) the selection or design of appropriate applications software, or computer programming;

(c) establishing the resources required to establish and operate a new system.

The sequence of activities in a systems analysis are similar to those involved in method study.

(a) Prepare a brief, defining the objectives of and constraints on the study itself.

(b) Investigate and record data on the current systems and procedures. This is done by flowcharting, as in method study, but with a greater emphasis on:
   (i)   inputs, processing operations (compilation, analysis, calculation, checks and so on) and outputs;
   (ii) the way information is recorded and/or stored – as forms, files and so on;
   (iii) documents: what they are for, who uses them and how;
   (iv) document routes: where they originate, who sees them, how many are used, where they go and where they end up.

    We give an example of a system flow chart in Figure 15.5.

(c) Prepare a specification for the new or modified system: what it will do and, broadly, how it will do it; whether existing computers could be used; what software would be required; what the costs might be.

(d) Design a new or modified system according to the specification.

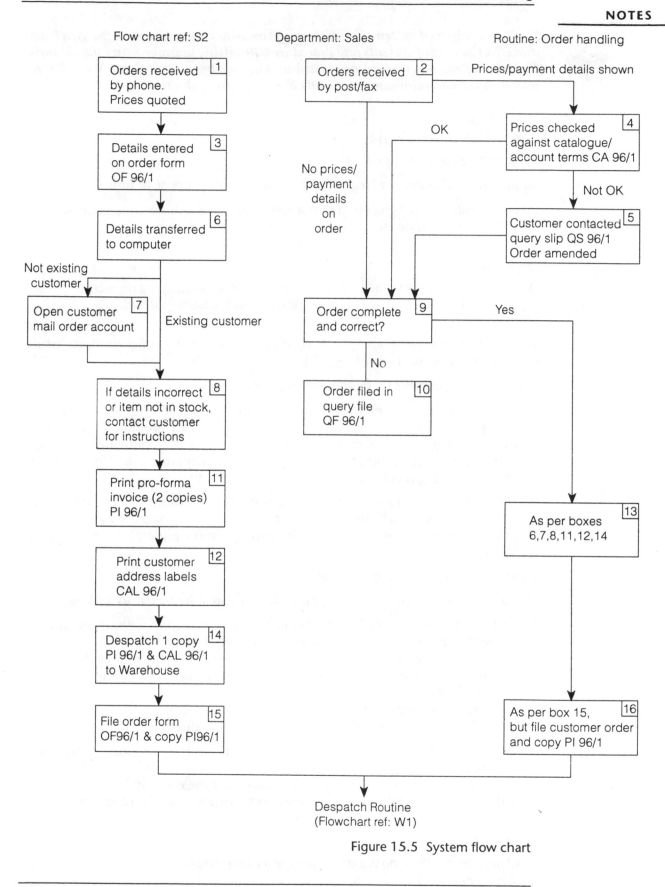

Flow chart ref: S2   Department: Sales   Routine: Order handling

1 Orders received by phone. Prices quoted

2 Orders received by post/fax

Prices/payment details shown

4 Prices checked against catalogue/ account terms CA 96/1

OK

No prices/ payment details on order

3 Details entered on order form OF 96/1

6 Details transferred to computer

Not existing customer

5 Customer contacted query slip QS 96/1 Order amended

Not OK

7 Open customer mail order account

Existing customer

9 Order complete and correct?

Yes

No

8 If details incorrect or item not in stock, contact customer for instructions

10 Order filed in query file QF 96/1

11 Print pro-forma invoice (2 copies) PI 96/1

12 Print customer address labels CAL 96/1

13 As per boxes 6,7,8,11,12,14

14 Despatch 1 copy PI 96/1 & CAL 96/1 to Warehouse

15 File order form OF96/1 & copy PI96/1

16 As per box 15, but file customer order and copy PI 96/1

Despatch Routine
(Flowchart ref: W1)

Figure 15.5 System flow chart

Activity 8   [30 minutes]

Think about applying for a job you have seen advertised in the local paper. Draw your own systems flow chart for the activities you will have to carry out.

Method study and systems analysis are primarily concerned with the efficiency and effectiveness of systems and procedures. Resulting improvements should have the effect of reducing costs – or at least making the best use of them. We will now look at a review technique specifically aimed at cost reduction.

3.3 Value analysis

Value can be classified as either:

(a) *use value* – the ability of a given item to achieve its purpose or function; or

(b) *esteem value* – the perception that a given item is worth owning, because of its status or reputation, say.

Definition

Value analysis is a cost reduction technique aimed at identifying unnecessary cost elements in an item, by analysing its function and design in detail.

The objective of value analysis is to maximise the value of a product, while minimising the cost involved.

Value analysis involves six basic stage, as follows.

(a) *Select the area(s) for analysis.* Value analysis is likely to reap greater savings (compared to the cost of carrying out the analysis) for products with a lot of parts or stages of production (some of which may be redundant), products which have 'been around' for a while without reappraisal, and products on which the margin between cost and value is currently low.

(b) *Define the product's function.* What do customers expect/want it to do? What does it do? What is it for? (The most effective definition is one with a verb and a noun: a vacuum cleaner 'removes dirt' perhaps, and a mineral water 'quenches thirst'.)

(c) *Record the components of the product.*

(d) *Calculate existing costs of making each component and the product as a whole.*

(e) *Consider alternatives which might eliminate some of these costs, without affecting the product's function or essential qualities.* Alternatives may include:
   (i)   eliminating or simplifying components, design features or operations;
   (ii) using standard parts and/or bought-in (rather than made) parts, if cheaper;
   (iii) using lower-cost materials or manufacturing processes;
   (iv) relaxing quality standards (short of affecting value).

(f) *Evaluate the alternatives and make recommendations.* There is clearly a trade-off between:
   (i) cost savings that can be made by a particular measure; and
   (ii) the extent to which the measure affects both use value and esteem value.

For discussion

What unnecessary 'frills' do you think there are on, for example:

(a) a Coca-Cola can?

(b) a Swatch watch?

(c) a top-range sports car?

(d) a food hamper from a 'quality' store like Harrods or Fortnum and Mason?

What cost savings could the manufacturers make? How would such savings affect the use value and/or the esteem value of the product?

This whole text so far has, in effect, been about improving performance: that is what managing is about. The following is a simple checklist of some of the programmes managers can implement to improve performance in three crucial areas.

4 IMPROVING PERFORMANCE

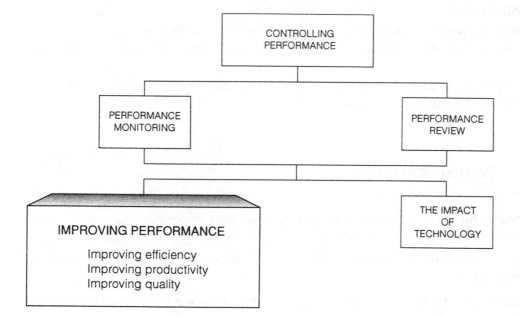

4.1 Improving efficiency

Efficiency (making best use of inputs to the organisation system) can be improved by:

(a) using method study to identify bottlenecks, unnecessary activities and poor co-ordination;

(b) eliminating unnecessary paperwork routines and forms, duplicates, checks and so on;

(c) speeding up, streamlining or redirecting work flows;

(d) solving specific problems such as bottlenecks, duplications and gaps in workload, or waste of resources;

(e) investigate opportunities for cost savings by using machines (especially for labour intensive tasks), product simplification, value analysis and so on;

(f) training staff in methodical, economical working.

4.2 Improving productivity

Productivity (the amount of output produced from organisational inputs) can be improved by:

(a) work simplification – eliminating unnecessary operations and movements;

(b) improving work environment, facilities, access and equipment – providing more efficient backup services, access to materials and tools, clear travel routes and so on;

(c) improving labour usage: employing fewer but better-quality staff, improving the skills of existing staff, improving management;

(d) better planning, scheduling, organisation, co-ordination and communication;

(e) mechanisation (speeding up human work through the use of tools and equipment) and/or automation (replacing human labour with machines or equipment);

(f) better motivation, incentives and productivity bargaining (negotiating with employee representatives to get agreement on work practices that will improve productivity in return for increased rewards).

For discussion

Malaysia has rejected 24-hour television programming, because 'studies by foreign countries have shown that all-day transmission has been a major cause of ... a plunge in productivity level'.

How broad do you think an organisation's attention to human factors can and should be, in the interest of improved performance?

4.3 Improving quality

Quality can be improved by:

(a) operating quality control and quality assurance procedures to ensure that unacceptable levels of errors/defects are identified and investigated;

(b) solving identifiable problems of control, methods, equipment, worker training and so on;

(c) training and involving workers in quality/service improvement issues;

(d) creating a culture in which quality and continuous improvement are key values;

(e) educating suppliers of materials and components, and retail outlets, in quality control and values;

(f) devoting resources to improving quality, if required.

Quality control is not a new idea, but recently it has been elevated into a philosophy that guides every activity within a business: 'total quality management', or TQM. The basic principles of TQM are:

(a) that the cost of preventing mistakes is less than the cost of correcting them, so the aim should be *to get things right first time*;

(b) that it is always possible to improve, so the aim must be *to get it more right next time*.

5 THE IMPACT OF TECHNOLOGY

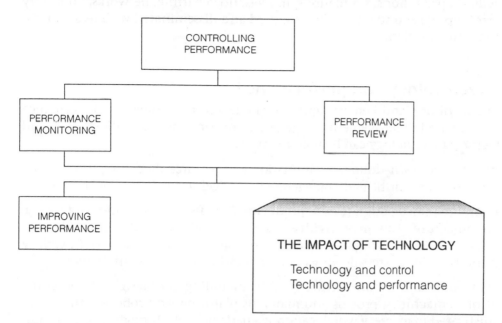

It is outside the scope of the guidelines for this module to discuss the enormous impact of information technology, in particular, on organisations and the future of work. We will merely touch on some of the applications of technology to performance review and improvement.

5.1 Technology and control

Technology can be used in the processes of performance review, monitoring and adjustment, in the role of sensor, comparator and even effector (see section 1.1 of this chapter). Computers, and related electronic systems, have had enormous impact on areas such as the following.

(a) *Automatic monitoring of processes, and the production of control reports.* We mentioned earlier the ability of word processors to monitor the keying-in performance of their operators. Similarly, think of the 'black box' recorders used in aeroplanes and trucks to monitor speed and operation. *Job reporting* by computer may be effected via terminals at each work station, linked to a central processor, which visually display job status (set up, start, interrupted, completed etc) and/or progress:

   (i)   for the manager or supervisor to allocate people or tasks to machines; and

   (ii) to notify the machine operator of his or her schedule.

(b) *Automatic monitoring and control of processes and machines.* Many manufacturing processes are now fully automated, with output and quality monitored and regulated by computers or robots.

   (i)   *Production monitoring* by computer keeps machines as smoothly and fully utilised as possible. Instruments in the machine tools are used to record the machine's on/off status, speed of operation, temperature, output rate and so on. The system can identify malfunctions or variances, produce exception reports, and adjust the operation.

   (ii) *Stock or inventory control* by computers allows usage rates and stock levels to be continuously monitored and updated; stock release to production teams, and re-ordering from suppliers, to be triggered automatically; and relevant documentation produced.

(c) *High-speed, high-volume, complex data processing for management control information.* As discussed in Chapter 13, on Management Information Systems, information technology allows data to be analysed, calculated, formatted and transmitted with far greater speed, accuracy and flexibility than is possible in human terms. Schedules, projections, simulations, models, flowcharting, networks, budgetary control reports and so on can be produced and disseminated with less and less human intervention.

5.2 Technology and performance

The same attributes and benefits apply to the use of technology in performance maintenance and improvement in general. Information technology (IT) and manufacturing technology can be used in several ways.

(a) In planning and scheduling, co-ordination and resource allocation, through the production of sophisticated management and decision-support information.

(b) In computer aided design (CAD), producing designs, drawings and data for use in manufacture. This may involve graphic models, simulation, engineering calculations and drafting and so on. It increases the organisation's flexibility and ability to innovate, allowing experimentation with different designs.

(c) In computer aided manufacture (CAM), including the design of tools, the control of machines, process and materials planning, and robotics (the use of sophisticated machinery which can move parts or tools through specified – but quite complex – sequences of motions). An integrated CAD-CAM system can be used to control entire factory operations, with great savings on labour and space, and associated costs.

(d) In the gathering, processing, storage, retrieval and communication of information. This is the greatest impact of the so-called 'second Industrial Revolution'. Electronic mail or 'E' mail allows computer users to communicate almost instantly, worldwide. The Internet allows access to a worldwide information database and communication channel. Meanwhile, even the smallest business has access to sophisticated technology in the 'electronic office'. For example:

  (i) facsimile transfer (fax) of text or graphics;
  (ii) 'smart' telephones with memory and switchboard facilities;
  (iii) wordprocessing, spreadsheet and other business application packages available off-the-shelf for use on microcomputers, or PCs;
  (iv) networks of PCs allowing the sharing of data and tasks;
  (v) the 'paperless' production and storage of data on disk; instant file retrieval and editing;
  (vi) documentation production with sophisticated text layout and graphics capabilities;

  and so on.

In all these areas, technology has the advantages of speed, capacity, versatility, reliability and accuracy. It can help the organisation to provide a faster, more accurate, more 'professional' service.

For discussion

Does technology offer the worker freedom from drudgery, a cleaner environment, an easier life, and new opportunities? Why is the introduction of technology so often resisted in the workplace?

Think about:

(a) job security – and perceived job security: do machines replace people?

(b) job interest: is the work more or less satisfying, and are the skills required more or less valuable and satisfying?

(c) personal competence and humanity: *do people feel threatened by machines, and is the environment and social system at work affected?*

(d) management and supervision: *who has a say in the planning and control of work when it is automated?*

(e) where people work: *is increased working from home, or on the move, a positive or negative experience for workers? Does it make life easier or harder for their managers?*

There are genuinely two sides to each of these questions. Try and stretch yourself to see both points of view.

Chapter roundup

- Control involves monitoring or reviewing performance, comparing actual results with expected/planned results and adjusting performance accordingly.

- A range of performance indicators and standards may be used as a yardstick for performance appraisal, including efficiency, effectiveness, economy, elegance and ethicality.

- Performance monitoring may be achieved by observation, reporting or the use of operational records.

- Performance review may be achieved using techniques such as: method study, systems analysis and value analysis.

- Technology offers benefits of speed, capacity, computational power, versatility, accuracy and predictability to the control process and also to operational and managerial processes.

Quick quiz

1 Outline two examples of control systems used in organisations.

2 Give six examples of non-financial performance indicators.

3 Give three examples of standards of ethicality.

4 Give three examples of financial performance indicators.

5 When might (a) activity sampling and (b) attitude surveys be used in performance monitoring?

6 What is 'activity sampling'?

7 What are the purposes of method study?

8 What questions are asked about an activity during a method study?

9 Name the four types of flow charts.

10 What are the four basic stages of systems analysis?

11 Distinguish between use value and esteem value.

12 What are the six basic stages of value analysis?

13 Suggest three ways of improving efficiency.

14 Give three ways in which quality can be improved.

15 Explain the terms 'production monitoring' and 'the electronic office'.

Answers to quick quiz _____

1 Budgetary control, stock control, production and quality controls.

2 Market share, quality, speed of response to customer, completion of projects on time, productivity per person/hour or per machine/hour, punctuality and professionalism.

3 Impact of operations on natural environment, hiring and promotion of staff from minority groups, non-reliance on contracts with military or political connotations.

4 Financial performance indicators include cost, profitability, return on investments, growth in earnings per share and many others..

5 (a) In varied work such as that in offices, canteens, warehouses, supermarkets.

   (b) If performance criteria relate to staff attitude, friendliness, responsiveness, clarity of information and professionalism.

6 Activity sampling means taking a representative number of observations of a work activity at random predetermined intervals.

7 It is concerned with how work could and should be done more efficiently.

8 What functions are performed when, how and by whom; what documents and records are used and where they 'go' at each stage; what resources are required by the system and where they travel in the course of it.

9 Man, machine, material, document.

10 Define objectives and constraints; investigate; record data on the current system; prepare a specification for the new system; design the new or modified system according to the specification.

11 Use value is the ability of a given item to achieve its purpose or function. Esteem value is the perception that a given item is worth owning because of its reputation or status.

12 Select areas; define product function; record product components; calculate existing costs; consider alternatives; evaluate alternatives and make recommendations.

13 Use method study, eliminate unnecessary paperwork and solve specific problems.

14 Operate quality control and quality assurance, train workers and devote resources to quality improvement.

15 Production monitoring keeps machines smoothly and fully utilised. In computerised systems all details of the machine's operations are recorded. Computers can identify malfunctions or variances and can adjust operations. Examples of an electronic office include sophisticated technology such as fax, 'smart' telephones, PCs and file storage on disk.

Answers to Activities _____

1 Obviously, there are many possible examples of disturbances to a planned business, but you may have come up with things like the entry of a powerful new competitor into the market, an unexpected rise in labour costs or scarcity of particular skills, the failure of a supplier to deliver promised materials or components, or even the tendency of employees to interrupt work for social chatter.

2 Ways in which your course is monitored include: your assignments and essays being marked; exam results; feedback from lecturers and tutors; end of year reports; and possibly peer assessment. You should, of course, be monitoring your own progress, for example by seeing whether your answers to questions in this book match up with ours (or are better than ours).

3 Goals where non financial performance indicators might be used are, for example:

   (a) less than 5% errors in output; less than 100 customer complaints per month;

   (b) market leader (biggest share of the market); 80% awareness of the organisation in the general public;

(c) 50 new products per year;

(d) lower rate of employee turnover than the industry average;

(e) a specific (low) ratio of inputs to outputs, ie efficiency in use of resources;

(f) target hirings/promotions from minority groups; target giving to community causes; reduction in complaints of infringement of regulations, eg on the environment.

4 Staff may not welcome task inspection for several reasons. Allowances may not be made for necessary interruptions, the need for rest and refreshment and so on: the staff may feel that the assessment of performance is not fair or consistent. The conspicuous nature of the monitoring may cause resentment, if staff feel they are not trusted.

5 For the given service qualities, BAA use the following mechanisms.

(a) Customer survey

(b) Customer survey; management inspection

(c) Customer survey; management inspection

(d) Customer survey; management inspection

(e) Customer survey; management inspection

(f) Internal fault monitoring systems

(g) Customer survey; internal operational data

6 Figure 15.3 seems to suggest wasted labour to have the movement to and from the bench between operations, and there are delays in the process where the sheets/part-finished booklets lie idle on the bench. Scheduling could be improved so that the sheets move continuously through the process.

7 To improve the layout in Figure 15.4, move the typist and the copier to between the manager and the files and the pot plant to where the typist used to be. Draw it like this and see what a difference it makes.

8 A systems flow chart for a job application might be as shown below.

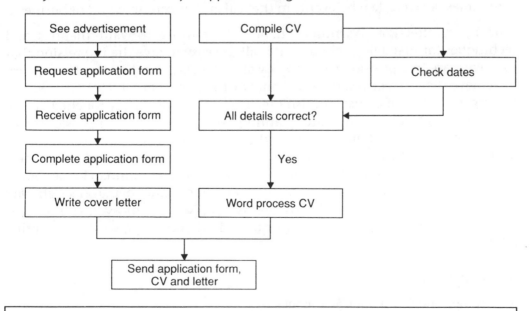

Assignment 15　　　　　　　　　　　　　[About 1¹/₂ hours]

Referring back to the problems of Pence & Sons (Assignment, Chapter 14), what methods of control, monitoring and review should the company introduce to improve and maintain their overall performance?

Chapter 16

CONSTRAINTS ON MANAGEMENT

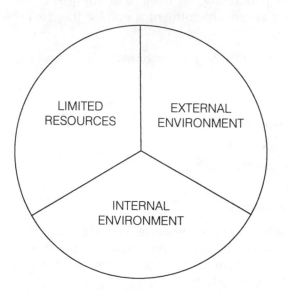

Introduction

We have occasionally had to insert 'Warning!' sections at the end of chapters, pointing out that the very best of theories, intentions and practices can sometimes be overtaken by events in the real and uncertain world of business.

This is, in effect, a 'Warning!' chapter. In putting forward theories and techniques for managing activities, it is all too easy to give the impression that managers are in a position to make any and all decisions they think necessary to achieve their objectives, bounded only by the scope of their authority within the organisation. Of course, this isn't really so. We have already touched on the uncertainty of forecasting and planning the future; the impossibility of gathering all relevant information; the fact that power and resources are limited; the need for compromise in interpersonal relations and in business decisions alike; the importance – and unpredictability – of human behaviour at work. All these factors act as constraints on the individual manager's right and ability to manage people and activities as (s)he sees fit, or even in the most effective way possible (in an ideal world ...). In this chapter, we draw together all these threads.

Your objectives

After completing this chapter you should:

- be able to identify the major constraints on the effective management of activities;

- understand how the management techniques learned in this text need to be modified in the face of these constraints;

- be aware of political-legal, economic, socio-cultural and technological ('PEST') factors in the organisational environment.

1 THE EXTERNAL ENVIRONMENT

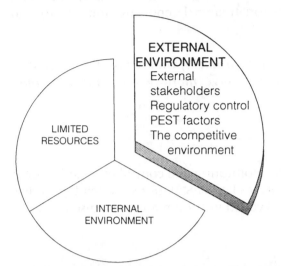

EXTERNAL ENVIRONMENT
External stakeholders
Regulatory control
PEST factors
The competitive environment

LIMITED RESOURCES

INTERNAL ENVIRONMENT

1.1 External stakeholders

Stakeholders are people or groups who have a 'stake' or interest in the activities and performance of an organisation and who impose certain obligations on its management. The external stakeholders of the organisation include:

(a) *its owners or shareholders* – the organisation, and its management, have a primary responsibility to look after the owners' interests and to secure them a return on their financial investment in the organisation; the shareholders of a public company have the right to vote on organisational issues in an Annual General Meeting and any Extraordinary General Meetings that may be called: ultimately, the shareholders have the say in what the organisation does and how it should be managed;

(b) *its customers* – the organisation's customers depend on it for the goods and services they need, and for the safety, value and honest marketing of those goods and services; in a free market economy, however, customers have the choice to accept or reject an organisation's offerings, and this gives them power: organisations need to tailor their products and their image to the values and wants of the market, if they are to survive competition;

Activity 1 [20 minutes]

What sort of issues have consumer organisations focused on in the attempt to influence businesses to protect buyers' interests and values? Suggest four examples that you are aware of.

(c) *the community, or society as a whole* – society depends on businesses for employment, investment, social responsibility (eg towards the environment) and so on. It also *provides* the organisation with labour, with potential customers and with a reputation which may affect the organisation's position in the market, so managers need to consider whether their decisions will be socially acceptable.

In relation to external stakeholders, an organisation has:

(a) obligations or responsibilities, which it may undertake voluntarily, but which do not form a part of its internal guidance or control mechanisms; for example, value for money, charitable donations, generous wages and so on; and

279

(b) boundaries or constraints on its managers' freedom to act as they see fit. For example, government legislation (on pollution, health and safety at work, redundancy and so on), regulation (on financial reporting and so on) and agreements with a trade union.

Society as a whole protects its own interests formally, via laws and regulations, designed to ensure that organisations behave morally (or ethically) and responsibly.

1.2 Regulatory control

Regulatory control involves the guidance, monitoring and control of organisational practices through formal mechanisms such as laws, regulations, 'watchdog' bodies and agreed Codes of Practice. These act as constraints on managerial discretion.

Laws

Organisations operate within a framework of laws which is very broad in scope, and deals with such issues as:

(a) *how an organisation does its business:* laws on contracts, selling and advertising practices, safety and labelling of goods, holding personal information on computer files and so on;

(b) *how an organisation treats its employees:* laws on employment protection (dismissal and redundancy), dealing with trade unions, health and safety, pay and benefits, discrimination and so on;

(c) *how an organisation deals with its owners and gives information about its performance:* laws on the duties of directors, reporting of results, constitution of meetings and so on;

(d) *how an organisation complies with criminal law* – on extortion, theft, assault, invasion of privacy and so on;

(e) *how an organisation discharges its responsibilities to government* – to collect and pay taxes, to provide information returns and so on.

In the UK, there is domestic legislation and also, increasingly, the implementation of Directives from the European Union, which are gradually being harmonised with legislation in the member states of the EU.

For discussion

Do you think it is necessary for governments to introduce legislation in areas such as:

(a) health and safety at work (obliging employers to provide a healthy and safe environment and procedures)?

(b) product safety (fire-retardant materials, no asbestos, safety belts in cars, health warnings and so on)?

If so, why? If managers were free to do what they liked or thought best for the organisation, what might standards be like? Do you think that laws encourage people to do only what is required, and not more – perhaps even lowering standards to what can be got away with?

Regulation

In some areas of decision-making, regulation has increased in recent years, where it has been felt to be in the public interest.

(a) Regulatory bodies oversee the activities of privatised utilities like BT, British Gas and the electricity and water companies. They can influence the company's pricing policy, competitive strategy (if they feel it is unfair) and so on.

(b) The financial services industry in the City is more heavily controlled than hitherto, though much of this is self-regulation carried out by the industry itself, with its own regulatory bodies and codes of practice, covering investment advice, 'insider dealing' and so on.

(c) Codes of Practice may be agreed by industry representative bodies, or published by other bodies, like ACAS. They allow monitoring bodies, like the Commission for Racial Equality or the Advertising Standards Authority, to measure the behaviour of organisations against defined standards.

(d) There is a body of regulations and standards covering the reporting of the financial performance of organisations and the verification of reports by auditors. For example, Financial Reporting Standards (FRSs) and other pronouncements by the Accounting Standards Board (ASB) and the Auditing Practices Board (APB).

Activity 2 [20 minutes]

What constraints do you think were imposed on employers when the Equal Opportunities legislation was introduced?

Try to think of three main areas which were affected and why.

A useful acronym, widely used in the UK to describe the external environment of organisations, is PEST: Political-legal, Economic, Socio-cultural and Technological factors.

1.3 PEST factors

The political-legal environment

Political-legal factors which managers must take into account include the following.

(a) Law and regulation, as discussed above.

(b) The power of the government, as the nation's largest supplier, employer, customer and investor. (Consider the effect of a change of government policy on defence for the defence industry, say).

(c) Political events at home and abroad. There may be trading sanctions imposed on states (as was the case with South Africa, Iraq and Serbia) by the international community. A war or change of regime can harm industries (as happened to airlines during the Gulf War) or build them (as in the opening up of commerce in Eastern Europe after the collapse of communism).

(d) Government economic policy – for example, on public spending, borrowing and taxation (*fiscal* policy) and on interest and exchange rates and control of the money supply (*monetary* policy). Businesses are affected by taxation, and by monetary policy: high interest rates, for example, increase the cost of investment and depress consumer spending.

(e) Government industrial policy – for example, encouraging exports (by subsidies or promotion), sponsorship of businesses in depressed regions, protection of domestic industry (duty on imported goods) and so on.

(f) Government social and foreign policy – on education and training of the workforce, trade promotion overseas, obligations towards the EU and so on.

The economic environment

An organisation is affected by overall economic conditions, as these influence:

(a) the demand for its products; and

(b) the cost of its supplies.

In times of boom and increased demand and consumption, the overall planning problem will be to identify the demand. Conversely, in times of recession, the emphasis will be on cost-effectiveness, continuing profitability, survival and competition.

A company's immediate *regional* geographical environment is also important. It might be located in a growth area full of modern thriving industry, such as Milton Keynes; or it may be located in an area of urban decay. The economic future of the area will affect wage rates, availability of labour, the disposable income of local consumers, the provision of roads and other services and so on.

The socio-cultural environment

Social and cultural influences on management decisions include the following.

(a) *Demography*, or demographics: that is, population trends.

Definition

Demography is the analysis of statistics on birth and death rates, sex and age distributions, ethnic groups and geographical movements within a population.

Conditions and changes in the local and/or national population can affect:
(i)   the availability of labour of the age and skills required by the organisation in its operating area; and
(ii) the demand for its products and services in particular areas (eg if population is declining or growing) or by particular groups (eg an increasing proportion of the population of a certain ethnic group, or over retirement age).

(b) *Culture*: the beliefs and values, attitudes, customs, language and tastes of a given society or social group.
   (i)   Organisations need to adapt their products, marketing approach and corporate image to the values of a given group. Language and other cultural barriers may have to be overcome, especially if the organisation is operating internationally. (The custom of giving gifts to business contacts is embedded in some cultures, for example – but would be called bribery in other places!)

EXAMPLE

1   When car-manufacturer Vauxhall launched its Nova in South America, it wondered why the response was poor. Finally, someone realised that 'No va' means 'doesn't go' in Spanish ...

2   In the 1980s, Coca-Cola decided to change its flavour to compete with Pepsi. Market research, taste tests and so forth elicited positive responses to the change, and so the new formulation was introduced. A small group of consumers vociferously opposed the change; and this opposition spread suddenly and rapidly like an epidemic, forcing Coca-Cola to re-introduce the old formula. It seemed that some consumers perceived Coke to symbolise 'American values', so changing the formula appeared to be an assault on them.

(ii) Organisations need to adapt their management styles and practices to the values prevailing in the culture from which they draw their workforce. (Having women in positions of authority is considered inappropriate in some cultures, for example.)

Activity 3 [30 minutes]

Give three examples of:

(a) products tailored to a particular cultural market; and

(b) employment and management practice influenced by culture.

The technological environment

Technology is not just *apparatus* (ie tools and machines), but also *technique* (skills and procedures for the use of tools and machines) and *organisation* (the social and work structure of tasks).

Technological *change* is extremely rapid, and organisations must constantly adapt to it. Technology can affect the management of organisations by:

(a) *presenting opportunities and threats in the market for the organisation's goods and services* – compact discs, satellite dishes and home computers are 'in': records, typewriters and heavy wooden-framed tennis rackets are 'out';

(b) *changing the possibilities for how products are made* – (for example, using computer-aided design and robots) – *and services are provided* (for example, cashpoint machines instead of bank tellers);

(c) *changing the way in which labour is utilised* – technology has facilitated the delayering and downsizing of organisation structures, and created a much more knowledge-based workforce.

In general, managers will be constrained to adopt new technology – especially if the organisation's competitors have done so – in order to cut costs, enhance quality, innovate and so on.

Apart from the PEST factors, which affect all organisations, a business organisation faces competition.

1.4 The competitive environment

Business organisations compete for customers and for labour – and the price of competitive failure may be the collapse of the business. The need to compete may constrain managers to:

(a) maintain or improve the quality of products/services;

(b) control the price charged for products/services;

(c) pay more to secure a reliable supply of high-quality materials from suppliers (particularly in specialised areas);

(d) pay more for selling, advertising, promotion, sponsorship and so on;

(e) pay higher wages, salaries and benefits;

(f) implement attractive human resource practices to attract skilled labour: welfare, training, workplace crèche or whatever.

These constraints will be particularly acute if there is a new or strengthening competitor in the market.

2   INTERNAL ENVIRONMENT

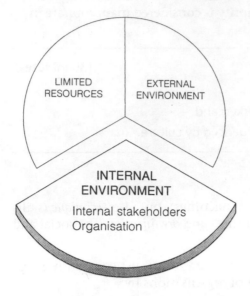

2.1   Internal stakeholders

The internal stakeholders of an organisation are its members or employees.

For discussion

Why do employees have a 'stake' in the organisation? What kind of things do they need or want from it?

The needs, wants and expectations of the employees will act as a constraint on management decision-making because the organisation may be concerned:

(a) to harness the energy and committed co-operation of its employees;

(b) not to lose skilled and experienced employees to competitors;

(c) to maintain a reputation as a responsible or generous employer, to secure a future pool of labour.

Activity 4 [20 minutes]

Give five examples of managerial decisions which might require careful thought because of their potential effects on the morale and attitudes of employees.

2.2   Organisation

The freedom of individual managers to make decisions as they see fit will be constrained by organisational factors such as the following.

(a) *The scope and amount of authority delegated to them*: their 'territory' and power within the organisation. A manager can only manage activities for which (s)he is responsible and has authority.

(b) *Plans, programmes, procedures, rules and so on*, which may already be in place. A manager is rarely able to plan activities and work methods from scratch: systems will have been developed for most routine sequences of activity. Managers often have to stick to plans and expenditure budgets which have been determined (with varying degrees of consultation) by more senior officials.

(c) *The existing organisation structure.* An individual manager is rarely able to organise work and workers from scratch. There may be no experience of multi-disciplinary teamworking to build on, for example, or departmental boundaries and job demarcation lines may be too firmly fixed to change.

(d) *The demand for co-ordination.* As we saw in Chapter 14, some tasks depend on others and have to be scheduled accordingly, and some processes and outputs need standardising in order to maintain co-ordination and consistency. An individual manager cannot make decisions for his or her own unit without reference to the requirements of the organisation system as a whole.

(e) *Organisation culture.* An individual manager is unlikely to be able to choose his or her own style of communication, motivation and management in general, without reference to the culture of the unit or organisation as a whole. A manager who does not 'fit' the organisational 'style' rarely lasts long ...

In section 2.1 above, we mentioned the constraints placed on management by having to maintain adequate supplies of a limited resource: skilled labour. Let's look briefly at some of the other limited – or scarce – resources which cramp a manager's style ...

3   LIMITED RESOURCES

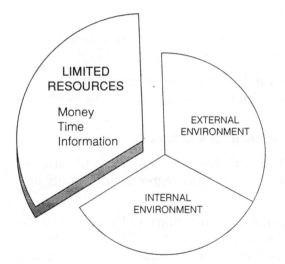

3.1   Money

Money, and the infinite variety of things it represents, is always limited and tightly controlled in organisations. Money allocated to different units represents cost to the organisation, whose financial objectives are likely to be profitability, return on investment and so on: in other words, to *maximise earnings* and *minimise costs.*

Individual unit budgets for expenditure are components of the overall organisational budget – like slices of a cake. A great deal of the politics and conflict within organisations is concerned with competing for bigger slices of the cake!

Limited financial resources therefore constrain managerial decision-making because:

(a) a limited budget can only be stretched so far, and the manager may not be able to obtain or retain all the other resources – quality materials, extra labour, new equipment and so on – that (s)he would want;

(b) a manager may be tempted to spend *up* to the allocated budget, even though it is not required, so as not to have the allocation reduced next time round.

3.2 Time

You may not have thought about it, but time is a limited resource.

(a) There are only so many working hours available. If these are not sufficient to accomplish everything a manager wishes, (s)he will be constrained to:
   (i) find extra labour or machine capacity, to cover the excess workload in the time available; or
   (ii) eliminate, or simplify, tasks or 'cut corners' in order to get high-priority work done with the existing workforce; or
   (iii) allow work to run late, and adjust the work plan for the knock-on effects.

(b) Deadlines may be imposed by customer requirements or internal co-ordination. Deadlines get closer: they make time both a limited and an *increasingly scarce* resource. Compromises of cost or quality may have to be made to meet deadlines.

(c) Time for information-gathering and decision-making is also limited. This may constrain managers to make decisions which seem riskier or less informed than they might be, or which have not been subject to as much consultation with team members as the manager's style might otherwise dictate.

3.3 Information

Information is a limited resource for several reasons.

(a) Time and money for gathering it may be limited.

(b) There is a limit to how much a person can take in and use effectively.

(c) Some information is simply not obtainable with any certainty – for example, how people are going to react, or what is going to happen tomorrow!

(d) 'Information is power', and individuals and units in organisations tend to hoard it if they think it will give them extra influence or a competitive edge over others.

Limited information constrains the management of activities because:

(a) decisions have to be taken on the basis of what is known: the full range of possible options can never be known, and a certain degree of uncertainty and inaccuracy remains;

(b) it is not possible to predict the outcome of all decisions and actions, nor the contingencies that might affect them. Changes in the PEST, competitive or physical environment of an organisation cannot always be foreseen and planned for.

If *management* information is not made available to a manager – for example, the objectives and results of the organisation, or the attitudes of employees – then the ability of the manager to make effective decisions will clearly be impaired.

Activity 5 [20 minutes]

How does scarcity of:

(a) money;

(b) time; and

(c) information

affect your management of your own activities? How are you constrained or limited by such considerations?

Chapter roundup

- Constraints on the management of activities include:
  - external stakeholders
  - regulatory control
  - political-legal, economic, socio-cultural and technological (PEST) factors
  - competition
  - internal stakeholders
  - organisational structures, systems and culture
  - limited resources
- The management of activities will be constrained by the limits and/or scarcity of:
  - labour
  - money
  - time and
  - information

Quick quiz

1. List the main external and internal stakeholders of an organisation.

2. Give three examples of (a) organisational practices constrained by law, and (b) areas in which regulatory bodies monitor and control organisational activity.

3. Give three examples of (a) political and (b) cultural factors.

4. How does (a) organisation structure, (b) co-ordination and (c) organisation culture constrain management discretion?

5. What resources do managers compete for in organisations?

Answers to quick quiz

1. External stakeholders include owners and shareholders, customers, the community or society as a whole. Internal stakeholders are its members or employees.

2. (a) Dealing with employees, entering into contracts, health and safety practice.

   (b) Activities of privatised utilities, financial services, industry, financial reporting and verification.

3. (a) Trading sanctions, war, change of regime.

   (b) Beliefs and values, attitudes and customs.

4. (a) Managers can only manage activities for which they are responsible and have authority.

   (b) Decisions are not possible without considering the requirements of the organisation system as a whole.

   (c) Decisions must 'fit in' to the organisational 'style'.

5. Money, time and information.

Answers to Activities

1 Aspects of business activity on which consumer organisations have focused include:

   (a) dangerous products and by-products (such as cigarettes and car exhaust emission);

   (b) dishonest marketing or promotion; in the UK there is legislation designed to deal with this kind of abuse;

   (c) the abuse of political and economic power by organisations (for example, ignoring international sanctions or trading with regimes with poor human rights records);

   (d) the availability of information. Consumers are anxious, for example, to be informed of any artificial additives in foodstuffs.

2 Constraints on employers as a result of the Equal Opportunities legislation would involve recruitment and promotion.

   In recruitment organisations can no longer specify that they only want, say male applicants (unless exempted for some reason).

   In promotion and training the same opportunities have to be offered in both these areas to all employees, regardless of sex, status, race or creed.

3 (a) Cultural products include: kosher food (to the Jewish community); magazines specifically for men, women or gays; low premium car insurance for mature drivers; cosmetics tested without cruelty to animals, for the 'green' market – eg Body Shop.

   (b) Employment practices affected by culture include: work hours to allow for religious holidays and observances; separate facilities and offices to differentiate managers and workers (not a cultural norm in Japan, for example); the extension of benefits previously given to 'spouses' of employees to 'partners' (including gay partners) – for example, by British Airways.

4 Managerial decisions requiring special care about morale and employee attitudes include, for example: office relocation; redundancies; change in work practices (eg introducing shiftworking); cut in benefits; cancellation of holidays in busy periods.

Assignment 16   [About 1¹/₂ hours]

Bunhams is a family firm manufacturing kitchen, floor and bathroom cleaning materials, weed killers and garden pest controls. The company now plans to change its products to become environmentally friendly. This will involve new working practices, products, advertising and marketing. Until the new products are established in the market place, profits may decline but Bunhams are firmly committed to this new concept. The company also feels that this is the right time to modernise operations by introducing new technology into the offices and the shop floor, which may reduce staffing.

(a) Which stakeholders will be affected by these new policies and why?

(b) What constraints will management have to consider and why?

ANSWERS TO ASSIGNMENTS

Answer to assignment 1

(a) You are asked to draw upon your experience and observation of what supervisors actually do and from this draw conclusions about what their roles are. The management writer Mintzberg came up with a useful list. He suggested that management fills ten roles, in three different categories.

    (i) *Interpersonal roles*

        (1) Figurehead – perform ceremonial and social duties as the organisation's representative.

        (2) Leader – perform the role of providing staff with motivation and direction towards reaching a goal.

        (3) Liaison – develop communication links with the organisation and with the outside world.

    (ii) *Informational roles*

        (1) Receiving information about performance of the organisation's operations.

        (2) Passing on information (to subordinates etc).

        (3) Transmitting information outside the organisation.

    (iii) *Decision roles*

        (1) Taking entrepreneurial decisions in order to meet the organisation's objectives.

        (2) Handling disturbances.

        (3) Negotiating (with persons or groups of people).

(b) It should be indicated to Dawn that in her present job as supervisor she is not expected to act in all these roles at once, but that some of them are to be found within her scope as a supervisor.

    (i) Liaison – Dawn's section communicates with the organisation as a whole through her, and it is part of her job to ensure that the assistance which her section requires is obtained from the organisation.

    (ii) Leader – she seems to be performing well in her role as leader of the section – the increase in output appears to be linked with her new duties, which must mean that she is motivating her team.

    (iii) Receiving information – she receives back reports on how effectively her section is carrying out its tasks and can take appropriate steps if the section's objectives (ie to get the work done) are not met.

Answer to assignment 2

(a) He is likely to encounter a lack of communication and co-operation, demotivated staff, resentment of his youth and an attitude of 'what does he know about things here?' amongst others. It may be difficult to get work done effectively as a result of these attitudes.

(b) Initially, it would probably help to hold a departmental meeting, so that Peter can indicate how he wants the department to run and invite comments. This will give both him and the staff the opportunity to 'weigh each other up'. This should be followed by individual meetings with each member of staff, encouraging frank and open discussion and, if necessary, attempting to solve any problems which members of staff may express.

(c) From the feedback received from the departmental and individual meetings, Peter may be able to determine which particular management style would be most effective. It would probably be advisable to start with the 'consult' approach, suggesting his own ideas and asking for comments. If this proves successful, he may gradually move further up the management continuum towards a more democratic style, although this may take some time. Looking at Blake and Mouton's managerial grid, he must aim for 9.9 and must not be tempted towards 1.9 in his attempts to improve relationships. At this stage he must be careful to strike the right balance between results and relationships. If he starts with a loose, friendly attitude, it will be almost impossible to tighten control if results are not forthcoming. On the other hand, tighter control can be relaxed as the team achieves its objectives and a greater degree of democracy can be achieved.

Answer to assignment 3

Your answer should cover most of the following points.

(a) The problems raised by the staff are symptoms of a deeper problem. A massive change was made without their knowledge. Familiar surroundings disappeared, resulting in resentment, insecurity and uncertainty. There may be a feeling of 'if they can do this without telling us, what else might they do?' People who were used to working in small groups of two or three now have to work with nineteen others and have to start building new relationships and learn different working practices.

(b) Overcoming the problems will not be easy. Management could start by explaining why the change was necessary or desirable. They need to sell the benefits of the change, but should concentrate on benefits to the employees rather than purely on those to the company. Deal with genuine problems. For example, if noise is a real problem, place acoustic screens in strategic places. This may also have the effect of creating more privacy.

(c) Discuss the change with those affected beforehand. Listen to comments and suggestions. Ensure that communication is free-flowing, both up and down. Sell the change effectively, giving reasons as to why it is necessary. Monitor results.

Answer to assignment 4

Your answer should cover most of the following points. (Note it should be in memo format.)

(a) Overall there appears to be an increasing lack of motivation and commitment amongst the workforce. This is probably the result of the tight management control, no prospects of promotion and poor, one-way communication.

(b) Possible action for improving the situation could be to re-organise working practices to encourage more team work (Maslow's belonging/social needs), to consider present employees for promotion (Maslow, Herzberg and Vroom), to introduce better communication methods and to encourage and act on feedback. Management should take a greater interest in their employees. Grievances should be dealt with as quickly as possible and people should be told when they are doing a good job.

By implementing these improvements, the workforce will feel that they are important to the organisation and not simply 'numbers on the payroll'.

Answer to assignment 5

(a) The management team must be briefed and an announcement of a general meeting should be placed on the noticeboards, Chris to give the information at this meeting. This should be followed immediately by departmental/section meetings with relevant managers. (If left too long, rumours will spread and reactions will worsen). Written confirmation could be given out at this point.

(b) There will probably be distortion, noise and overload, when people are unable to take in the full implications. Reactions may include anger, frustration, fear, resentment to change, blaming management, uncertainty and shock.

(c) At the departmental/section meetings, managers must give employees the opportunity to ask questions. At this point, if not already done, written confirmation should be handed out. With this amount of information, it can be difficult to remember all the points. After the meetings have taken place, people directly affected by redundancy or retraining must be interviewed individually, either by their direct superior, or the personnel manager. The information they receive regarding dates and procedures to be adopted should also be confirmed in writing.

Answer to assignment 6

Your answer should include most of the following points.

(a) A group is informal and loosely structured. A team is a formal work group brought together to achieve an objective.

(b) Giving the group a greater sense of identity as a team, encouraging solidarity and encouraging the group to commit themselves to shared work objectives.

(c) Expressing solidarity, encouraging interpersonal relationships, controlling conflict and intra-group competition and encouraging inter-group competition.

(d) Clearly set out objectives; involve the team in setting targets and standards; provide necessary information, resources, training and environment; give regular, clear feedback; encourage feedback and ideas; give positive praise and reward; and visibly support the team in the organisation.

(e) High levels of labour turnover, accident rate and absenteeism; low output and productivity; poor quality of output; individual targets not achieved; time wasted and lost.

Answer to assignment 7

(a) It is not really effective. It has too many headings, most of which are unquantifiable. Employees may be reluctant to 'react' to and 'comment' on the appraisal. It has too many performance classifications. Unless the employee completes his/her own self evaluation form prior to the appraisal, it could become a very one-sided meeting which would not encourage the employee to make comments or suggestions.

(b) Rather than referring to 'weaknesses' it would be more positive to indicate 'opportunities for improvement'. The number of performance classifications should be advised as should the number of 'skill' headings. Performance criteria should be quantifiable wherever possible.

(c) Ensure the appraisee is informed of the results of the appraisal, carry out agreed actions, monitor the appraisee's progress and check that all necessary actions have been carried out. Take necessary steps to ensure that improvements are possible (this may include training, guidance, obtaining feedback, altering work methods or whatever else is required).

(d) If follow-up action is not taken, employees will feel that appraisal is all talk and just a waste of time and that efforts to improve action on their side will not be appreciated or worthwhile.

Answer to assignment 8

(a) *General considerations*

Training has two purposes. Its main purpose is to raise performance standards and competence in the production and marketing of goods and services. Also, from the perspective of the employee, it is part of career development to motivate the employee to personal growth. (It is sometimes argued that overall levels of training in an economy can affect long-term economic performance – as an investment in knowledge.)

With this in mind – that training should serve both the organisation and the individual – we can identify general considerations for any training program.

One way of so doing is to take a systems approach, which compares the situation before and after training.

Identify training needs

Analyse the job to be done (in terms of physical and mental skills, roles to be played, existing job descriptions), and then the potential trainee's current performance and skills. The difference between the job's demands and the individual's capacity to satisfy them is known sometimes as the training gap.

Some training requirements are automatic (eg new legislation affecting organisational practice in key areas).

Set objectives

It will be helpful to specify the objectives of the training program. The reason is so that the trainer can know what is expected, the person being trained has an idea as to what he or she is to be taught, and the trainee's boss can know what skills the trainee can be expected to have acquired at the end of the course. It encourages training relevance.

Monitor result

So that the effect of the training can be measured, some monitoring of the result can be useful. This could mean assessing the employee's actual performance before the training, and asking for the employee's comments on the training program.

(b) In Bruce's case, the manager has a choice. There is a four week gap between the date Bruce joins and the date that Fiona, Bruce's predecessor, leaves. The problem involves making the most effective use of this time for Bruce's training.

An important factor determining how this time can be used is Bruce's learning style. It is possible to identify four types of learning style.

(i) Theorists like to learn basic principles and by analytical methods. Such people like structured training.

(ii) A reflector learns slowly, by observation, research and experience from which conclusions can be drawn.

(iii) Activists require hands-on training, and get bored with theory

(iv) Pragmatists like training to be directly relevant to the task in hand.

Bruce is evidently a reflector. Bruce thus needs time to become acquainted with the job, and he might be a slow learner. So, he needs a gradual induction.

Throwing him into the job at the deep end would be unfair. It may be that he needs as much tuition from Fiona as possible, as there is no one else from whom he can learn directly. On the other hand, without formal training, he will be working for five months without any overview.

It is possible that Fiona can teach him the job's essentials. This will enable Bruce to get by with the bulk of his work. Fiona could also be asked to write detailed step-by-step instructions for the routine tasks, to maximise the effectiveness of the learning time.

The manager should assess the content of the formal training program. Is it a standard course, with elements that could, if necessary be left out for the time being? Or is all of it directly relevant to Bruce's task?

Whatever happens, the manager should set proper targets for the training, and in terms of what is expected from Bruce's performance on the job. This will make it easier for Bruce to get to grips with it. The manager should supervise Bruce's work fairly closely, and perhaps should set him particular tasks that assist learning as well.

Answer to assignment 9

Your answer should cover most of the following points.

Lateness, absenteeism, and minor infractions of work rules will result in a first warning which will be oral but be recorded on the employee's record. If there are further occurrences of a similar nature, a second warning will be issued. This will be written and a copy will be retained on the employee's file. Any further breach will result in a final written warning. If there is yet another breach, it will result in dismissal.

At all stages the employee will be interviewed by the relevant manager and given the opportunity to state his/her case. The employee has the right to be accompanied by a fellow worker or trade union representative. The right of appeal is relevant at all stages and any appeal must be lodged with the relevant manager within 10 working days.

Answer to assignment 10

(a) They must plan in order to co-ordinate the members and resources so that everyone knows what they have to achieve and their deadlines. Everyone should be fully involved with no duplication of effort or idle time.

(b) They should consider what resources are required, such as materials for the presentations, possibly maps for those carrying out field research, availability of computers for processing the report, visual aid equipment such as overhead projectors or flip-charts. They will also have to consider task scheduling and contingency planning. (What if it is raining when the field researchers are out? Do they struggle on or change their location or return to base?) Time limits and priorities will also be of prime importance.

(c) The group will probably first select a leader or co-ordinator who will ensure the deadlines are being met, deal with problems and generally monitor progress. It is important to identify all the skills and abilities within the group. Is there someone with artistic ability who would be able to concentrate on the visual aids? Are there people who would enjoy talking to others during the field research? Some members may prefer to carry out desk research or to concentrate on the written presentation. It is often surprising to find how many talents, skills and abilities exist within one group.

(d) Reverse scheduling would probably be the most effective method. The assignment deadline is set, therefore it is possible to estimate how long each activity should take and allocate time effectively. It would be useful to use a wall planner charting the various time stages for each activity.

Answer to assignment 11

(a) Problems include the following.

   (i) Consultants do not contact the office regularly.

   (ii) Office staff are not familiar with the visit areas and possibly do not plan visits as effectively as they could.

   (ii) Management is unaware of consultants' whereabouts. Jim is unable to 'pin down' consultants when urgent matters arise.

(b) Jim should insist on regular weekly meetings which all consultants must attend. Area maps should be provided to office staff so that visits can be organised on a more effective basis. Consultants must telephone the office daily to give and receive information. A wall chart would show where each consultant was on a daily basis. Jim and the office staff should use checklists to ensure that all necessary information is given or received during the phone calls from the consultants. Rather than ploughing through all the visit reports, Jim should delegate this task and adopt management by exception, thus saving time. A diary system would help him to monitor progress and completion deadlines.

Answer to assignment 12

(a) In both cases the projects have no specific objectives or time spans. Case (1) is hampered by continually changing specifications, an aircraft which is too small for the task and technology which is not yet developed. Therefore it would be impossible to identify fixed specifications, budgets or time.

Case (2) has similar problems as no real decisions have been made as to what kind of event is required. This involves many companies, a large site and no specific direction.

(b) First, a decision has to be made about the actual 'event', after which a budget needs to be set and a final deadline for completion. Then it becomes possible to break down the overall objective into smaller projects such as planning sites, building design, landscaping and approaching interested parties who may wish to participate in an exhibition. It would also be necessary to gain necessary planning permissions and meet any other legal obligations.

Once everyone knows what the broad plans are and the smaller projects have been decided, budgets and time can be allocated to each and progress can be monitored. A start has been made recently: the main site will be Greenwich.

Answer to assignment 13

(a) There are two types of communication method.

   (i) Oral communication, which includes meetings (individual and groups), telephone contact, briefings and the informal 'grapevine'.

   (ii) Written communication which includes instructions, letters, memos, formal and informal reports.

Whatever methods are used, the main purposes are to give and receive timely, accurate and understandable information, instructions and feedback.

(b) Effective downward communication can maintain the ability and willingness to carry out orders and instructions. It provides positive and negative reinforcement by praising and encouraging. Dissatisfaction can be indicated along with the re-emphasis of required standards; constructive criticism can be given. Leaders can communicate the values and beliefs (culture) of the organisation. Performance feedback can be given to enable employees to know how they are doing personally and how results are progressing, compared to the plans and standards set by the organisation.

(c) Tactical level MIS enable management to gather information from a wider range of sources, which can cover external information from the environment as well as internal sources. It can filter out unnecessary detail which is not required. It can investigate, analyse and otherwise process data received from the operational level and can apply it to tactical decisions.

Answer to assignment 14

(a) The overall results are: an increase in costs due to lost machine time and increased overtime, poor customer relations caused by delays and conflicting information which may result in lost business; and a clash of interests, where the sales team is increasing orders which production is unable to handle effectively. These factors will have a demotivating effect on staff, who cannot achieve objectives and who are subject to constant change. It may become more difficult to persuade them to work overtime.

(b) Management should ensure that the organisational objectives are redefined and restated to all staff. Everyone needs to know exactly what is to be achieved. The parts situation has to be resolved by reorganising the ordering system so that parts are available as required. The sales and production departments must liaise closely so that orders and deliveries are processed to agreed dates. Tasks must be prioritised and management should introduce an MIS (or use one more effectively). Monitoring is vital to this organisation to ensure there is no repetition of the present situation.

Answer to assignment 15

Budgetary control is probably already in place but is not being used effectively, therefore it is important to look again at departmental and overall budgets to ensure that variances can be identified and dealt with promptly. There is certainly a need for a stock control system to be introduced so that parts are available as required. Production control is required to eliminate down time and bottlenecks, and a quality control system of some type must be present.

By using the 'E' factors of organisational performance it would be possible, once the organisational objectives have been re-established, for management to carry out comparisons and highlight any weaknesses.

Time sheets may also be useful at this point for production management to be able to establish precisely where the holdups occur.

Method study may be required to ensure the most effective and efficient methods are being used. Flow charts and movement charts may indicate further improvements to be made. Therefore by thoroughly analysing the present situation, recommending improvements, implementing improvements and continually monitoring, it will be possible to achieve and maintain performance.

Answer to assignment 16

(a) The owners, who are aware that, until the new products prove successful, there is likely to be a decline in profits will be affected. Existing customers may not like the changes and switch to other products, although new customers may be gained. Society may find the new environmentally-friendly products more acceptable. Employees may lose their jobs if the new technology reduces labour efforts. They will need to be retrained to operate the new machinery.

(b) Management need to consider legislation regarding redundancy, health and safety, selling and advertising practices, product safety and labelling of goods. They will also have to consider the present fiscal and monetary policies and the economic environment, as they may have to take out loans to finance the new machinery. They are being constrained to introduce new technology to reduce costs and increase efficiency. They will need to consider the competitive environment, their own organisation structure and existing culture.

All these factors can affect the rate at which decisions are made and implemented and the possible need for compromise in their business decisions.

GLOSSARY

Activity scheduling Provides a list of activities, in the order in which they must be completed (called 'task sequencing' in part of this book).

Added value An accounting term for the difference between the cost of raw materials and the sales price of the finished product; ie the value that is perceived to have been added to inputs by processing within the organisational system.

Attitude A mental and neural state of readiness exerting a directive or dynamic influence upon the individual's response to all objects and situations with which it is related.

Authority The right to do something, or to get others to do it.

Bias A mental tendency or inclination to see things in a particular way. It is used mainly to refer to irrational preferences or dislikes, usually a form of prejudice.

Brainstorming A process whereby people produce spontaneous, uncensored ideas, sparked off by a particular problem or task.

Budget A statement of desired performance, usually expressed in financial terms (expenditure, revenue, profit and so on).

Communication The transmission or exchange of information.

Control The overall process whereby goals and standards are defined, and performance is monitored, measured against the goals and adjusted if necessary, to ensure that the goals are being accomplished.

Co-operation Working or acting together

Co-ordinate To plan, or take action to improve, the interrelationships (especially of timing and methods of communication) between a number of various activities, which contribute to the achievement of a single objective, so that they do not conflict and the objective is achieved with a minimal expenditure of time and effort. (*Dictionary of Management*).

Counselling A purposeful relationship in which one person helps another to help himself. It is a way of relating and responding to another person so that that person is helped to explore his thoughts, feelings and behaviour with the aim of reaching a clearer understanding. The clearer understanding may be of himself or of a problem, or of the one in relation to the other. (*Rees*).

Criterion (plural: **criteria**) A factor or standard by which something can be judged or decided. For example, 'meeting output targets' is one criterion for judging work performance.

Data Are the raw material of information: facts and figures in an unprocessed state.

Deadline The end of the longest span of time which may be allotted to a task: in other words, the last acceptable date for completion.

Decision support system (DSS) An MIS (usually computerised), designed to produce information in such a way as to help managers make better decisions.

Delegation The process whereby superior A gives subordinate B authority over a defined area which falls within the scope of A's authority.

Demography The analysis of statistics on birth and death rates, sex and age distributions, ethnic groups and geographical movements within a population.

Development Job experience and learning from other employees, particularly one's immediate superior.

Discipline A condition in an enterprise in which there is orderliness, in which members of the enterprise behave sensibly and conduct themselves according to the standards of acceptable behaviour as related to the goals of the organisation.

Education The process which results in formal qualifications up to and including post-graduate degrees.

Effectiveness The measure of how far an organisation, and its managers, achieve their output requirements, as defined by performance objectives and targets.

Efficiency The relationship between inputs used and outputs achieved. The fewer the inputs used to obtain a given output, the greater the efficiency. Efficiency can be expressed as:

$$\frac{output}{input}$$

Empowerment Making workers (and particularly work teams) responsible for achieving, and even setting, work targets; with the freedom to make decisions about how they are to be achieved.

Evaluation Comparing the costs of a process against the benefits which are being obtained.

Formal organisation An organisation which is deliberately constructed to fulfil specific goals. It is characterised by planned division of responsibility and a well-defined structure of authority and communication. The organisation structure provides for consistent functions and roles, irrespective of changes in individual membership.

Grievance Occurs when an individual feels that (s)he is being wrongly treated by a colleague or supervisor: picked on, unfairly appraised or blocked for promotion, or discriminated against on grounds of race or sex.

Group Any collection of people who *perceive* themselves to be a group.

Incentive The offer or promise of a reward for contribution or success, designed to motivate the individual or team to behave in such a way as to earn it. (In other words the 'carrot' dangled in front of the donkey!)

Influence The process by which an individual or group exercises power to determine or modify the behaviour of others.

Informal organisation One which is loosely structured, flexible and spontaneous, fluctuating with its individual membership. Examples are colleagues who tend to lunch together and 'cliques'. Informal organisations always exist within formal organisations.

Information Data which have been processed (selected, sorted, analysed, formatted) so as to have meaning for the person who receives it, and be suitable for a particular purpose.

Job analysis The determination of the essential characteristics of a job.

Job enlargement The attempt to widen jobs by increasing the number of operations in which a job holder is involved.

Job enrichment Planned, deliberate action to build greater responsibility, breadth and challenge of work into a job.

Learning The process of acquiring, through experience, knowledge which leads to changed behaviour.

Management Information System (MIS) A system designed to collect data from all available sources and convert it into information relevant to managers at all levels, for the purposes of planning and control of the activities for which they are responsible.

Method study The systematic recording and critical examination of existing and proposed ways of doing work, as a means of developing and applying easier and more effective methods and reducing costs.

Motivation The process by which the behaviour of an individual is influenced by others, through their power to offer or withhold satisfaction of the individual's needs and goals.

Organisation 'A social arrangement for the controlled performance of collective goals'. (*Buchanan and Huczynski*).

Perception The psychological process by which stimuli or incoming sensory data are selected and organised into patterns which are meaningful to the individual.

Personality The total pattern of characteristic ways of thinking, feeling and behaving that constitute the individual's distinctive method of relating to the environment.

Potential review The use of appraisal to forecast where and how fast an individual is progressing.

Power The ability to do something, or to get others to do it.

Prejudice A 'pre-judgement'; an opinion formed before all the relevant facts are known – particularly an unfavourable opinion.

Project An undertaking, often cutting across organisational and functional boundaries, and carried out to meet established goals within cost, schedule and quality objectives.

Quality circles Groups of (typically 6–10) employees from different levels and/or disciplines, who meet regularly to discuss problems of quality and quality control in their area of work.

Reward A token (monetary or otherwise) given to an individual or team in recognition of some contribution or success.

Responsibility The liability of people to be called to account for the way they have exercised the authority given to them. It is an obligation to do something, or to get others to do it.

Systems analysis The process of analysing methods, procedures, sequences of activities, paperwork flows and the inputs required and outputs expected in operational or informational processing systems *which are based on computers*.

Task sequencing See Activity scheduling

Team A formalised group to achieve particular objectives.

Time scheduling Adds to Activity scheduling the timescale or start and end times/dates for each activity in a sequence.

Training (**1**) The systematic development of the attitude/knowledge/skill/ behaviour pattern required by an individual in order to perform adequately a given task or job (*Department of Employment*). (**2**) Formal learning activity which may not lead to qualifications, and which may be received at any time in a working career; for example, a course in counselling skills (*Constable and McCormick*).

Validation Observing the results of a process (for example a training scheme), and measuring whether its objectives have been achieved.

Value analysis A cost reduction technique aimed at identifying unnecessary cost elements in an item, by analysing its function and design in detail.

INDEX

3

360-degree feedback, 133
3-D management grid, 41

A

ABCD method of in-tray management, 202
Ability, 60
ACAS, 165
ACAS guidelines, 165
Accountability, 228
Action plans, 198
Activity sampling, 262
Activity scheduling, 186
Added value, 20
Affluent Worker, 83
Age, 59, 64, 91
Allocating tasks, 189
Analysis paralysis, 242
Appraisal, 129
    follow-up, 136
    improving the system, 138
    interviews, 136
    procedures, 132
    purposes, 129
Aptitude, 60
Argument, 98
Assertiveness, 102
Assessing training schemes, 148
Assistant to positions, 147
Attitudes, 43, 58, 100
Authority, 10, 14, 285

B

Bar charts, 199
Bar line charts, 210
Barnard, 4, 75
Barriers to communication, 94
Behaviourist or stimulus-response
    approach, 62
Belbin, 113
Bias, 90
Blake and Mouton, 40
Brainstorming, 111
Briefings, 232
Bring forward systems, 202
Budget, 183
Budgetary control, 218, 259

C

Career development, 154
Cash incentives, 83
Challenge-support matrix, 153

Change, 67
Checklists, 162, 195
Class, 59
Classical school, 14
Closure, 57
Coaching, 151
Cognitive or information processing
    approach, 62
Commanding, 9, 225
Committee work, 147
Communication, 92, 251, 252
    routes, 228
    skills, 101
Competition, 98
Competitive environment, 283
Computer aided design, 274
Computer aided manufacture, 274
Computer-based training, 146
Computers, 239
Concentration, 201
Conclusions, 235
Confidentiality, 161
Conflict, 97–98, 116, 251, 253
Content theories, 75
Contingencies, 187
Contingency approach, 17, 38, 45, 123
Contingency planning, 184
Continuum of management styles, 37
Contribution profile, 122
Contributions to group, 120
Control, 7, 180, 227
Control systems, 181, 240, 258
Controlling conflict, 98, 253
Co-operation, 96
Co-ordination, 9, 178, 227, 249, 285
Cost estimating, 217
Cost reduction, 270
Cost scheduling, 217
Counselling, 160
Counselling session, 161
Courses, 137
Crash cost, 219
Crash times, 219
Crashing, 219
Criteria for assessment, 130
Critical activities, 213
Critical path, 213
Critical path analysis (CPA), 213
Culture, 6, 20, 65, 282
Customers, 279

D

Data, 239
Database systems, 241

Deadlines, 185
Decision support systems (DSS), 241–242
Decision-making, 227
Delayering, 19, 26
Delegation, 10, 42, 193
Demography, 282
Development, 149
Disability, 91
Discharge, 165
Disciplinary action, 165
Disciplinary interviews, 166, 167
Disciplinary layoffs, 165
Disciplinary situations, 164
Discipline, 164
Discrimination, 91
Distortion, 94
Divisions, 188
Dorming, 114
Downward communication, 230
Drucker, 9, 150
Dummy activity, 212

E

E factors, 260
Economic downturn, 19
Economic environment, 282
Economy, 260
Education, 150
Effective work group, 123
Effectiveness, 179, 260
Efficiency, 179, 260
Electronic office, 274
Elegance, 260
Employee development, 150
Empowered teams, 111
Empowering, 161
Empowerment, 24, 81, 110, 234
Environment of leadership, 29
Environmental factors, 77
Ethicality, 261
Evaluation, 149
Expectancy theory, 78
Experience, 150, 156
External stakeholders, 279

F

Face-to-face communication, 230
Fayol, 9, 14
Feedback, 93, 117, 130, 148, 234
Financial performance indicators, 261
Financial resources, 286
Flat structures, 19
Flexibility, 21, 22, 24
Flexitime, 22
Float, 211, 214, 218
Flow charts, 266
Followership, 34, 46
Formal communication, 228
Formal groups, 109
Formal organisation, 5

Formal report, 236
Formal training, 146
Forming, 114
Forward scheduling, 186, 198
Functional authority, 11
Functions of management, 9

G

Gantt charts, 200, 215
Gender, 58
Goals, 6, 64, 100, 194
Goldthorpe, Lockwood, 83
Good information, 243
Grading, 132
Grapevine, 229
Grievance, 168
Grievance interviews, 169
Grievance procedures, 168
Group norms, 118
Groups, 109
Groups in decision-making, 119
Guided assessment, 132

H

Half open door, 201
Halo effect, 90
Handy, 38, 42, 80, 98, 123
Hawthorne Studies, 15
Herzberg, 15, 77, 80, 82
Hierarchy of needs, 76
Human Relations, 15, 74
Human Relations theorists, 80
Hygiene factors, 77, 82

I

Idiographic approach, 52, 54
Impact of technology, 273
Improving communication, 95
Improving co-ordination, 252
Improving efficiency, 271
Improving productivity, 272
Improving quality, 272
Incentives, 74, 81
Indicators of potential, 128
Induction, 137
Ineffective work group, 131
Influence, 33
Influencing skills, 102
Informal communication, 229
Informal groups, 123
Informal organisation, 5
Informal report, 237
Informal talk, 165
Information, 234, 239, 286
Information needs of employees, 226
Information needs of management, 226
Information outputs, 228
Information overload, 242
Information systems, 19
Information technology, 273

Institute of Personnel Development, 160
Instructions, 231
Intelligence, 61
Inter-group competition, 116
Internal stakeholders, 284
Interpersonal skills, 99
Interruptions, 201
Intra-group competition, 116
Inventory control, 259, 273

J

Jay, 110
Job analysis, 131
Job descriptions, 131
Job design, 80
Job enlargement, 80
Job enrichment, 80
Job management, 193
Job reporting, 273
Job rotation, 147
Job satisfaction, 75, 80
Job specification, 131

K

Key results, 181

L

Labour turnover, 144
Laws, 280
Leadership, 33
Leadership traits, 35
Learning, 62
Learning cycle, 62
Learning organisation, 20
Learning theory, 147
Likert, 45
Limited resources, 285
Line authority, 10
Linked bar charts, 210
Lists, 194
Livy, 144

M

Management by exception, 201, 234
Management by walking around, 109
Management development, 150
Management Information Systems, 239
Management style, 35
Management succession, 150
Manager's time, 192
Managerial authority, 10
Managerial Grid, 40
Managerial roles, 11
Maslow, 15, 63, 76
Matrix organisation, 188
Matrix structure, 23
Mayo, 15
McCormick, 150
McGregor, 43
Mead, 54

Medium for communication, 93
Memorandum, 231
Mentoring, 152
Method study, 264
Mintzberg, 11
Mission, 6
Modelling, 242
Morale, 65
Motivation, 65, 73, 74, 233
Motivation and performance, 74
Motivation theory, 75
Motivator factors, 77
Movement charts, 267
Multi-disciplinary teams, 23
Multi-skilled teams, 24
Multi-skilling, 21

N

Needs, 63
Negative discipline, 164
Network analysis, 211
Network diagram, 211
New Organisation, 18
Noise, 94
Nomothetic approach, 51
Non-cash incentive schemes, 81
Non-financial performance indicators, 261
Non-monetary rewards, 79
Non-verbal communication, 93
Norming, 114

O

Objectives, 117, 147, 179, 182
Observation, 261
Official warning, 165
On-the-job training, 146, 147
Operational decisions, 240
Operational level, 182
Operational level MIS, 240
Oral communication, 230
Oral warning, 165
Orders and instructions, 231
Organisation, 4
Organisation as a system, 16
Organisation culture, 5, 285
Organisation manual, 217
Organisation structure, 5, 253
Organisational chart, 14
Organisational politics, 95
Organising, 9, 178, 188, 227
Orientations to work, 74
Outward bound courses, 150
Overall assessment, 132
Overcoming resistance to change, 68

P

Participation, 148
Pay, 74, 82
Pay as a motivator, 82
Pedler, Burgoyne and Boydell, 152

Perception, 56
Perception and work behaviour, 57
Perceptions, 100
Perceptual organisation, 57
Perceptual selectivity, 56
Performance, 74
Performance appraisal, 129
Performance monitoring, 128, 259, 262
Performance review, 259, 262, 264
Performance standards, 181, 260
Personal Development Plans, 151
Personality, 52, 130
Personality and work behaviour, 54
Personality development, 54
Personality trait tests, 53
Personality type, 53
Persuasion, 102
PERT, 219
PEST factors, 281
Peter, 137
Peter principle, 137
Planning, 9, 177, 180, 227, 252
Planning horizons, 183
Policies, 182
Political-legal environment, 281
Politics, 252
Positive reinforcement, 117
Potential, 137
Potential assessment, 137
Potential review, 137
Power, 10
Precedence network, 197
Prejudice, 90
Primary working group, 110
Priorities, 181, 195
Priority, 185
Problem-solving approach, 136
Procedures, 182
Process theories, 76
Production control, 259
Production monitoring, 273
Programmed decisions, 240
Programmes, 182
Progress control chart, 210
Progressive discipline, 165
Project, 207
Project management, 207
Project planning, 207
Purpose of management, 8

Q

Quality circles, 111
Quality control, 259

R

Race, 58, 59
Race Relations Act 1976, 91
Rackham and Morgan, 121
Rating scales, 132
Recognition schemes, 81

Recommendations, 236
Reddin, 41
Regulation, 280
Regulatory control, 280
Reinforcement, 148, 233
Reporting by exception, 263
Reports, 235
Reprimand, 165
Resisting change, 67
Resource allocation, 184, 186, 215
Resources, 250
Respect, 44
Responsibility, 10, 14
Results-orientated approach, 133
Results-orientated schemes, 133
Reverse scheduling, 186, 198
Reward, 74
Role ambiguity, 88
Role incompatibility, 88
Role models, 89
Role set, 88
Role signs, 88
Role theory, 88
Roles, 100
Rules, 182

S

Scalar chain, 14
Scheduling using the critical path, 214
Scientific management, 13
Selecting team members, 112
Self, 54
Self discipline, 164
Self image, 54
Self-concept, 60, 65
Self-development, 151
Sensitivity analysis, 242
Sex, 60
Sex Discrimination Act 1975, 91
Social perception, 89
Socio-cultural environment, 282
Socio-technical system, 16
Specialisation, 14
Spreadsheets, 242
Staff association, 113
Staff authority, 11
Stakeholders, 7, 279
Standardisation, 182, 253
Stereotyping, 53, 90
Stock control, 261, 273
Storming, 114
Strategic decisions, 241
Strategic level, 181
Strategic level MIS, 241
Strategies, 182
Stress, 66
String diagrams, 267
Structures, 188
Subjective probability, 78
Suggestions, 234
Surveys, 263
Suspension, 165

Symptoms of poor co-ordination, 250
Symptoms of stress, 66
Systems analysis, 268

T

Tactical decision-making, 240
Tactical level, 182
Tactical level MIS, 240
Task importance, 195
Task inspection, 262
Task scheduling, 184, 198
Task sequence, 184, 194, 196
Task urgency, 196
Task-centred structures, 184
Tasking sequencing, 184
Taylor, 13
Team development, 114
Team effectiveness, 122
Team identity, 115
Team roles, 113
Team solidarity, 116
Teambuilding, 115
Teams, 108–9
Teamworking, 23, 111
Technological environment, 283
Technology, 24
Technology and control, 273
Technology and performance, 274
Telephone, 230
Tell and listen method, 136
Tell and sell method, 136
Temporary promotion, 147
Temporary working, 22
Terms of reference, 236
Theory X, 43
Theory Y, 43
Tight and loose styles, 38
Time, 286
Time management, 192

Time scheduling, 186
Time sheets, 263
Timetables, 199
Trade union, 112
Training, 143, 150
    and education, 146
    evaluation of, 148
    groups, 112
    methods, 146
    needs, 143
    needs analysis, 144
    objectives, 145
    system, 143
Trait clusters, 53
Traits, 52
Trust-control dilemma, 42
Tuckman, 114
Two-factor theory, 77

U

Unity of command, 15
Unity of direction, 15
Upward appraisal, 134
Upward communication, 136, 234

V

Valence, 78
Validating a training scheme, 148
Value, 270
Value analysis, 270
Vroom, 78

W

Work breakdown structure, 108
Work organisation, 202
Work planning, 184
Written communication, 230

REVIEW FORM

NAME ....

COLLEGE ....

We would be grateful to receive any comments you may have on this book. You may like to use the headings below as guidelines. Tear out this page and send it to our Freepost address:

BPP Publishing Ltd, FREEPOST, London W12 8BR

Topic coverage:

Summary diagrams, signposts, definitions, exercises, discussion topics, chapter roundups and quizzes:

Student friendliness:

Errors (please specify, and refer to a page number):

Other:

Learning Resources
Centre